Making Meaningful Lives

CONTEMPORARY ETHNOGRAPHY

Kirin Narayan and Alma Gottlieb, Series Editors

A complete list of books in the series
is available from the publisher.

Making Meaningful Lives

Tales from an Aging Japan

Iza Kavedžija

PENN

UNIVERSITY OF PENNSYLVANIA PRESS

PHILADELPHIA

Published by
University of Pennsylvania Press
Philadelphia, Pennsylvania 19104-4112
www.upenn.edu/pennpress

Printed in the United States of America on acid-free paper

10 9 8 7 6 5 4 3 2 1

A catalogue record for this book is available from the Library of Congress

ISBN 978-0-8122-5136-4

For all those in my circles of care

Contents

Note on Conventions

All personal names in this book are rendered using the Japanese custom of writing the family name before the given name. Rather than using Mr. or Mrs., I use the suffix *san* when referring to my interlocutors. All names, including the names of locations within Osaka, have been changed. Romanization throughout the book follows the Hepburn system. During the period of fieldwork in 2009 the exchange rate for Japanese yen was approximately ¥100 for one U.S. dollar.

Chapter 1

Subjects of Care

Must an anthropology of the elderly be about aging? There are many things we can hope to learn from a study of older people, and in particular we might expect to find out more about aging itself and how it is experienced; aging is, after all, a process that affects us all deeply. Paying close attention to the changes it entails often seems to lead to a consideration of the challenges that arise—including, especially, issues of loss and decline. To be sure, for some, these can be important or even defining facets of life in older age. For the Japanese men and women who are the focus of this book, however, the experience of aging was not a primary concern. Anthropologists tend naturally to be interested in what the people with whom we work care most about; and while my interlocutors did occasionally speak about aging, at times in a reflexive way, they simply did not define themselves in terms of their old age, or allow it to overshadow how they thought of themselves or their companions. Life in older age is not all about senescence, as they reminded me constantly through their actions and attitudes.

Approaching the end of life does, however, often seem to bring to the fore certain existential questions concerning life, death, and connection to others. In this sense, we might think of an anthropology with the elderly as, among other things, a kind of existential anthropology, exploring life lived and experienced: life as it is thought, but also as it unfolds in practice. As such, it deals explicitly with questions of how people see their lives—whether as a whole or in fragments—in relation to the world that surrounds them, and the role of stories in framing and shaping a life and crafting the wider sociality in which it is imbricated. In leading a meaningful life, what is it that people most care about, and how do they compare their cares of today to those of yesteryear? How do people deal with existential issues, and how do they come to an understanding of what makes life worth living?

A Purpose in Life: Ikigai

A central concern of this book is the complex relationship between the good life, or what it means to live well, and one's sense of meaning or purpose in life. In the Japanese context, a useful starting point for exploring this issue is the concept of *ikigai*. This can be translated as "that which makes one's life worth living," or what makes life "livable," as it were.[1] One might or might not "have" an *ikigai*—in which case the term refers to a particular motivation to live or a purpose in life. In the past, *ikigai* was related to the social value of a person's life, but since the nineteenth century the usage has changed somewhat and now incorporates a sense of happiness in life (Wada 2000). Despite this gradual shift in meaning, however, the earlier idea of social significance or sense of contribution to the larger social whole appears to have been preserved (Koyano 2009). A line from the well-known text *Ikigai ni tsuite* (About *ikigai*) captures this sentiment nicely: "People feel [that they have] *ikigai* mostly when they think that their own wishes and duties (to others) are in agreement" (Kamiya 1966, cited in Koyano 2009:23). The genealogy of the term helps to highlight the intrinsic link between happiness, meaning in life, and the fulfillment of a social role.

Interestingly, however, *ikigai* is widely seen by Japanese as problematic, or as an especially pertinent issue for certain social groups. The elderly, in particular, are seen as vulnerable in this regard.[2] Here is an excerpt from an interview I conducted with the organizer of "Ikigai Classroom," a series of one-year courses for the elderly: "In the case of the elderly, *ikigai* refers to enjoying life. . . . Young people have a stronger *ikigai*, their work or child becomes their motivation [*gendōryoku*] for life. But the elderly lose that, don't they? They retire from work, and stay at home, deal with everyday things like eating and sleeping. That's why we want to make their life more fun, enjoyable. That way they can also live longer [*nagaiki*]." The organizer's words indicate how something seemingly as personal as *ikigai* is nevertheless a matter of public concern. Run by the Department of Lifestyle of Senior Citizens, Suita City Hall, the courses offered in this particular program included calligraphy, flower arrangement, singing, and physical exercise, among many others. Elderly (over the age of sixty-five) can enter the courses but must subscribe well in advance by filling out a form, committing them to attending for a year with the same group of people. The intention is that elderly people improve their well-being by participating in a group activity. Furthermore, the structure of the course implies their commitment and responsibility, while the official purpose of the course focuses on public concern with the *ikigai* of individuals.[3]

If the *ikigai* of the elderly is seen as particularly problematic and older people are seen as vulnerable to its loss, this opens an existential question that is both personal and social. If one's role as a mother or a valued employee provides one with an *ikigai* in the form of a child or work, *ikigai* becomes an issue when one's role is unclear. Longer life expectancy means that people spend more time in what Ernest Burgess (1960) referred to as the "roleless role." *Ikigai* thus becomes a social issue, a matter of concern, when it no longer "naturally" unfolds from the social role itself. While this does not mean that the elderly have no social role to perform, it is likely that this role is changing due to economic and demographic circumstances.[4] These new circumstances mean that there are fewer models for a meaningful older age, fewer "cultural scripts" that provide a sense of older people's position in the society. The older people in Shimoichi and elsewhere, by drawing on a range of available scripts and crafting their own stories of life well lived, are at the forefront of a social change. If social change is sometimes seen as a domain of the young, the case of my older friends shows that the elderly can change that story too. One story that they were actively rewriting is that of the elderly as a burden and those who need care.

For many of my interlocutors in Shimoichi, care emerges as a central concern: care not only as a form of embodied work in support of older people, but also as an attitude, or a form of attention to others underlying social relationships between the inhabitants of Shimoichi—among neighbors and friends, and not restricted to the family or professional carers.[5] An attitude of care not only makes life possible for those it supports and nourishes, it also provides a sense of meaning for those who do the caring.[6] In this broader sense, care indexes what matters, not in the form of static or clearly delineated, abstract values alone, but through practice.

What and who one cares for is then closely related to purpose in life, sometimes considered the basis of *ikigai*. In this sense, *ikigai* can refer to a more general form of well-being and pleasure in life, especially when used in relation to the elderly. This raises certain existential questions in relation to older age: does maintaining a particular purpose in life, a well-defined source of meaning, remain possible or even necessary in older age? Indeed, do even younger people have or need such a well-defined purpose? To what extent are life stories relating to meaning and purpose in one's life related to stories of expectations and values in the broader society? In short, I argue that the issues of aging and the good and meaningful life are inextricably connected.

Companionship and Meaning

Early one afternoon in the Shimoichi Fureai salon in downtown Osaka, Kato-san shared a little story with her friends. A slim, lively lady of ninety, she had a glint in her eye as she waited patiently while everyone settled around the large wooden table with their cups of tea. "Last week," Kato-san explained, "Yamanaka-san came in and joined us here for a cup of tea. She's in good health, and delighted that her great-grandson has enrolled in university. Unfortunately, she had to return home a little early. She was feeling tired and her back ached a bit. She had these pretty white sandals with a bit of a heel. 'You know,' I told her, 'you really shouldn't wear those. Once you're past ninety, it gets harder to walk around in high heels!'"

Though her comment was not really meant as a joke, everyone around the table laughed warmly. The conversation continued and more people joined in, greeted by cheerful smiles as some of the ladies rushed to find them chairs or order tea and coffee from the salon's volunteer staff. But if Kato-san's anecdote seems light and mundane, it should not be seen as out of place in a discussion of what makes for a meaningful and good life. My interlocutors often strove for a light touch in their relationships with each other and cultivated a certain sensibility for the uneventful, which may be situated against the backdrop of hardship they suffered earlier in life. The stories people told their companions, stories such as this one, formed the beating heart of sociality in the salon. More than this, though, I hope to show, following Frank (2010), how stories are also themselves companions of a sort. They accompany people in their daily existence and their meaning-making activities. Like any companion, stories can be both good and bad, flexible and rigid, malleable or unrelenting witnesses to the way one leads one's life.

A daily routine for some, a weekly treat for others living farther away, the Fureai community salon always got particularly busy in the early afternoon, with up to twenty people gathering around two large wooden tables. Nestled away in a small townhouse in bustling Shimoichi, a downtown neighborhood in Southern Osaka, the salon was at the time of my fieldwork especially popular among the elderly living in the vicinity, and had been since its opening some two years earlier, in late 2007. I joined the salon as a volunteer and enjoyed making countless cups of coffee and tea for the visitors, while savoring the opportunity to listen to and join in their wide-ranging conversations. As already mentioned, these conversations rarely focused on topics like feeling unwell or being old, and even less frequently about death. Instead, they revolved around topics like daily news, politics, family, mutual acquaintances, plans for the following days, changes in seasons, or seasonal festivities. Like my friends in their twenties, the salon attendees could spend hours talking about the best place to buy clothes, or about a new *okonomiyaki* restaurant they had found near Dōtonbori, describing in great detail how to get there through the complicated maze of streets, alleys, shops, and bars that make up downtown Osaka. In particular, people loved to talk about food: the kinds of food they like, regional specialties they had tried while traveling, seasonal foods and dishes, restaurants and places to eat around downtown Osaka, or about eating together. At first I dismissed such talk about food as irrelevant to the larger goals of my research. Yet over the course of several months, I began to see how these seemingly mundane conversations were an essential part of a people's broader concern with what we might call "the good life." Clearly, the salon was not merely the venue for the expression of ideas about the good life but itself a central component of it. As one of my interlocutors put it: "This salon is the source of our well-being."

Related Lives

Tokuda-san was a lady in her late eighties when I met her. One cold winter's day she arrived in the salon soon after opening time, while it was still empty. She sat down at the table, and after ordering a cup of tea, she revealed to me that her husband had been hospitalized with a serious heart condition. "I am alone now. Now I live alone. Do you know, before, people used to live with their children, especially with their oldest son. But not anymore. I have two daughters, one lives in the vicinity with her family and the other lives in Kyoto. Most people coming here [i.e., to the salon] are living alone. Their husbands and wives have passed away. At least I have two daughters. At least sometimes they invite me for dinner." It became clear to me in later conversations that Tokuda-san felt that other women who had lost their husbands some time ago did not really understand her, and that made her feel isolated. She was feeling anxious: about her husband's condition, about the possibility of his death, and about her own days drawing to an end. But more than anything, she was facing the fear of loneliness.

Most people, in the course of their lives, face some existential issues; they ask themselves questions about their lives. According to the existential psychotherapist Irvin Yalom (1980), these issues include death, freedom (with its flip side, responsibility), isolation, and meaninglessness. In the Western world, most contemporary psychopathologies are centered around one of these existential anxieties and surface when they become so powerful as to appear as some other fear or problem. It is noteworthy that existential anxieties are thought to surface in relation to some major event in one's life or one related to the life course: a childbirth, a serious illness, retirement. The freedom desired so strongly by human beings refers, in existential terms, to a lack of structure and guidance, which emphasizes personal responsibility (Yalom 1980:8).[7] Certain life stages or life situations may leave one feeling an intense sense of isolation: of being left alone to deal with one's problems. This is not always a consequence of being alone, for one need not always feel lonely when alone, but it can reflect the feeling that one's values or actions are at odds with the expectations of others.

Existential anthropology can be understood as an investigation of the ways in which people try to make their lives their own in the face of adversity and constraint. Writing about such a pursuit, Michael Jackson (2005) calls for a focus on events in order to avoid perils of generalization and to attend to the interplay between the personal and the interpersonal or shared. How to go about this when nothing much seems to happen? Spending numerous hours with the people who allowed me into their lives in Osaka, very often in the welcoming space of the community salon, life appeared to proceed at quite an even pace. Here, existential dramas did not play out in the form of ruptures or discrete events, but quietly, in everyday life.

Older people living in the vicinity of the salon would often pop in for a cup of tea or coffee, but more importantly for a chat and companionship. For a first-time visitor, it can easily seem like not much is happening there: just a group of people sitting together around a table and telling stories. For an ethnographer convinced of the importance of praxis, of observing what people do and not just what they say, this can be frustrating, simply because not much "doing" seems to take place. Yet from another perspective, every narration, every story, is an event. People come to the community salon precisely because, as they themselves put it, "there is always something going on." And that "something," to a large extent, means exchanging stories. Big news stories broadcast nationally to millions of people across the country mix and interact with personal stories from the spheres of the everyday, the mundane, and the intimate. Storytelling can be entertaining, a way of passing time with others, but it can also provide an opportunity for reflection, a chance for making sense of things by relating them to other people and also to each other, to other events or happenings. *Meaning in Life* brings together the cheerful chatter of the downtown Osakan café and the silences, both solitary and shared, in the lives of older Japanese.

Links of Care

A short piece of string, with a triple loop on one end and a safety pin on another, passed hands. As she held it, a simple three-part plait, bright green and smooth, Ueda-san looked questioningly at Kato-san, unsure as to what she'd just received. Kato-san had crafted the simple device the day before after a conversation about misplacing keys: "You attach the keys to the loop and pin it inside your bag, then you can't drop them," she chuckled. More than twenty years Ueda-san's senior, she was well versed in the business of being old and a touch forgetful, but was certainly no less caring. The disposition to care ran deeply in this nonagenarian with a stubbornly positive attitude.

Beyond the institutionally organized support, care took various forms in Shimoichi, crafting ties of different kinds between people. Not limited to the family circle and kinship, nor to the institutional provision of nursing and support—both of which were undeniably important to my hosts—care was a crucial part of the creation of moral subjects in Shimoichi (Kleinman 2009). The issue of care is woven through this book, from the state-level policies and local care provision by a variety of organizations supported by the national long-term care insurance (LTCI), to the personal involvements of community members in giving care to others. The ethnography presented here reflects an abiding sense of concern for others among staff members, volunteers, and elderly salon goers. They express it through giving gifts, offering measured statements that are polite yet friendly, dropping in on each other, giving information and recommendations, taking up volunteering, and helping out in the salon, among other things. Beyond a merely practical recognition that support is necessary if people become frail, the active everyday involvement of many of these people in caring for others in their community might be seen as reflecting a more basic human trait. This *disposition of care* encapsulates acts of kindness and concern for others as well as an expectation and desire to be cared for and looked after, and includes, in the most general sense, the tendency to extend oneself toward others. In existential terms, care is intimately related to the idea of purpose in life, as these entwinements with others so often lie at the very heart of one's sense of a meaningful existence. In this sense, care is much more than the one-sided relationship of dependency that so much of the popular discourse on anxieties related to an aging society would seem to imply, and it involves a complex interplay of relationships and tendencies that must be held in balance.

Understood in this broader sense, which extends far beyond the limits of nursing care and other physical acts in the support of life, care offers a different depiction of agency of the elderly and subjectivity. My older interlocutors not only seek care or enact care for others; indeed, by crafting caring relationships in their neighborhood, they create a community of care. If care relationships are often asymmetrical, they are most noticeably so in situations of radical dependency in dyadic relationships between a carer and a person cared for. The distribution of care practices makes the debt and obligation circulate in a broader field, beyond a dyad, thus complicating the account of the reciprocity and burden of care.

Care itself reminds me of the bright green string of the key keeper—it links and is pleated from more than one interaction, more than one kind of material. Ueda-san poured tea as a volunteer for Kato-san and her friends and helped her sister find a nurse when she fell ill, while Kato-san recommended a dentist for Ueda-san's nephew and arranged for a neighbor to fix her leaking tap. At their best, links such as these are smooth, almost frictionless, crafted from small and subtle enactments of care that inevitably draw in others, opening out in numerous loops.

Chapter 2

Aging Communities

According to neighbors, the nondescript house on the riverbank in a residential area of Tokyo, surrounded by a lush wall of trees, always had the rain shutters closed. The secret that the house held was quite unexpected. Inside, in late August 2010, police discovered the mummified body of an old man, who was supposed to be 111 years old. His family, who still lived there, later confessed that he had withdrawn into his room in November 1978, saying he wanted to attain Buddhahood during life (*sokushinjōbutsu*).[1] They did not report his death, and even after his wife's death in 2004, his daughter, aged 81, continued to receive his pension. The daughter and granddaughter were arrested, and the story was widely reported in all major media outlets (e.g., *Asahi Shinbun* 2010a). The local welfare commissioner had visited the household many times since 1992, and each time she inquired about the man, she received an answer such as "he's down with a cold at the moment," or that he was at a facility for the elderly in another prefecture. When she once attempted to get the details of the institution, she was told he had returned to his old family home. After several attempts to acquire a valid address, something seemed odd and she began to suspect he had died (*Asahi Shinbun* 2010b).

In preparation for the annual celebration of the Respect for the Aged Day in late September, the municipal governments scoured their data looking for centenarians, who on this occasion receive small tokens of appreciation. For the next couple of months, while the search continued, numerous stories appeared about the unknown whereabouts of some centenarians, and there were a few morbid cases of unreported deaths and bones found in people's houses. While the efforts of welfare commissioners were appreciated, as in the case of the missing 111-year-old man (*Asahi Shinbun* 2010c), these cases raised concerns over the growing elderly population and the lack of relevant information. As one welfare commissioner usually covers an area of several hundred households, each commissioner is in charge of a growing number of elderly as a consequence of the aging population. Furthermore, according to a sample survey conducted by the Ministry of Health, Labour, and Welfare, in around 15 percent of areas the commissioners are not supplied with the personal information of the people in their jurisdiction because of concerns to protect privacy. Yet, as some pointed out, it was precisely thanks to the efforts of the welfare commissioners that the truth was uncovered in this case (*Asahi Shinbun* 2010c).

This story resonated through the media space during the last months of my research visit in 2010, but was preceded by many less bizarre but no less saddening stories of elderly people dying alone with nobody noticing for quite some time afterward. I propose that all these stories might be understood as contemporary versions of the story of Obasuteyama. This legend has many forms, but always refers to a mountain to which old relatives were taken to die. Here is a version recounted to me by a friend:

> "The time has come," a mother told her son on a cold winter evening. The son sat in silence, refusing to take note of what was said to him. "Other people of my age have already been taken, and such is the rule in the village," the mother insisted. Confronted, the next morning the son took his mother on his back to the mountain, struggling all day up steep paths and through dense shrubbery. After a long climb they reached the peak. "It will get dark soon, you must get back," said the mother, and urged her son to return. Reluctantly, the son started making his way down the mountain but soon got lost as the darkness and mist thickened. Some twigs cracked underfoot and he managed to find his bearings, realizing that his mother must have strewn some twigs on the way up to mark his way back. Moved, he could not leave his mother to die on the mountain, but instead took her home.

A longer version of this story also mentions that the local ruler set the villagers a series of tasks that they found difficult to fulfill. The man's mother suggested solutions to all the tasks, and when the man was confronted about how he could find all the solutions, he admitted that his old mother helped him. Recounting the events on the mountain, the son explained that he could not bear to leave his mother, when she cared for him so much that she left the markings for him not to get lost. "Old people may not be able to work, but their wisdom is much greater than ours," the son said to the lord, who ruled that from then on, no old people would be taken to die on the mountain again.

This version reaffirms the social role of the elderly and the need to respect them in a society founded on their wisdom rather than their economic productivity, while stressing the importance of filial duties. Other versions may not have a happy ending at all. For instance, a Noh version by Zeami tells of a woman left to die on her own in the mountain, who turned into a ghost troubled by the shame of her abandonment (Danely 2008:14). The newspaper coverage of stories about elderly dying alone and their families being unable to confirm their whereabouts may similarly be read as a warning against the mistreatment of the elderly and an admonition to treat them with respect.

The Setting: Two Neighborhoods in Kansai

My research was conducted in an urban setting in the Kansai region over a period of fourteen months from September 2009 until December 2010. Kansai or Kinki region is located on the southern side of the central part of the main island, Honshu. While the Kansai region includes Mie, Wakayama, Hyogo, Shiga, Nara, Kyoto, and Osaka, the research was conducted exclusively in the latter two prefectures. The Kansai region is one of the two most urbanized regions of Japan, the other being Kanto region (where Tokyo is situated), to which it is often compared. The city of Osaka, where the bulk of the research was conducted, has a long urban history. Already in the early modern period (sixteenth-seventeenth centuries) Osaka was one of the two largest cities and an economic center, the second largest after the capital and political center of Edo, or modern-day Tokyo (Tsukada 2012:1). It has been argued that Western and Eastern Japan (with Kyoto and Tokyo as their respective centers) have distinct cultural styles due to their different political and economic positions in history: "Comparatively, Tokyo maintains warrior-style local culture with the marks of formality, hierarchy, and face-saving, while Osaka retains a merchant lifestyle with an emphasis on practicality, informality and pragmatism" (Sugimoto 2010:65). While Japan has often been described as a "vertical" society, with a strong emphasis on hierarchy (e.g., Nakane 1970), Sugimoto (2010) draws on a number of community studies to make the case that this is more characteristic of Eastern Japan, and that relationships characterizing social life in Western Japan were somewhat less formal, hierarchical, and patriarchal, with women having comparatively higher status (than in the east), and the family having a more independent position within the local community. The majority of studies of urban Japan to date have been conducted in the Tokyo area, followed by Kyoto, two cities that are both in many way atypical in the context of Japan.[2] It has, in fact, been argued that despite a certain degree of homogeneity in Japanese mass society, regional variations play an important role in the everyday lives of Japanese (Daniels 2010).

In this light it is clear that Osaka, despite its size and importance, has been somewhat neglected in Japanese studies. Furthermore, given the fact that many more Japanese live in three-generation households in rural areas than in cities, the experiences of aging may differ considerably in rural as compared to urban settings (cf. Traphagan 2000). Despite living in a large urban center, Osakans nevertheless feel that their area is in a state of decline, with business developments and administration functions centralized in Tokyo. Many of my interlocutors' families had moved to Tokyo for work, and some mentioned the increased feeling of lack of hope and prospects, especially for the young, in Osaka. However, as an old merchant city that developed around trade, Osaka has attracted many newcomers over the course of its history, many of them in search of work. Due to the large numbers of migrants, workers, and unskilled laborers, which led to problems related to unemployment and poverty, Osaka was one of the first places where social welfare provisions emerged (see Goodman 1998:141).

The main field site was located in Shimoichi, an old merchant *shitamachi* (downtown) neighborhood in the southern part of central Osaka, south of the central area of Namba, one of the two central transport hubs and a major shopping area.[3] The neighborhood, lying south of this busy shopping and central business district, boasts its own small shopping arcade that once pulsed with activity; despite its decreasing popularity, it was still full of small shops and attended by many shoppers from the local area. The shopping arcade (*shōtengai*; Figure 1), in the very heart of the neighborhood, used to attract customers from a much larger area but was now used mostly by local elderly and housewives living nearby, as it now has to compete with several large supermarkets and convenience stores with long working hours. The shops in the arcade mostly specialize in just one kind of good, such as tofu, seaweed, meat, fish and sushi, vegetables and fruit, green tea, pottery, clothes, or small household appliances. Older people in the area often pointed out to me that they could easily compare the prices and quality of goods in different

Figure 1. Shimoichi shopping arcade (*shōtengai*) on a typical morning.
Photo by author.

shops and that they enjoyed the personal contact with the sellers, many of
whom they have known for many years. As one of the staff in the organization
running the community salon in Shimoichi, Nakajima-san, told me: "For
some elderly who live alone, the chat in the arcade is very important—on
many days they would otherwise have no reason to open their mouth to anyone." The salon that became the focal point of this research is located in the
shopping arcade in an old, refurbished shop.

The neighborhood itself has a rather old-fashioned *shitamachi* feel to it,
as many of the houses survived the World War II bombings. Some of the inhabitants had roots in the area that spanned many generations, while others
had moved there in the period immediately after World War II, when they
bought the houses that remained standing. Wide, busy roads frame an or-
thogonal grid of inner-neighborhood streets, which are very narrow and quiet

Figure 2. An older couple walking in Shimoichi. Photo by author.

with hardly any traffic. Most of these are lined with narrow-fronted two-story
family houses, a mixture of prewar wooden structures and newer, mostly pre-
fabricated ones. In recent years some larger apartment blocks were built in
the neighborhood, mostly on the large roads framing the area, close to the
underground station. The brightly lit chain cafes, supermarkets, hairdresser
salons, and ubiquitous convenience stores and high-rise concrete structures
of these large avenues stand in quite a stark contrast with the atmosphere of
the inner-neighborhood streets and alleys (Figures 2 and 3), where housewives
tend the potted plants on their doorsteps and air their futon mattresses, and
children can be seen playing in the street. The neighborhood has a very high
proportion of elderly.[4]

My interlocutors often described it as a very good area for older people
to live in, not least because the streets were quiet and flat, with the shopping
arcade in walking or cycling distance, a multitude of community links in the

Figure 3. Quiet streets in Shimoichi. Photo by author.

area, convenient transport connections, and a special free bus service for the elderly (available throughout Osaka). Finally, because of the large numbers of older people in the area the services typically required are abundant and easily accessible: physiotherapy and chiropractors, health clinics and dentists, hairdressers and stylists, shops with clothing in styles popular among older people. My older friends often pointed out that the neighborhood was indeed very convenient and easy to live in (*sumiyasui*).

My second field site figures less prominently in the ensuing chapters but informs many of my discussions and analyses as a point of comparison. It is located in a suburban neighborhood that I will refer to as Awara, in Suita, a city in Osaka Prefecture on gentle slopes just north of Osaka. The urban landscape in that area continues uninterruptedly from Osaka past the outer boundaries of the city, stretching almost without a break to Kyoto in the north and past Sakai in the south, and stretching from Kobe in the west all the way to Nara in the east. Awara is a relatively new town on the fringe of Osaka that underwent rapid development in the early 1970s. A large road passing through the middle of the neighborhood at the fringe of the town connects it to train stations on several lines, to the local center, and to Osaka. The area is hilly, and behind some larger *manshons* (condominiums or residential blocks of apartments of a higher class, built from ferroconcrete) lining the main road lies a network of small, winding streets and alleys and, surrounded by newer buildings, the old Sugiyama village, with its old-fashioned houses whose inhabitants are unused to seeing a face unknown in their parts, let alone a foreign one. On the other side of the main road, large buildings of schools, *danchi* (a large cluster of apartment buildings typically built in the 1950s, 1960s, and 1970s as public housing), *manshons*, a town hall, and a library dominate the landscape, obscuring a large and well-maintained park in the valley.

While a certain sense of local recognition and pride was exhibited by my interlocutors in Awara, the local allegiance was more to the neighborhood and local community of Awara rather than to the wider administrative unit of the city of Suita; all of my interlocutors from the area saw themselves as inhabitants of Osaka. This is unsurprising, as the good train connections allow for a quick commute to Umeda, the northern center of Osaka, in under thirty minutes on either the JR line or Hankyu line, with quick and reliable bus connections to the train station from within the neighborhood. Furthermore, as the neighborhood expanded and developed its current urban form in 1970, during and immediately after the 1970 World Expo, many of its current inhabitants moved in from other parts of Osaka and perceived it as a new satellite town for commuting. Eyal Ben-Ari (1991:15) distinguishes two kinds of suburban residential areas in Japan: the older rural centers that were integrated into larger administrative units, whose inhabitants mostly replaced agricultural pursuits with employment outside; and new housing estates (*danchi*) developed by public or private companies, whose inhabitants usually commute to white-collar jobs elsewhere. Awara combines both of these characteristics, as it was rapidly built up and expanded in the 1970s as a commuter town around an older core. The old village of Awara sits in a small but deep valley in the middle of the neighborhood, surrounded by steep hills and even higher apartment blocks (Figures 4 and 5).

Whereas Shimoichi is a part of the ward of Osaka with an above average proportion of the elderly and rather large numbers of elderly over the age of seventy-five,[5] the population of the city of Suita can be said to be aging but

Figure 4. Urban landscape in Awara: the old village in the valley and new apartment buildings on the surrounding slopes. The mass of electrical wires is not an unusual sight in residential areas of Japan. Photo by author.

not nearly as old,[6] possibly due to its status as a "new town." Many of my interlocutors in Awara suggested that a large majority of their neighbors moved in at the same time as they did, mostly as young adults, and subsequently had children. There were then two large kindergartens in the area, only one of which is still operating. The building that used to house the other is now used for communal activities, including the community salon that became my second field site. These people, who were in their twenties and early thirties in the 1970s, were recently retired or about to retire around the time of my fieldwork. Many of these young retirees were very socially active, and community activities in Awara flourished: hobby groups (including a photography club, a watercolor painting club, hula classes, a male choir, baking classes, and a local history group); a theater troupe that puts on free performances in the local temple during the summer; an abundance of voluntary organizations (nonprofit organizations, or NPOs, but also smaller, unregistered groups), such as a large group of park volunteers who maintain the local park and organize learning tours for children; a group of people in their sixties who read stories aloud to the children; a group of older people who play an instrument and visit the day care centers for the elderly in the neighborhood to play for them on a weekly basis; and a group of older men who do gardening with elementary school children on a small plot of land set aside for the purpose by the school.[7]

The citizen groups and NPOs are actively involved in the organization of traditional community events, such as the Bon dance,[8] where many set up their own stalls with refreshments as a way of raising money for other activities, and a local festival organized by the local community association and the voluntary fire brigade. While many of my interlocutors said they were aware of the distinction between the old and the new Awara, the newcomers are so numerous and active in community activities that they did not feel marginalized. As I did not have an opportunity to speak to any of the inhabitants of the old Awara village, I have little insight into their perspective. Many of the citizen groups and voluntary organizations in the neighborhood make one of their aims to "build a community" and "make Awara a pleasant place to live" by creating connections in the neighborhood, and to help people who have moved to the area to settle in and feel at home. Having themselves once been newcomers to the area, many of my interlocutors implied that they knew what this meant and made a particular point of being welcoming.

A new generation of younger families with small children moved to the area after some large, new apartment blocks (*manshon*) were built in recent years, providing relatively affordable accommodation as compared to central Osaka. Inoue-san, a young mother in her early thirties, told me how much she liked living in Awara, where there were many parks and lots of greenery and the streets were quiet and safe. She and her husband used to rent a place near Osaka Castle, in the center, which was very convenient for commuting and rather fun when they used to go out. But things changed when their daughter was born; suddenly, Inoue-san felt somewhat lonely as there were few mothers with children in the area, and at times she felt unsafe taking her daughter for a walk in the pram, past all the homeless living in the park and the often rowdy youth walking the streets in the evenings. She told me she feels that Awara is a much better place for them to live in, with its lively community and greenery, and they even managed to rent a small allotment from the municipal government and spend their weekends growing vegetables

Figure 5. The old village of Awara, surrounded by hills and high-rise apartment buildings (*manshons*). Photo by author.

as a family, socializing with other families and older people, who use the municipal facilities for a very small, symbolic fee.

From Inoue-san's description one might imagine a suburban dream, and while this is perhaps true to an extent, this is not a typical quiet suburban idyll as a Western observer might imagine it. While there are some small detached houses in the neighborhood, many of these young families live in enormous high-rise structures over ten stories high and containing hundreds of apartments, often with an small enclosed inner yard. The apartments are often finished to a high standard and are relatively spacious, with good views (especially from the higher floors). This makes for rather efficient high-density living, though to an unaccustomed observer the sheer size of these buildings and the numbers of apartments may seem disconcerting (see a high-rise structure in the background in Figure 5). The heavy traffic on the main roads, lack of space for lawns and gardens, as well as the footpaths in many of the narrower streets in the neighborhood make it seem less friendly for small children, who cannot often be seen playing in the streets as they do in Shimoichi.

Furthermore, *manshons* with many inhabitants are seen to change the nature of social relationships in the neighborhoods, as it becomes more difficult to know most of one's neighbors' faces. Saito-san, a young woman in her thirties, told me that even in Shimoichi, where the majority of the houses are still old-fashioned, small townhouses, parents are becoming more reluctant to let their children play outside without supervision. In the past, almost everyone knew which child is from which house, and neighbors were able to look after them merely by glancing through their kitchen windows. This different mode of neighborly life was commented upon by Yamada-san, a tall and handsome lady in her early sixties. Like many other older people whose children have moved out of their homes, Yamada-san and her husband moved from their larger house into a smaller apartment in a nearby *manshon*. This allowed them to save some money for later life, in case they might need care when they get older, and made housekeeping easier, while staying in the same familiar area. Yamada-san told me that compared to her previous house, it was much harder to meet her neighbors in the massive *manshon*, where she shared a staircase with dozens of other families. While high-rise structures and large new developments with many newcomers with few links to the area undoubtedly have an impact on the local community, it would be facile to draw a conclusion that the rise of the *manshon* is a sign of community decline. Indeed, the case of Awara with its unusually vibrant community life and large number of volunteer-run activities, clubs, and classes, encouraged and supported by the local authorities, may offer insight into the life of communities beyond the traditional village model.[9]

In this respect, Awara is perhaps similar to Hieidaira and Yamanaka, two communities in Kansai region described by Ben-Ari (1991). Ben-Ari contrasts the "breakdown of community" approach (where ties of loyalty and cooperation are dissolved as a consequence of processes of modernization) with the "transfer of community" approach (1991:4–7), associated with the "group" model of Japanese society (see, e.g., Nakane 1970), which posits that people interact within a hierarchically organized group within which there is a strong emphasis on harmony and loyalty to a leader, which the latter repays by benevolence and care. According to the latter approach, loyalty to the local community gets transferred to the company, while local ties become shallow and lose importance. Ben-Ari suggests that both of these models capture something important about social changes in recent history, acknowledging

Figure 6. A shopping center in the newer part of Awara, built in the 1970s.
Photo by author.

that "there is no doubt that Japanese communities in the 1970s and 1980s are 'weaker'—i.e. less integrated, less capable of collective action" (Ben-Ari 1991:8). Yet he calls for a different approach, one which examines different modes for community action and collaboration that may have emerged in these new contexts. In the case of Awara, it could therefore be argued that the citizens' groups and voluntary associations in the neighborhood complemented and to an extent replaced the older community networks and ties based on personal acquaintance with one's neighbors in the street and quarter.[10]

A Close-Up: Two Community Salons

The bulk of my research was conducted in the community salon in Shimoichi, which as I have discussed is located in an old townhouse in the shopping arcade, managed by a small NPO that I will refer to as NPO Fureai.[11] The community salon functions as a space open to everyone, with a couple of large wooden tables seating at least six, but often many more as spare seats are brought when more people wish to join. It resembles a coffee shop, with a salon volunteer always present to serve a hot drink, but differs in at least four respects. First, the prices are kept low, as the cost of the venture is covered by other activities run by the NPO and the volunteers are unpaid. Second, one can stay as long as one wishes, and this is indeed encouraged by the policy of not charging for any second servings of drinks and allowing people to bring their own lunch. Third, it is not unusual to see guests chatting freely regardless of whether or not they know each other, unlike in a café, where one is usually expected to converse only with people one has previously arranged to meet. Finally, the community salon was created mostly with older people from the neighborhood in mind, although it is open to all and some younger people visit occasionally. Most of the salon visitors are in their seventies, eighties, or even early nineties, which makes it a very convenient location for fieldwork with older people who live in their own homes rather than in an institution such as a nursing home.

I found the NPO Fureai with the help and support of the staff of the Osaka volunteer information center, who introduced me officially to the NPO staff after conducting an interview with me and asking for further details about my research over the course of a couple of weeks. The process may have been somewhat protracted, but they found an extremely well-matched NPO for my project and supported my case with initially somewhat reluctant Komatsu-san from NPO Fureai. After the initial interview for the volunteer position at the salon, at which I was accompanied not only by the young lady who helped me find the NPO but also her superior, Komatsu-san's concerns about the ability of a foreigner to help in the salon were dispelled and I was warmly accepted and supported in all my endeavors in the NPO and the salon.

I volunteered in the salon twice a week and visited on other days, which provided me with an opportunity to meet older people in the neighborhood and listen to their conversations. The salon volunteers are not treated by the customers like waiting staff in a commercial enterprise but rather like a member who happens to be on duty and could at other times be a guest herself, as they often are—arriving earlier or staying after their shift, or just dropping by for a hot drink. As a consequence, like the other volunteers, I was often encouraged by the guests to sit with them at their table and join the conversation. I was therefore able to participate in conversations, sometimes leading them in a particular direction of interest, or just asking for clarification, but I was also in a position to listen unobtrusively to peoples' conversations as they spontaneously unfolded. At first, my presence there was very noticeable and was itself a frequent topic of a conversation, but as time passed most customers grew accustomed to my presence and did not pay me much attention, other than upon my arrival (just like anyone else's, I should remark—most familiar faces were greeted very loudly and cheerfully). Finally, I was also able to conduct several one-on-one interviews with some of the salon customers and volunteers and to collect six life stories, typically in a series of consecutive interviews. These interviews took place outside the salon, either in the homes of my interlocutors, if they invited me, or in a quiet, secluded room in the office space above the salon, and once in a quiet neighborhood café. I also had the opportunity to talk to the NPO staff on many occasions and to interview all of them.

The salon in Awara, my secondary field site, was established by the local authorities in a building that used to house a kindergarten, which closed due to a decline in the number of children of kindergarten age. The local authorities assigned the building for community use, and its numerous rooms can be rented for meetings and classes, while the management of the building is entrusted to a volunteer group. The largest room on the ground floor, facing the inner courtyard, was assigned to the community salon, also managed by volunteers. As mentioned earlier, Awara is a community with an unusually vibrant social life and a large number of volunteer-run activities, clubs, and classes, encouraged and supported by the local authorities. This is reflected in the structure and membership of the salon: there are around fifty active volunteers, approximately two-thirds of them female and one-third male. Men were reluctant to serve hot drinks but were encouraged to help with organizing woodwork classes or to offer handyman services to the members. On all occasions when I visited (twenty times over the course of six months) volunteers made up roughly half the visitors to the salon. Many of these volunteers mentioned that they felt like joining the salon, not merely visiting it, as it gave them more opportunities for involvement. Initially I came as a visitor myself, introducing myself as a researcher to the volunteers and soon having a chance to talk to the organizers and interview them. This was followed by an informal chat with other volunteers and guests present, and after the volunteers posted a photograph of me in their online newsletter (a blog they jointly edited), I found that most volunteers and frequent visitors knew who I was before I even had a chance to introduce myself. One busy afternoon I was asked if I would be interested in helping out as a volunteer, which I happily accepted, and I had the opportunity to help out on several occasions.

The visitors to Awara salon are mostly in their sixties, several in their seventies and fifties, and a few are young mothers with small children. The group in charge of running the Awara salon is not registered as an NPO, but as they are directly responsible to the local authorities who established the community salon they have a large burden of paperwork, including a meticulous daily count of all visitors to the salon categorized by age and gender.

Overall, the demographic and spatial characteristics of the communities and the way the salons were organized under the direction of the local governments made for the largest differences between the respective salons, including the settings, events and activities organized, users, and volunteers. With more *manshons* being constructed, large numbers of newcomers are coming to Awara. The salon explicitly targets newcomers by offering a place to make acquaintances in the community, get advice informally about local amenities, and the like. Via the salon one can participate in local festivals, such as Bon Odori or Summer Festival, thus creating a bridge toward the more traditional local associations. Most of the volunteers in the Awara salon moved to the area in the 1970s and are therefore well aware of newcomer issues. They try to make the community appear open and welcoming and make an effort to inform people who recently moved to the area about their activities as well as other events and local facilities. The details of the community salon as a place to find out more about local events and facilities are available on the internet, through leaflets in the local municipal office, posters in the library, and the internet page of Suita City Hall.

Over the course of fieldwork I managed to obtain a considerable amount of relevant background information in a variety of ways. For example, I attended public lectures and seminar series related to aging, well-being and *ikigai*, care for the elderly, and housing options for the elderly, mostly organized by municipal authorities or local NPOs; I conducted interviews with some of the seminar attendees and organizers, as well as with city hall officials in charge of welfare of the elderly. Finally, an additional but very welcoming and fruitful field site that I regularly attended was a women's discussion group in the Kansai region (in a town on the southern outskirts of Kyoto), attended by approximately twenty women aged between forty-five and seventy. Many of these women, it turned out, cared for aging family members. I was introduced to the group through a mutual friend, and the group members immediately accepted my presence in a warm and friendly manner. In addition to participating in their weekly discussions and more informal conversations over lunch after each discussion session, I conducted semistructured interviews with all the regular members of this group.

As anyone who has conducted ethnographic research in an urban setting will be well aware, it can be difficult to maintain the sustained contact required for creating the rapport and participant observation that are among the primary characteristics of in-depth ethnography. One way of counteracting this problem is to find more or less bounded groups one can visit on a regular basis, something both of the salons and the women's discussion group provided for me over the course of my fieldwork. In a highly literate, industrialized society like Japan, with an incredibly high circulation of texts in newspapers, books, magazines, pamphlets, and brochures, it is impossible to ignore the content available to most people in this form. While I have not undertaken systematic and large-scale content analysis of any one of these sources, I have attempted to provide relevant background to the discussions in the chapters that follow by quoting newspaper stories or outlining the information provided in newsletters and brochures available to my interlocutors. Without doubt, written media are not the only relevant sources of information in Japan, and radio and television have an important place in the lives of many of my interlocutors. Nevertheless, due to time constraints I have not followed the content in either of them systematically, judging that my time was better spent talking to people and attending events rather than watching TV at home.

This may be a good place to comment on my decision to change the names of all of these organizations in spite of the good work they are doing and the recognition they deserve. I considered asking for permission to publish the names of these organizations, and after having received such a high degree of support and cooperation in all of them I was relatively confident that permission would be granted.[12] I spent a lot of time in informal conversation with many members and obtained insights into many of their private matters, which was invaluable for a deeper understanding of the issues discussed in this work. All of these organizations were small, and if their names were published it would be very easy to find out who the individual members were even if I changed their names. I have therefore changed the names of all the persons involved as well as of the organizations and neighborhoods, as even specifying the name of the neighborhood would make finding the organization very easy.

The Socialization of Care: Long-Term Care Insurance

Efforts within these neighborhoods to rekindle community feelings and establish new networks of support should be seen against a backdrop of a widespread feeling of weakening community ties. With changing demographic situations, the ability of families to care for all their aging members has declined over the years. One major response by the government to this perceived weakening of community ties and the limited capacities of families to care for the elderly was the introduction in 1997 of long-term care insurance (LTCI) (*kaigo hoken*), which went into effect in April 2000. As the beneficiaries (depending on their needs) are all those above the age of sixty-five, this includes all of my older Shimoichi and Awara interlocutors. Furthermore, the organization of which the Shimoichi salon is a part provides some of the services covered by LTCI, which in turn funds the expenses of running the salon and organizing other activities. Finally, as will become apparent in the ensuing discussion of the system itself, by providing rather extensive support for the elderly through a variety of providers (public and private, making it possible for the older people in need of support to avoid full institutionalization or total reliance on the family), LTCI has important consequences for the conceptualizations of independence among older people. In view of the above, a brief overview of this (admittedly somewhat complicated) system and its characteristics provides important background for the discussions to follow.

The Japanese program is considered to be the largest and most radical compulsory long-term care insurance program in the world. This is considered unexpected given previous welfare developments and the reliance on family care (Campbell and Ikegami 2000:27), as sometimes implied by the term "Japanese-style welfare state." The change was not as sudden as it may seem, as it followed a series of measures in the 1990s that supported the increased use of public professional services, in a transition away from an exclusively private, family-based care for the elderly (Robb Jenike 2003:178). What was the reasoning behind the change of attitude? According to the Ministry of Health and Welfare, the aim was "to establish a system which responds to society's major concern about aging, the care problem, whereby citizens can be assured that they will receive care and be supported by a society as a whole" (Ministry of Health Labour and Welfare 2002:1). The creation of LTCI is, therefore, a move toward the socialization of care, which is argued to be necessary in light of social changes: the lengthening and the degree of seriousness of care for elderly people, the aging of caregivers, the declining proportion of elderly people living with their children, and an increase in the number of working women.[13]

Despite such convincing arguments and visible pressures, some authors point out that there was curiously little debate over the cost of such a system before the LTCI law was passed in 1997. John C. Campbell and Naoki Ikegami (2000, 2003) emphasize that the introduction of this system should be understood in its historical context, with the first large financial commitment for long-term care services embodied in the so-called Gold Plan in 1989, which came at the time of an economic boom. This program grew rapidly to respond to increasing demand and was followed up by an expanded New Gold Plan of 1994, introduced at a time when the government was trying to stimulate the economy with large-scale spending. Concerns over budget pressures eventually surfaced, but LTCI was planned as a system with its own revenues (Campbell and Ikegami 2003:23).[14] Debates about the shape the system should take primarily concerned the services to be provided and whether it should provide cash allowances for family care. The latter suggestion was opposed by welfare professionals, who called for a rapid expansion of formal services, which could only take place if the demand was high, and by officials who pointed out that everyone eligible would be likely to apply regardless of need, thus increasing the need for extensive financing soon after the introduction (Campbell and Ikegami 2003:30). Perhaps most interestingly, many feminists argued that "the allowance would just go into the family budget, and family caregivers would continue to be exploited" (Campbell and Ikegami 2003:30), a criticism that seemed to have a serious effect on the final decision.

So, how does the LTCI system work? The beneficiaries (everyone aged sixty-five years or older, and persons aged forty or older with an age-related disability) apply to their municipal government, the officials of which assess the level of care needed using a standardized questionnaire entered into a computer system and confirmed by the physician in charge. The levels of needs initially identified five levels of care (yōkaigo) (ranging from level one for minimal care to level 5 for maximum care) and one level of support (yōshien) for the independent elderly in need of assistance (Ministry of Health, Labour and Welfare 2002). This later changed to four levels of care and two lower levels of support. The benefits (in year 2000) ranged from JPY 61,000 to 358,000 per month (roughly USD 560-3,260) (Campbell and Ikegami 2000:33). For community-based care (such as home helpers, visiting nurses, and day care) the beneficiaries can choose the provider and draw up a care plan with the help of a care manager (Campbell and Ikegami 2003:22). The insurance is financed by premiums (which are mandatory for all citizens aged forty or above), copayments for the services by the users (a fixed amount of 10 percent), and from general revenues (50 percent national, 25 percent each from municipalities and prefectures; Campbell and Ikegami 2000:31).

The LTCI system is based on the provision of formal services, and cash allowances were not included. The insurance covers services both in the home and in institutions, which include "long-term facilities for the elderly, day-centres, respite care facilities, visiting nurse stations, home-help services, care houses, housing for assisted living, and group homes for dementia patients" (Coulmas 2007:68). The range of services allows for a more flexible way of meeting the needs for care than under the previous system, which was fo-cused on the home or a hospital, and proved to be very costly, too, while pro-viding a high level of care for many (Coulmas 2007:67–68). Campbell and Ikegami list several important aspects and aims of the new system: "(1) shift a major responsibility for care-giving from the family to the state; (2) inte-grate medical care and social services via unified financing; (3) enhance consumer choice and competition by allowing free choice of providers, in-cluding even for-profit companies; (4) require older persons themselves to share the costs via insurance premiums as well as co-payments; and (5) expand local government autonomy and management capacity in social policy . . . leading to a major expansion of community based care" (2000:31). My inter-locutors generally had a rather positive view of the support provided by LTCI but also pointed to some problems with the scheme. The volunteers and staff at NPO Fureai were convinced that the potential of increased cost of the system will lead to stricter screenings and that it will be harder to get the ser-vices covered. Some of my older interlocutors with little income found the cost high when more services were needed, as individuals are expected to con-tribute 10 percent of the overall cost; if they needed to move to a care facility, the cost would be very high compared to their low incomes or small savings. As the majority of the salon visitors were in good health they were rarely en-titled to the care element of LTCI, but most of them qualified for support levels and could use the entitlements to cover most of the cost of home help-ers once or twice a week, who would come and tidy around the house. Ikeda-san once told a group of other ladies how she stopped using the service as she and her sister would spend the whole morning tidying before the arrival of the helper, as they found it too embarrassing to have a stranger enter their house when it was less than tidy, even though they knew well it was the helper's role to do the cleaning. Some of the ladies laughed and remarked that they often feel the same way. One lady wearing bright pink lipstick and a colorful blouse then said how she liked having all the help she could get, as that freed up the time for her to do other things. In order to get the highest possible entitlement, on the morning of the visit of the person who was supposed to asses her needs, she "forgot" to put on her clothes, to brush her hair, and to put away her bedding, and opened the door in her nightgown. She advised the others that making sure not to apply any makeup and appearing a little confused was the best way of getting many hours of help at home. Other ladies disagreed, however—as they commented afterward, when the lady in question left—but merely softly remarked how they prefer not to allow strangers into their homes. This issue was a real concern for many, but in general the impression of the support offered through LTCI was rather positive.

Tsui No Sumika: The "Final Abode"

In the context of the family changes touched on above, it may be unsurprising that there is an increasing number of elderly living alone or with their partner rather than in the three-generation household.[15] The data from a national survey indicates that older people living alone have more concerns regarding their health, care issues, loneliness, and finances (Cabinet Office 2009:7). In other words, one need not be frail to feel uneasy about living on one's own, and the decline in one's abilities makes this feeling even more acute. This is a situation in which many older people look for a suitable housing solution with an appropriate level of support and care. The new welfare framework under LTCI allowed for a diversification of care and support arrangements, or "solutions," by covering services in the public, private, and not-for-profit sectors. This provides important background for understanding the living conditions of my interlocutors in Shimoichi, and for understanding the issues of autonomy and dependency.

The feature theme of the March 2010 issue of the magazine *Consumer Information* (*Shōhisha johō*) is entitled "*Tsui no sumika*" or "final abode." It deals with the question of how to choose a "comfortable" and "appropriate" place to spend one's final years and runs through various housing options for the elderly. It implies that the place one chooses will be a place one can comfortably stay in, a solution to one's problems. While the term "final abode" has a strangely spiritual ring to it, it is not unusual to see it used in the context of addressing a mundane matter of housing.[16] At the same time, the proliferation of kinds of supported housing for the elderly in Japan makes the decision about where to move a difficult one to navigate.

However, most of my interlocutors in Shimoichi (and some in Awara) had lived in the same place for many years and had not considered moving, as they valued highly their links in the neighborhood and had come to rely on them. Kato-san, a cheerful ninety-year-old lady, lives in a narrow two-story prewar townhouse in a small alley branching off from the shopping street, together with her younger sister, Ikeda-san, who moved in after she had fallen ill. At the front of the lower story there is a small kitchen and dining space, which leads to a narrow four-and-a-half-tatami[17] room that houses a large wardrobe, and this room leads to a larger eight-tatami room with a low table and two low armchairs and a TV, and a refurbished fitted bathroom. (The bathroom had been fitted a decade ago, though the sisters still often prefer to visit the public bath around the corner, which they find more sociable and much warmer than their small bathroom.) The second story houses two large bedrooms, one at the front and one at the back of the house, with a couple of small rooms filled with large chests of drawers full of kimonos, and a couple of Western-style wardrobes. Despite the narrow staircase, the sisters have no problems walking up and down the stairs, and their neighbor, Murata-san, helps them with small repairs around the house and by taking out the trash twice a week.

Some of the salon goers live in similar houses in the neighborhood with their families, as does Sato-san, who lives with her son and grandchildren, for whom she frequently prepares meals and makes cakes. Other houses have been newly built on old plots of land, and some of these have been designed to house two generations in two separate apartments within the same house. This type of housing, called *nisetai jūtaku* (two-generation housing), has become popular for practical reasons, including high land prices and because it offers the possibility for mutual support (Brown 2003).[18] These housing types are not the new options presented to the elderly as a solution for their "final abode" and are, in fact, the first and only family house in which my interlocutors have lived over the course of their adult life, rather than a separate place to which they have moved for the final stages of their life. Nevertheless, these new housing options are there on offer, and for many other elderly they may provide a chance for pursuing independent living, with some organized support. In this sense, housing options provide an important background to discussions of the category of the elderly and issues of autonomy and dependency, so crucial to many of my interlocutors' understandings of their lives.

Okuma-san, a white-haired lady who wears sporty polo shirts and slacks, lives on her own in a rented *manshon* flat. She used to rent elsewhere in the neighborhood in a smaller apartment block, but that had to be demolished and she was relocated to the big apartment block just a few steps from one end of the shopping arcade, on a corner of a warmly lit pedestrian street lined with small shops. While most regular salon goers vaguely know where others live, they do not know their precise address but rather speak in terms of areas ("on a corner near the post office," or "in the alleyway past a hairdresser, but not as far as the futon store"). This meant that when Okuma-san did not show up in the salon for a while and Kato-san wanted to check up on her, she found the large apartment block but had no idea which entrance gate or which apartment it would be, and the downstairs gate was firmly locked. The benefit of Okuma-san's new accommodation included a concierge service on the ground floor, meaning that there was always someone she could call for help by pressing an emergency button in her apartment (in case she felt suddenly ill, for instance). The concierge and the locked front door also meant that not everyone could come in easily, which was an added safety benefit. Nevertheless, what was advertised as an important security point in the housing seminars also meant a degree of separation from the neighborhood networks of informal support. In short, while many of my interlocutors in Shimoichi continued to live in their own houses where they have spent much of their lives, this was in part made possible by more or less formal networks of support in the neighborhood.

Finally, many of my interlocutors who lived on their own had the material means of moving into one of these supported housing options, as most owned their own houses, which they could presumably sell. If they were aware of supported housing (some of them may well not know about it, even though information is abundant, or precisely because so much information about all kinds of things is surrounding them) and yet continued to live in their own houses in their neighborhood, the explanation for this gives some indication as to the kind of life that is considered preferable. First, it should be noted that an overwhelming majority of my Shimoichi interlocutors were in good health and almost entirely capable of living on their own (most of them qualifying for support but not care, according to long-term care insurance criteria, "support" referring to two of the lower levels of LTCI). Second, the choice to continue living in the neighborhood, or even lack of interest in other options (at least so long one is not forced to contemplate issues of nursing care), would indicate the high value placed on the social relations one has built in the neighborhood, as well as emotional attachment to place and the functioning support network in the area. The NPO running the community salon lies at the heart of one such support network, comprising a variety of formal and informal relationships.

Chapter 3

Mutual Help

It is a cold, crisp, sunny morning in February. I am walking from the underground station toward the community salon where I have been volunteering since November. I walk down the wide road lined with tall buildings and large apartment houses (*manshon*) and dotted with glossy new shops: a large, brightly lit supermarket on the corner; a convenience store with an ATM; a shiny, stylish hair salon; a bakery selling French-style bread and pastries; a shop with high-tech toilet seats, air conditioners, rice cookers, and other small electric appliances. As I turn into the small streets just off the main road, the surroundings change radically. Most of the buildings are small, old family houses sitting close together. The streets are quiet and few cars pass by. A group of children are laughing as they play with a ball in an alley. A small three-wheel truck passes by with the driver announcing through a megaphone that that he is collecting old paper. The farther I walk into the narrow streets, the less traffic but more activity there is to be seen on the streets. A young woman is hanging out the bedding on her small balcony to air; an old lady is repotting the plants on the curb of the road in front of her house; a young man and his son are washing the family car. I finally enter the shopping arcade (*shōtengai*) in which the salon is located—a narrow, roofed street lined with small shops. There are a few older shoppers buying vegetables, but some shopkeepers are still busying themselves with preparations for their first customers of the day.

Many of the shopkeepers are elderly: a short, sturdy lady with her hair dyed black in the dry goods shop with a darkened, dusty interior; a delicate, white-haired lady in the shop selling tea leaves—a particularly charming old-fashioned wooden shop, not unlike the Edo-period replicas in the Osaka Housing Museum: the same dusty, cramped space with large wooden boxes with goods and containers with tea on rough wooden shelves, dimly lit with just one bare light bulb. A few steps farther, I pass a brightly neon-lit bookshop, neat but overflowing, owned by an old couple in their early seventies who are listening to the radio and doing sudoku. A fishmonger with a sushi stand attached, recently refurbished, is run by a relatively young married couple, and their produce sells steadily throughout the day. A lively old man standing outside a shop with ladies clothing is cheerfully greeting all passersby. His goods are all carefully arranged on hangers and hooks outside the shop: rows of jackets in subdued colors; comfortable trousers with elastic waistbands, of the kind that the older ladies in the salon often sported with floral blouses; and dozens of sensible hats, warm and pretty. A few doors farther down on the other side of the arcade, two middle-aged ladies are making *okonomiyaki* and *takoyaki*[1]—Osaka street-food favorites—on one of the stands where visitors to the salon would often buy boxed lunches, alternating between sushi, steamed rice with vegetables, and *okonomiyaki*, and occasionally buying instant noodles from the supermarket when the shops were closed on Wednesdays.

As I slide open the door of the salon with a greeting, a chorus of lively voices replies cheerfully. I step inside and see Saito-san, a young volunteer in a pretty yellow skirt, listening politely to the conversation at one of the two large tables seating guests in the salon. In the background I hear the barely audible regular buzz of a photocopier emanating from the office above the salon. Kato-san and her younger sister are cheerfully chatting to Abe-san. Two small children stop to look at the ornate dolls displayed in the window for the upcoming Hina Matsuri,[2] much to the delight of the older guests in the salon. Kato-san rushes to the door and beckons them in for a cup of tea. The children and their mother enter somewhat hesitantly, encouraged by nine smiling older faces and loud greetings, followed by a commotion to find them three seats on the same side of one of the two big wooden tables. Only after their coffee was served did they have a chance to look around the warmly lit interior with its exposed wooden beams, just large enough to accommodate up to twenty people around the tables, with additional chairs lined up against the walls on left and right, and a small kitchen counter and a toilet in the back of the salon, which was once a fish shop. The children found a small wooden shelf at the back where various crafts, including colorful origami, were on display, and before long a packet of colored paper appeared on the table. Suddenly everyone seemed to be making paper dolls for the young visitors, chatting casually to their mother.

By the time I started work there, the salon had won recognition in the local neighborhood as a place to enjoy a conversation or just a quiet morning in the company of others. It began operations in late 2007 as a part of Fureai, an NPO established in early 1995.[3] After years of running its services, including a volunteer home-helper system, from the founders' own apartments and from rented rooms, it now had an office and a space for community activities. The salon gradually emerged as both a place and a social network: a physical site as well as an ideological project of community help and mutual support.

While voluntary activities in the community have usually been discussed in relation to the state, its responsibility, and intervention in the voluntary sphere (see, e.g., Avenell 2010), and the influence of the government agenda on the opinions of Shimoichi welfare workers and volunteers should not be underestimated, this chapter instead focuses on the perspective of volunteers who established Fureai and their concern with the well-being of others. These volunteers, now managing the NPO (and referring to themselves as staff), are well educated, highly reflective, and very aware of the wider societal context, including trajectories of demographic change, the deficiencies of the medical system and care services, and the atomization and perceived decline of community ties. This sets them apart from other volunteers, with whom they nevertheless share some motivations.

"Helping and Being Helped"

Nakajima-san was involved in establishing Fureai from the very outset. She told me the story of its early days:

> It all started sixteen years ago. At that time, in 1994, there was no long-term care insurance system in Japan, and the local administration had just started a program of support visits to households in need of help [e.g., looking after a sick child while the parents had to go to work, looking after a sick relative or an older person, etc.]. The level of support provided in this way was quite low, and it was difficult to get an immediate response; for instance one family whose grandfather suddenly became bedridden applied for help, since they were finding it hard to balance out all the other obligations with full-time care. They waited for two years, and finally a letter arrived from the government saying they'd been allocated a helper a few weeks after the grandfather had passed away. This was quite terrible, of course, and some of us started thinking about what we could do to help somewhat. We

were thinking of help by fellow citizens [*shimin dōshi*], a form of mutual help [*tasukeai*]—healthy people could help those who needed support in times of trouble, and the people who had a hard time, if they got better in future, could do some . . . volunteering themselves. We were wondering if there was something like that we could do.

Around that time, Hotta Tsutomu-san appeared in a television talk show program called *Tetsuko's Room*, by the well-known actress Kuroyanagi Tetsuko. Hotta-san talked about the Sawayaka Welfare Foundation [Sawayaka Fukushi Zaidan] and proposed the creation of mutual help [*tasukeai*] in every neighborhood, calling out to the people suggesting that if everyone does this then the creation of a costly system funded by taxes won't be necessary. Komatsu-san, a lady who now sometimes volunteers in the salon, had watched this program and thought that it would be good if people in the neighborhood would do such a thing. She was involved at the local Parent-Teacher Association (PTA) in my children's primary school, where I was serving on a committee, when she brought up this topic and asked what we thought about it. We thought of it as a challenge and decided to give it a go. We started a learning group, at first some forty-two of us gathered to find out more about the mutual-help system and establishing an organization. In Tokyo there were several organizations involved in mutual help since about thirty years ago, fifteen years before we started, so we organized a visit to a branch of one of those organizations in the Kansai area. I wanted to find out more about the good aspects of the system and the parts we might want to do differently, and by cobbling those bits and pieces together we started Shimoichi Fureai, this NPO. By then, it was not all forty-two of us who participated in the learning group, but nine of us. The nine of us gathered at Komatsu-san's place, where we rented a room on the second floor. After we had our phone line sorted out, we started our activities on the thirtieth of May, sixteen years ago.

Over the past sixteen years, NPO Fureai has engaged in a wide variety of activities: starting with a volunteer project (*tasukeai*, mutual help), later developing a home-helper service registered as a care provider under the long-term care insurance system; collaborating with other institutions in the field and supporting some of their projects; up to opening a community salon and activities in the neighborhood in 2007. I will now briefly describe the content of these various projects and the actors involved. I will then present the main characters of the story of the salon—the members of staff of the organization—and the story of their involvement and how it influenced their lives and ways of thinking.

NPO Development, Structure, and Activities

Tasukeai: Mutual Help

The organization started its volunteer activities in 1995 under the banner of tasukeai, or mutual help. Tasukeai is a volunteer system based on Hotta 's idea of creating networks of exchange in local areas through exchanging coupons for small-scale volunteer help with things like household cleaning, cooking, or looking after children; helping with the commute to the hospital for a check-up; or tending to a garden. Many of my interlocutors have heard Hotta speak on the television, and some of the NPO staff members have read about his work—it was the story that inspired them to start up the NPO. The proposed system is simple: members register with the local organization, pay an annual registration fee, and gain the right to use the services and provide them. The coupons—worth 300 yen for half an hour—are purchased in advance, and volunteers can themselves exchange them for services or for money. Bookings are made per hour, with two additional coupons for transport expenses. The organization does not charge additional expenses for overhead or for coordinating the users and volunteers, apart from a small annual fee. The users and the volunteers are treated in an equal manner, even if their equivalence, or interchangeability, was more a theoretical possibility or a normative ideal than practice. After the Tasukeai system gained momentum, various kinds of people joined up, from young mothers in their early thirties whose children had just started kindergarten, to much older people. While the majority of the volunteers are housewives, there are also people working part-time or with jobs that permit other involvement (for instance, one school teacher helps out during the school holidays), who volunteer in the afternoons or on weekends.

Anyone who wishes to become a member must call up the office and arrange a time for a staff member to visit them at home for a short interview. They are informed about the details of the services, and after registering they are carefully matched to a volunteer and are entitled to make their appointments by telephone. The users of the services are either the elderly or young people who need someone to mind their child for a short while. These days there are around ten regular users of volunteer help services and several more who are registered. In some cases, older people who are hospitalized need some help, as long-term care insurance does not cover helper support during their stay in the hospital. They may need laundry done, for example, or small shopping services, if they have no family members who could assist them.[4] Furthermore, older people sometimes book services not covered by the long-term care insurance home helpers: tidying the garden or cleaning rooms they are not using personally, or doing their spouse's laundry. Some people feel uneasy about going to the hospital on their own and, if they have no one else, ask for a volunteer to accompany them.

At the time of my fieldwork *tasukeai* had just ten active volunteers, though there were many more on the register. There are times when they are too busy and have to decline requests from users, which they do if it is not an emergency. In the event of an emergency—for instance, if someone living on their own suddenly falls ill, or having returned from hospital feels weak and needs some food—rather than trying to find an available volunteer, the staff members rush to their aid.[5] At the peak of their volunteer activities Fureai had up to ten bookings a day and such things would happen on a weekly basis. According to the NPO records, they had accumulated 38,000 paid volunteer hours by September 2007. These days they have one or two time slots booked a day, as the number of users and the hours they book has decreased significantly over the years. The main reason for this is the introduction of the long-term care insurance (LTCI) system. According to Kuroki-san, another member of staff, the situation has changed considerably due to economic circumstances putting a strain on family budgets:

As you know, we had a recession here in Japan for the last ten or twenty years. As soon as their children are old enough to go to school, many women start working, looking for paid employment to supplement their husband's income. Also, from the users' perspective, since the introduction of long-term care insurance the economic burden of getting a helper through the insurance system is somewhat lighter than asking for a paid volunteer to come over. Among volunteers, whoever could get a helper certificate did that, in the hope of earning a little money. Some of those who started working as helpers stayed with us, and some moved to other organizations. Therefore, those who are left are mostly women in their sixties and seventies. . . . In terms of content, they only provide support with things they can do. Before the establishment of LTCI, volunteers not infrequently did things that helpers now do—changing diapers for bedridden people, or wiping the body with a cloth. This all changed some ten years ago with the introduction of LTCI and the long recession.

Home Helpers

In 1999 the Fureai organization obtained legal status as a not-for-profit corporation (*NPO hōjin*), and after the introduction of long-term care insurance the following year it launched its Golden Star Care services—home helper services funded through LTCI.[6] The home helpers must possess a certificate (awarded after taking a short course, something the Fureai NPO does not organize itself) and are paid 1,200 yen per hour. The users have their needs assessed and their care plan drawn up by a care manager, who helps them to choose services from different providers (including the private provider and NPOs). The NPO in this case matches the users with helpers, runs support sessions for the helpers, and coordinates the activities on a weekly basis. The number of helpers with Fureai has recently decreased significantly, something that worried my interlocutors very much. While at the peak of their activities they had around twenty, there are presently twelve. Despite the low numbers of helpers, Fureai tries not to decline any requests from users. Only when users require that they only come on weekends every time, then they might decline.[7] The helpers have different and flexible schedules and many work just one day a week, on average around four hours a week. While some places allow users to book for hours in several bursts over the day, this is something that Fureai cannot do due to the lack of manpower. As the helpers only receive remuneration per hour of work, the commuting and preparation time are not included and this breakdown of hours of work would be very inconvenient for the helpers. Among the helpers at Fureai, there are many housewives, as it is a job that can be easily taken up with little specialist experience. It mostly involves housework, but it requires sensitivity and patience, as one is required to be responsive to the user and to perform the duties while amiably conversing with them, should they wish that. Komatsu-san, a staff member at Fureai in charge of the helper organization who also organizes support and training meetings for the helpers, put it this way:

"One can't get engrossed in the work and forget that the beneficiary is a person."

According to Komatsu-san, there are several reasons for these dwindling numbers:

After a while [some helpers'] personal circumstances have changed—they need to care for their own parents, or they've had a baby. Also, well, the helpers' job is a service: they go there, to the [customer's] house for a couple of hours. But, as I often tell helpers, it's ultimately an interpersonal service. Yet, the older people sometimes have a different idea about how things work. How shall I put this . . . there are issues of compatibility. Not everyone is grateful [*mina san wa kansha shite kureru wake dewanai no ne*], there are cases when they just take the fact that they come for granted. . . . Some elderly have dementia, and it takes a lot of energy and patience to work with them. Some people get very stressed from this and at times they decide they can't continue their work anymore. It seems there are many helpers with a certificate, but it's also a job with the highest rate of turnover. Moreover, when they leave the job once, they don't come back. Furthermore, as the helpers are paid through the long-term care insurance system, their remuneration is fixed. Even though many men have helper certificates, the income is nowhere near the income most men are accustomed to receiving. So there might be good intentions, willingness, but at times it just isn't viable, when they get married and if they have a child. When they think about the future, people want proper [*chanto shita*], regular employment with an insurance. Everywhere in the care world these days, most places have trouble finding full-time helpers. Mostly, like us, they have one or two full time, and a few more for shorter stints on the register. . . . One more reason is that the helpers need to take notes on the user's records, and those who aren't good with words can't keep working, so they leave. The majority of those who work with us are the ones who've been with us for over ten years, those who joined in the beginning.

There is also the possibility of taking a state certificate (from the Ministry of Health, Labor and Welfare) of care worker [*kaigofukushi-shi*] and moving one's career ahead. . . . Large institutions, such as old people's homes [*tokubetsu yōgo rōjin homu*] have been increasingly hiring them.

Komatsu-san's explanation, just like those of my other interlocutors, emphasized the low wages and lack of security of the helper job, which makes it hard to earn a living if one is not supported by someone else. Mostly, as in Fureai, this is a job done by either young people or housewives. If something changes in their personal circumstances they may become unable (or unwilling) to continue this work. The issue of low payment, but remuneration nevertheless, is not irrelevant. The low levels of remuneration have consequences for the perception of this work as having low prestige. On the other hand, as it is not remuneration-free, it can be perceived by the users as something they are entitled to and thus taken at face value. The care and support jobs are very demanding and psychologically and emotionally exhausting, as Murata-san, a man in his late sixties who had worked as a helper in a day care center for the elderly, told me on more than one occasion. Many of the other helpers from that center shared his opinion, as I learned during a visit (Kavedžija 2015).

The Fureai-run Golden Star Care has around forty users using the services of helpers. Some of them have a long-standing relationship with Fureai (*nagai otsukiai*): they have been using the services of volunteers through Tasukeai (the mutual help system), and after the introduction of long-term care insurance they started using its helper services, so there are some users in their eighties who have been users since their seventies. The users differ somewhat in the levels of support and care required, but the majority are healthy and require just the minimal level of support (LTCI levels 1 and 2), while just under half are classified as care levels 3 and 4. Those requiring higher levels of care usually live with and are cared for by families.

Networks and Associations

Fureai is involved in various forms of social education and operational support for other similar institutions, as well as in the work of networks and associations in the field. It is a member of an association of paid volunteer organizations in Osaka comprising eight NPOs and three volunteer groups throughout the city, all cooperating with the Osaka volunteer information center. NPO Fureai is also a member of an Osaka City association of old people's homes and group housing, which draws together community salons, day care centers, small retirement homes, and group housing for the elderly. Furthermore, it took over responsibility for the administration of a volunteer organization in the neighborhood called Open House, located in a small, empty, two-story old-style family house owned by one of the members of that organization, who wanted to put it to good use by refurbishing it and opening it up to the people from the neighborhood to use for informal meetings, playgroups for children, and as a space for community activities. NPO Fureai coordinates the volunteers who open the house in the morning and take turns in keeping it open to visitors.

Commercial Activities—A Cleaning Service

In 2005 NPO Fureai launched a new project, a commercial cleaning service that they named Golden Star Cleaning. NPOs are permitted to run commercial activities so long as the profit is used for another activity rather than distributed among its members. In the beginning, as with the other activities, there was a lot of preparatory work, mostly done by Sakamoto-san, one of the newest staff members. She set up the system, arranged the legal and accounting side of things, spoke to prospective customers, and found interested workers. Sakamoto-san's enterprising attitude was made clear to me on several occasions, as when she explained the reasoning behind this development:

> As you know, the NPO operates Tasukeai which doesn't earn any income, and Golden Star Care. Many of our users, users of Golden Star Care, told us that unless one has family to help out, the care provided solely by LTCI is insufficient. While Tasukeai volunteers can help out with some of the easier tasks, many of them aren't young and fit enough for more demanding kinds of housework. So the idea came to us, perhaps we could earn some income by providing for these needs. That way we could create a third pillar of support for our organization. At the time when Fureai started thinking about new options and activities, I was working here only one day a week and the rest of the time as a career consultant providing work advice. At that time, after the economic bubble had burst, many middle-aged people lost their jobs in the restructuring and found it very hard to find another job. That's when we got the idea to open this activity and offer the job to some of these people who lost their jobs but have no special skills or certificates.

At the time of fieldwork, Golden Star Care had six employees: some in their sixties; a few in their thirties with small children, who work a little on the side; and one in full-time employment but who wants an additional income and claims she really enjoys cleaning. On average they work some four hours a week, or a couple of cleaning jobs, as one job consists of a two-hour time slot, and receive 900 yen per hour, while the service costs 4,000 for a two-hour slot. Golden Star Cleaning has eight permanent customers who receive one or two cleans a week, or one slot every two weeks. Mostly the customers are families in which both parents work or an elderly couple needs help but only one of them qualifies for LTCI; there are also some older people living alone and some single-parent households. Employees sometimes do one-off jobs, such as spring cleaning or cleaning after a move, but they are hoping to get more work through their networks and recommendations.

Salon

At the end of 2007, after having found a space in an old two-story townhouse in a shopping arcade (*shōtengai*) in their neighborhood, the NPO started a community salon and finally acquired its own office space. The house they bought was previously a shop, and they had it refurbished with the help of an architect specializing in the restoration of old townhouses in the area, in a mix of minimalist contemporary and rustic traditional style. They had only enough money for the most basic work and had to paint the walls themselves with the help of a few volunteers. They thought carefully about the furniture and decided to get two large, heavy wooden tables. These two tables are indispensable actors in many of my field notes, as the dynamics between the visitors could be almost perfectly mapped onto the seating patterns around them. At first, the tables were joined and served as one long surface, but as tensions grew and some of the newcomers felt it was difficult to join in the conversation around a big table immediately after entering the salon, they were separated into two tables with six chairs each. Of course, when more people joined, the number of chairs increased. The tables are heavy and one can lean onto them while getting up from one's chair without the threat of it overturning.

All in all, the space is very accessible yet has none of the institutional atmosphere of an standard accessible space, with its ramps, railings, linoleum-covered floor, and industrial finish. The lavatory in the corner of the room has a sliding door, wide enough to accommodate a wheelchair. The space around the entrance is left empty for any strollers to be parked or large shopping carts and bags to be left, and there is a parking space for bicycles at the front. The aim of the careful refurbishment was to make a space that is inviting for everyone, a place where one feels comfortable (*ibashō*). Here one would be able to have a tea or coffee every day between 10 a.m. and 5 p.m., or come to an event such as a concert, *rakugo* (traditional comedy performance), a singing or origami class, a children's book-reading session, or a film screening, all of which were held on a regular monthly or weekly basis.

Most visitors to the salon live in the neighborhood and arrive on foot from the little streets branching out from the *shōtengai*. Not infrequently, they would decide to pop back home for lunch or an afternoon nap, and return again in a couple of hours. While the majority of the visitors are older, above the age of sixty-five, and the oldest three ladies are in their nineties, some young women would come for a cup of tea while shopping in the arcade with their children, and a few middle-aged women would meet regularly in the afternoons for coffee, once or twice a week. Some of the older people were coming from a little farther away, some by underground train; one couple would come on the "red bus," a free bus service for the elderly funded by the local administration; and several cycled. According to a survey conducted by the NPO staff, the average age of visitors was eighty-eight. The majority were women with an elementary school education, and only a few had a junior-high-school education, which according to Nakajima-san would have been fairly unusual for girls at the time of their youth. Many of these women are widowed, and while some lived with their families, most lived on their own. In terms of their financial situation, it is likely that some would have savings but (according to the NPO staff) most would be receiving a low old-age pension from the state in the vicinity of 50,000 yen.[8]

The volunteers in the salon are mostly in their late sixties (seventeen of those working regularly, and another six or seven helping out on occasion) and typically work one or two times a week for three hours. After a while, I realized that volunteers in the Tasukeai were not volunteering in the salon, even though they sometimes visited the office upstairs or on occasion came to the events held in the salon. As it sometimes happened that someone had to cancel their shift in the salon at the last moment, I would wonder why the staff never asked one of the Tasukeai volunteers to help out. The answers I got suggested that there was no need for this, as there were many more salon volunteers on the records who were willing to take up short time slots once every few weeks and were not regularly scheduled. But there was also a feeling that it was a good idea to keep different activities separate. This meant that the Tasukeai volunteers were recruited separately (and as mentioned earlier, they had to become members and pay a membership fee), as there was always the danger of gossip. According to Komatsu-san, it was important to protect the privacy of the users of Tasukeai services, as well as the evaluative comments of the volunteers and helpers among the salon visitors. Furthermore, Komatsu-san and other staff members did not want to restrict access to the salon to the users of other services but wanted it to be used more freely.

Changing Welfare Frameworks

"Tasukeai" refers to mutual aid or cooperation, but it was used by my interlocutors as a keyword to refer to a particular type of volunteer organization, as promoted by Hotta Tsutomu of the Sawayaka Welfare Foundation. It is a form of cooperation based on a ticket system, where the tickets or money vouchers are exchanged for services for a set duration of time, usually in thirty-minute intervals. Fureai founders have studied the setup of Sawayaka and based their organization on this model but have not mirrored all aspects of it, being well aware of some differing circumstances. For example, as Hotta was a prominent public figure who gained public attention during his time as a public prosecutor, Sawayaka had been receiving significant amounts of money in donations, which was not something Fureai could rely on. One of the more interesting differences in the institutional organization of Fureai is the absence of a single leader: all six staff members reached their decisions together, by consensus. Upon establishing an NPO they elected a nominal president, for legal reasons, a position they all used to take in turns until they offered it to a sympathetic professor of social welfare who was aware of the nominal nature of the appointment and agreed to take it as a way of increasing their social visibility. The program's lack of a leader and democratic way of making decisions had one downside, as the members somewhat reluctantly admitted to me: it was more time consuming, as they had to confer on most issues.

The decision to register as an NPO was strategic and linked to the introduction of long-term care insurance in 2000. The introduction of this system brought about a significant change in the provision of the care for the elderly, in which not all the voluntary citizen groups did equally well. For instance, one of the organizations based on the model provided by the Sawayaka Welfare Foundation had ceased to exist as a mutual-aid system five years after the introduction of LTCI. The case was well known to the staff at Fureai, as they had visited it prior to the establishment of their group in order to learn more about the ticket system. As Nakajima-san explained:

Throughout the country Tasukeai organizations mushroomed [in the 1990s], but then LTCI was introduced by the state. At that time, they all split up in two camps: some organizations continued their Tasukeai based on volunteer activities and started to provide the helper services through LTCI, while some decided to keep their activities volunteer-based as a citizens' group [*shimin dantai*]. The latter were thinking that, being a national initiative, LTCI and helpers were the government's business, or somehow profitable and not for them, and they continued to provide volunteer services with all their might. Those organizations that provided support through LTCI started receiving profits and gradually forgot about their initial aim of providing Tasukeai, and so these organizations split into two categories. Surprisingly, our Fureai continued both activities. The group where we studied had gone the LTCI way and stopped the Tasukeai activities.

The government's introduction of LTCI thus had a significant impact on Japanese civil society, especially on welfare-oriented organizations. It could be argued that the introduction of LTCI (allowing for the provision of welfare services by private institutions and nonprofit organizations) co-opted the voluntary sector efforts for the state aims. However, Japan's voluntary sector and the state have historically been intertwined and do not conform to the simplified understanding of civil society as separate from the state or as a site of resistance (see Hann and Dunn 1996). Volunteers were recruited throughout the 1970s for various welfare-related tasks and cooperation was established with earlier voluntary associations in the local community, such as neighborhood associations or *chōnaikai* (Garon 1997:172; Garon 2003; Avenell 2010). While the academic literature on civil society often posits its separation from the state (Hann and Dunn 1996:1–26), my interlocutors emphasized their close relationship to the state and to various level of local government.[9]

Mori-san, one of the staff members, emphasized the role of the state in promoting tasukeai through education and believed the state had a responsibility to support various mutual-aid endeavors of the kind Fureai was engaged in. She was convinced that the state could create more room for social engagement, primarily in the school curriculum (which is currently focused on examinations and preparations for entering the university), but also in people's daily lives: "It is not enough for it to be recognized [by the government and in the society] that this is a valuable activity, because if there is no room in one's daily life, and mentally no leeway to engage in this activity, then it will be impossible to continue with the operation, even if people know that it can be socially fulfilling and good for health." Nakajima-san, another staff member, explained the complex relationship between the NPOs and public administration in the provision of welfare:

> It is believed that if one could create links between ordinary citizens, public administration [gyōsei], and NPOs, that would make for an ideal civil society where all cooperate on the same level, equally. In reality, the NPOs have way less power, and as it is, the space of cooperation is not as large as one would hope for, but this could change, if the NPOs grew and gained power. For this to happen the NPO have to be recognized [as partners] by the administration, which would provide funding. It would be good if they could suggest what things NPOs could do to help to receive more money, or to raise funds from the private sector. The administration is happy to request things and ask for cooperation, but it needs to do more in return. There are not many NPOS that receive recognition from the administration.

While there is little doubt that the state is delegating responsibility by mobilizing people through NPOs and other voluntary organizations to provide the services that are expected from it,[10] it is easy to overlook the attitudes of the actors toward the role of the state and the relationship of the voluntary sector to the local authorities. Nakajima-san was not only aware of the links of the NPO sector to the local government but also hoped that these links could be strengthened, albeit on more equal footing, as partners. Both she and Mori-san were calling for more, rather than less, engagement with the state.

Ogawa Akihiro, in his ethnographically rich study of an education-oriented NPO in Tokyo, argues that the power and involvement of the state in the voluntary sector is not on the wane and moreover "continues to be strong, and NPOs—a product of the state's deliberate institutionalization of civil society—are now even synonymous with the state. The state is an unusually strong actor, retarding development of a healthy, dynamic civil society" (Ogawa 2004:4). While the involvement of Fureai (and similar NPOs in the field) in grassroots policy formation is very limited, not least because of lack of interest among its members, it retains a high level of autonomy in its operation and managerial freedom in pursuing the values chosen by the staff. Rather than focusing on the ability of NPOs to influence policy change, one might begin by asking if this is even a concern or aim for them. Ogawa notes that, unlike the members of some social movements, citizens (*shimin*) involved with NPO activities are typically apolitical (Ogawa 2004:106) and often did not realize that they are being mobilized or used by the government (Ogawa 2004:100, 117). While certainly not interested in revolutionary movements or subverting state agendas, my interlocutors had clear ideas about the social values they held in high esteem and worked toward them, thinking of the state as a resource or a source of support, rather than as an antagonist. The role of the state and the local government, its support and guidance, are seen as desirable, and Komatsu-san mentioned on several occasions that state support, funding, and policy input were very important. On other occasions, when Nakajima-san or Komatsu-san criticized the actions of the local government, this was often precisely because of the lack of intervention or appropriate action rather than too much intervention. In close contacts with government officials, NPO staff—especially Nakajima-san and Komatsu-san (who did most of the direct liaising)—often found the attitude of officials deficient and somewhat stern and unyielding. This could be ascribed to a power structure differential, the officials demonstrating clearly who wields greater power. Nakajima-san explained that she did not mind this much, as it was understandable that they were representing powerful systems. What she did begrudge was the lack of effort to conceal it, and lack of signs of genuine attempts to take the suggestions that stemmed from their long-term experience in the field with appropriate consideration. Overall, though, Nakajima-san and Kuroki-san found that with increased visibility and prolonged contact with the officials their relationship improved, as the officials themselves started to rely on the favors of the NPO staff, including running seminars or giving public lectures that were organized by local institutions and authorities, including the shakaifukushikyōgikai (or shakyō), the local welfare council.

Community and NPO

Shimoichi is an old downtown Osaka neighborhood with a long tradition and an unusually high proportion of older people, with almost a quarter of the population above the age of sixty-five. Interestingly, there are also quite a few young couples and families in their twenties or thirties but, a fact pointed out to me by Nakajima-san, there are relatively few people of her generation, in their fifties. She was increasingly aware of this as the numbers of volunteers and helpers in the NPO were dwindling, and this was the group that did most support activities, unlike young families who had small children to look after and often require volunteer support themselves (such as babysitting). Demographic circumstances of this kind vary greatly between different parts of Kansai, or even Osaka, with considerable impacts for the NPOs and provision of support for the elderly. Furthermore, class may be an important factor, as most volunteer and community activities are undertaken by professional housewives, who are for the most part supported by their husbands in adequately remunerated employment.[11] On the other hand, the downtown neighborhood of Shimoichi has been described to me as having a fair proportion of family-run businesses as a main source of employment. Like Kuroki-san, some young wives are helping with the family business, and most of the women in the area knew each other and occasionally helped out in times of need, but had limited time for or interest in the elaborate community activities of more middle-class areas. As Kuroki-san put it: "There aren't many housewives in my neighborhood. There are many families in which everyone is involved in the business, which means that the relationships were not as closely knit [*bettari no otsukiai dewanai desu*]." Yet, to an outsider like Sakamoto-san, the community relations in Shimoichi seemed close and caring (*ninjō ga aru*).

There are many prewar houses still standing in the neighborhood, and some neighborly links between families stretch over several generations. Nakajima-san said that she never felt a sense of belonging fully; many of her children's classmates' parents and grandparents went to the same school and knew each other well. Despite being born and brought up in the neighborhood, she did not feel entirely an insider. That said, many people moved to the area after World War II or even more recently and felt accepted, even if not fully on the "inside." By way of example, she mentioned people's habit of referring to each other not by surname but by nicknames, or by mentioning what their grandfather did for a living, which would be quite incomprehensible for a newcomer. Sakamoto-san, originally from a large satellite town in Kansai region, felt that the dynamics of native and newcomer was much more pronounced in this kind of place than in more recently developed areas. It could, under these circumstances, be argued that those with less developed links in the community would be more interested in joining a volunteer group or an NPO. According to Ogawa, those who moved to the community in Tokyo where he worked found the NPO a good way to build community links, especially if they found the local territorial-based organizations, such as neighborhood associations, difficult to join (Ogawa 2004:26). This may have been the case with both staff and volunteers at Fureai, as well as visitors to the salon. At the same time, those with strong connections to the neighborhood thought of volunteering as an extension of existing networks, and moved freely between them. This ability to create relationships that seamlessly blended with the old ones while also having a somewhat new form is at the core of the work of a community NPO.

Hedgehogs, or, the Burden of the Gift

When I asked Nakajima-san, one of the founders of Fureai, about the purpose of the NPO, she gave me a little set speech that was clearly well prepared: "The purpose, or what one may call the mission of this NPO is to make the neighborhood a nicer place to live, a place in which it is easy to live. In a way, it has to do with making a place where people want to be and stay. More specifically, it is about creating a place, like the salon, where people can gather, and raising the consciousness of the people, fostering the public spirit [kōkyōshin], and a spirit of mutual help, thinking about the way everyone can live together well. We have various activities, organize lectures, connecting different generations from babies to the elderly."[12] She then began to elaborate, and as the pauses in her speech grew longer, she gave a more personal account with a smile: "So that people wouldn't become isolated, live somewhat spaced out, private. . . . You see, while hedgehogs might want to pile up for warmth, they might also feel uncomfortable when they are too close. . . . We want to create a place where people can cordially live together [minna de nakayoku kurashite] while still maintaining a sense of distance [kyōrikan], that is our purpose." Other staff members described the purpose of the NPO as fostering relationships in the neighborhood. Kuroki-san emphasized having fun and creating a comfortable living environment (sumiyoi), and "creating links between people." She believed that if people came to the events and to the salon they might be able to make acquaintances, to get to know people by sight. Similarly, Sakamoto-san thought that the purpose was specifically to create a place where one could widen one's social horizons in an urban environment, creating a place for oneself. This may at first seem like a programmatic statement, especially when uttered in terms used by local government and prevalent in funding applications: sumiyoi machizukuri (making a town good for living). Nevertheless, the sentiment repeatedly expressed by my interlocutors, in various forms over the course of my stay, seemed genuine: they felt a need to create certain kinds of relationships in the neighborhood, but in some ways quite different from the old "traditional" community, that resembled a village despite being in an urban neighborhood (see Knight 1996:220). The neighborhood was seen as a very cohesive social group with responsibility shared by the members of the community, for instance through the local neighborhood association (*chōnaikai* or *jichikai*) (see Sugimoto 2003: 273–274).

Watanabe-san, one of my interlocutors from a women's discussion group in Kyoto, described her neighborhood as "rural" in terms of social relations. When I once asked her to tell me more about her daily activities, she started by explaining how much her daily routine has changed in the previous three months:

> Until now I was really busy with raising children and neighborhood duties, things like being a neighborhood association officer, organizing events for children, helping out, there were always things to do. This year there is none of that, for the first time since I got married I'm free, I have some time on my hands. . . . Before, I served as an officer [*yakuin*] [in various roles]. Last year I was an accountant for *jichikai*, and because I live in the countryside [*inaka*], it was really busy, like having a proper job. The neighborhood *jichikai* duties are done on a rotation basis, like distributing the newsletter, the removal of rubbish. . . . Accounting is a lot of work, because all the fees or contributions need to be recorded and a receipt issued to everyone who contributed. When an event is organized and the food and drinks bought, all the receipts need to be collected. The summer festival is the biggest, and that is a lot of work—it involves a lot of stalls with various snacks and games for children, for which we issue coupons and then these can be bought. Then there is the Sports Day [*undōkai*], and other festivals. . . . It's unimaginable, I'm from Kobe and we don't have so many there. Most of these officer positions are done on a rota basis, which with twelve houses means you won't need to do it again. But I didn't have a job so I was asked to do the accounts last year. Not entering the association is not an option, you wouldn't receive the newsletter, your rubbish wouldn't be taken away and. . . . you probably wouldn't be able to live [normally] [*tabun seikatsu dekinai*]. . . . Otherwise we are all on good terms, the neighbors—everyone knows where everyone lives and so

on. When I get off the bus it is hard to get to the house without talking to several people: "Oh hello, what are you up to today," "Where
are you going," someone would shout out, "Oh, isn't that Watanabe-
san?" another person would call out.

Watanabe-san, who is not originally from the suburban neighborhood she
now lives in, explained later how she felt surprised at the abundance of these
ties and obligations and various communal activities. Being from Kobe, she
thought of her new neighborhood as in this respect quite like a village (*inaka*).
While she appreciated the support and involvement of her neighbors she frequently found the intensity of social relations to be rather onerous.
Watanabe-san's account gives us some flavor of the old-style, village-like
community relations, sometimes described as "sticky" relations in the community (e.g., Imamura 1987:65), and invoked by Nakajima-san in her reference to "hedgehogs."[13] In such a place, relations between neighbors are close,
which can be pleasant but also constraining. One probably "wouldn't be able
to live" there, as Watanabe-san said, if one were to opt out of the neighborhood association and the obligations it involves. Kuroki-san, and all the other
staff members at the salon, mentioned the need for having community relationships but made clear that overly close relationships in the neighborhood
are undesirable, as they are *okorisuru yōna*, annoying, or literally, prone to
cause anger.

On numerous occasions, they mentioned the importance of privacy, using the English-derived word *puraibashī*, and noting that people nowadays
find this important. This is also a term that some of my older interlocutors
used when explaining why they were wary of strangers entering their houses,
even as home helpers. In this case becoming a member of the same organization, like this NPO, was a solution, as the NPO guaranteed privacy (which
is why separation of home-helper-service users and salon guests was seen as
important, and why helpers were not to discuss private living circumstances
of the people in whose houses they were helping out). The system set out clear
expectations of reciprocity and set boundaries on the interactions. Since the
members were all part of the same organizations, this in turn meant that
people entering their houses were not, technically speaking, strangers. That
this was an important concern is confirmed by the fact that when I initially
suggested that I would be interested in visiting some older people in their
homes through the NPO network as a part of my research, this was greeted
with a polite but firm refusal on the part of the NPO staff. Furthermore,

during the *chotto tasukeai* seminar a session was dedicated to the discussion of important issues regarding helping out a little in the neighborhood. Participants were divided into six groups, which were supposed to brainstorm on a couple of case studies and then were invited to give comments. Independently, four out of six groups mentioned the issue of privacy as an important concern and at the same time as a great obstacle: it is difficult to enter older people's homes in order to check on them and see how they are doing, as they feel reluctant to let strangers in. In this sense, privacy seems to refer to a protection from imposition, from the judging gaze of a stranger, of one outside the immediate social circle of kin and friends. And yet, as many of the friendly relationships required proper behavior, it was difficult not to feel the imposition even when one's friends were visiting or staying overnight. This was reflected in a statement by Okuma-san to the effect that she was exhausted after her friend visited her for several days, which kept her very busy, trying to do everything the way it should be (something that she did not do for herself when she was alone). Distance, or a certain degree of separation, is required to maintain harmonious but cordial relationships, and avoid sticky relationships that can prove to be too onerous.

Volunteering and Meaning

The year of the Great Hanshin Earthquake, 1995, is often dubbed the First Year of Volunteering (*borantia gannen*). The term *borantia* (volunteer) is a loanword that has since been in frequent use.[14] Even though numerous volunteer activities and efforts long preceded both the earthquake and the introduction of the NPO law in Japan soon thereafter, a new era of volunteering was expected to ensue.[15] The new volunteers were expected to be different: not enlisted by the state but self-driven through local government initiatives or institutions. The separation of these new volunteer efforts from the state has since been shown to be questionable, as it has been facilitated by the state and coaxed in the direction of state agendas (Avenell 2010). Nevertheless, in contemporary usage, the term *borantia* preserves a sense of newness and difference, as implied by its foreign origin. I would like to argue that use of the term *borantia*, and the related activities of volunteering, is aimed at reforming relationships within the community, albeit not in the ways envisaged by its early advocates (e.g., Nakata 1996), promoting the development of a civil society as a sphere separate from the state and even as a site of resistance to government agendas. As I have already noted, community volunteer groups like Fureai seek out and actively cultivate their relationships with the local government. The reframing of relationships and community ties that is sought by these volunteers is rather more subtle, aimed not merely at reinvigorating the community and bringing back its tightly knit networks, but at establishing altogether new kinds of relationships, under the old banner of community.[16] I will explore this subtle change with respect to ideas of exchange and obligation.

Undoubtedly, neighborhoods such as Shimoichi pride themselves on multiple community ties supported by relationships of exchange, where the items exchanged include travel gifts, seasonal gifts and "meaningless" gifts (Rupp 2003:29), in addition to gifts given on important ritual occasions such as weddings and funerals. While seasonal gifts may be given to some members of the community who have played a patron role in one's life, such as helping one or one's child to find a job or a marriage partner, ritual gifts may be exchanged with neighbors, with the gift varying in monetary value depending on the "gravity" and closeness of the relationship. Yet the somewhat neglected class of "meaningless" gifts may be the one that is most important for the constitution of neighborhood community. It is precisely these small gifts of food, prepared meals, and distribution of surplus delicacies one had received or managed to acquire while doing the shopping that supports the numerous loose neighborhood links. Visitors to the salon would often bring cakes and sweet treats that they had made themselves, or perhaps a surplus of mandarins to share with everyone present. "Meaningless" gifts are labeled as such because they are not necessarily given in return or as a part of a set exchange (unlike the seasonal or life-events-related gifts; see Rupp 2003), and they do not require a formal return exchange within a set period of time. A number of little favors can be classified within this kind of relationship. Yet while they may not demand an elaborate response, they may still require some form of kindness, perhaps an offer of a hot drink, or a small thank-you gift on a later occasion.

The volunteer-user relationship seeks to minimize this kind of obligation felt by the receiver, as it is often perceived as burdensome. As the volunteer help and support activities usually take place at the receiver's home, the formalized polite relationship might require the receiver to offer a cup of tea and a snack to the visitor, and to have the house in a presentable state—something that a few of my older interlocutors in the salon gave as a reason why they did not use the services of volunteers and home helpers. Being too embarrassed to receive them in a messy house, they always spent the morning tidying and preparing for their arrival, and so were more exhausted on the days they had such "visitors," as Tamura-san explained laughingly on one occasion. The volunteer system is aimed at changing this dynamic, not necessarily by making the interaction much less formalized but by explicitly changing the rules of the game. When signing up, both the volunteers and the users are given booklets with guidelines. The volunteer booklet describes the procedure when visiting the user, designed to minimize awkwardness and chances for misunderstanding. It suggests that one always make all the arrangements through the coordinator, and notify them of any changes, to make sure they understand precisely what the task requested involves and to pay attention to how the user likes things done—where the utensils are kept, what quantities of spices they like in their meal, and so on—to pay attention to safety, to check that they have switched off the stove and appliances before leaving, and to check the time when they begin the work and to announce it to the user. Furthermore, they are warned not to give their address and phone number to the user, even if they are asked, and not to accept any hot drink, such as tea. Similarly, the users are asked to make all the arrangements through the coordinator, not to change the services once requested through the coordinator without contacting them, not to ask the volunteers directly to stay longer or to come again tomorrow, as they may feel uncomfortable declining, and not to offer them any hot drinks. In this way, the Tasukeai system aims to minimize the sense of personal obligation and the burden felt on either side.

The avoidance of burden is often invoked as one of the main reasons behind the introduction of the voucher system, or "paid volunteering." Kuroki-san explained this to me as follows:

> Basically, things that were done in the neighborhood, connections, now every family does itself, . . . These things were something that used to be just normally done amongst neighbors. . . . So borrowing from that system we started our mutual help—doing a little bit instead of your family, helping and being helped, that is what we had hoped to put together. Why paid volunteering [yūshō borantia], one may ask. Well, as I'm sure you've heard from Nakajima-san and others, even in close friendly relationships, if you keep asking for favors there's a feeling of burden [futan]. . . . So we thought, let's get rid of that feeling of burden from the beginning, that's why we introduced the voucher system. When the volunteering is free, totally free, the users

are the ones who are concerned [*ki wo tsukatte*], and put some money
in an envelope, or prepare things. . . . So we charge both volunteers
and users a membership fee, as one never knows when one might oneself need some help. . . . And there are many cases when someone
who was a user wants to help out, for instance someone who needed
help with babysitting, and the child is now going to school—so we
make it an equal relationship, we make membership "flat."

Kuroki-san mentioned the decline in community ties and in help between
neighbors but did not seem to think that things were all rosy in the past, or
that old neighborhood relationships should be resurrected. She mentioned
the concern and care expressed by users: *ki wo tsukau*, or literally "using one's
spirit," which involves gifts and formal expressions of gratitude. This expression of concern and gratitude for a service or help received is quite pervasive
in Japan. For instance, some hospital wards have a sign advising against "*ki
wo tsukau*," or in other words, against giving presents to the hospital staff.
Patients' families often circumvent this rule by sending presents directly to
the doctor's house (Ohnuki-Tierney 1984). This kind of relationship can be
seen as vertical or hierarchical as it creates an inequality, something that is to
be avoided. Indeed, the fees paid by both the users and providers of services
within the Tasukeai system are equal and indicate that these roles, at least
theoretically, could be swapped. In contrast to a vertical relationship of obligation, the emphasis is on keeping them equal and membership being "flat."
    This resembles the explanation Mori-san offered for the disappearance
of the old neighborhood sociality (*mukashi no kinjo tsukiai*), when the mutual help occurred "naturally":

Well, there is the issue of privacy [*puraibashī*], but also of concern—
Japanese are very concerned [*sugoku ki wo tsukau*] and restrained [*enryo suru*]. And this became larger and larger: one helps someone a bit
and there they are, coming with a thank you gift, showing concern
[*ki wo tsukau*], so the small help became very difficult. Before, the
neighbors used to help with the funerals . . . helping with the preparation of food, all of that was taken care of by the neighbors. But people
started feeling reticent, restrained [*enryo*], and stopped getting help.
The same happened with other kinds of help, even very small favors.
Really, when one now has a little problem it feels like one has no one
to ask. Neighborhood sociality had its good sides but also its bad sides:

the gossip, being told things by one's neighbors [about one's behavior], annoying things like excessive meddling [in one's affairs]. Trying to avoid these annoying things, people stopped doing it.

While it is easy to romanticize the communities of the past, with their caring character and thick networks of relationships, the inhabitants of Shimoichi, one of the more "traditional" neighborhoods in Osaka, found these burdensome.[17] The salon visitors negotiate the links and burdens carefully. As is apparent from the above explanations, finding ways to balance community ties and associated burdens was a central concern for many of my interlocutors, and it provided a motivation for the NPO staff members to establish the group and mutual help system, Tasukeai. While volunteering efforts such as Tasukeai aim to reduce the burden felt by the recipients of support, they do not aspire to turn it into a "free gift," an idealized gift (in this case, of goodwill), with no strings attached and no expectation of reciprocity (Laidlaw 2000:627).[18] Recognizing the difficulty, or indeed impossibility of a free gift, Tasukeai instead introduces token payment for its volunteer services, thus distinguishing itself from a semblance of charity and the necessity to reciprocate by gifts or in kind in future. It is still "volunteering" as it is not based on one's duty or a feeling of responsibility stemming from a personal relationship, nor is it perceived as commodified: a service provided for an adequate remuneration. The aim is to make the relationships lighter, less "sticky," something that is as important for the users as it is for the volunteers, who might otherwise feel that to be a part of a relationship is as obliging for them as it is for the users and may find it difficult to withhold additional favors.[19] Tasukeai seeks to make these relationships less personal, and the sense of reciprocity and benefit more generalized and diffused.

In other words, in their attempts to create a good community, of a kind where one can "live well" without friction, NPO staff and residents of Shimoichi grapple with the issue of separation. This may be considered as an important aspect of the existential issue of autonomy and dependency. In his work on separation and reunion in China, Charles Stafford proposes that we can understand separation as a universal human constraint, of which death is just one type (Stafford 2000:1). He notes that physical separation generates crises of relatedness, with two aspects: "We are often obliged to part with those with whom we wish to remain, and often obliged to stay with those with whom we wish to part" (Stafford 2000:13). Yet the broad-ranging material in his book largely deals with the undesirable separations and desirable reunions. In everyday relations in Shimoichi, and probably other urban neighborhoods in Japan, a degree of separation is nevertheless highly valued, as reflected in the emphasis placed on privacy, a notion to which I will return shortly. The Shimoichi material forces us to take seriously the importance of separation for harmonious relations.

Ideas surrounding the relationship between the self and others would seem to be crucial for understanding anxieties such as isolation anxiety, as well as their opposite—the need to maintain a separate identity. In contrast to Western notions of selves as essentially separate, Roy Wagner (1977) writes of the Papuan ideas of relationships as given, and of the social order as innate, rather than crafted or created. Eduardo Viveiros de Castro (2004) offers a similar insight in his writings concerning the difference between Western and Amerindian ontologies. Where Westerners assume that we are individuals and have absolutely singular minds (it is our biological bodies that are similar), Amerindians assume the opposite. To put it simply, we tend to assume that while our physiology and bodies work in similar ways, our character and "mind" is separate from others and utterly our own. Amerindian thought, by contrast, presupposes the interconnectedness of selves and the similarity of characters, but bodies are more problematic. This leads to very different kinds of anxieties: "Our traditional problem in the West is how to connect and universalize: individual substances are given, while relations have to be made. The Amerindian problem is how to separate and particularize: relations are given, while substances must be defined" (Viveiros de-Castro 2004:476). Not only is the difference in ideas of the innate based in very different understandings of the body, but we could also imagine it has consequences for the understanding of the relationship of self to others. If one assumes that relationships are "given" and the link to the other is assumed, the task is to distinguish oneself from others, and one fears incorporation or assimilation. With the boundedness of a personal unit, as in the West, unique identity is a given, but one must strive to build bridges toward others. The Shimoichi case holds both of those tendencies in balance, striving both for connection and separation, as the relationships in question are not understood to be given in the way ties of kinship might be, and the community ties can no longer be taken for granted.

This relates to a changing sense of public and private, with privacy often invoked as something that precludes the old kind of "thick" (Knight 1996) communal relationship. In its extreme form, it could lead to isolation, as mentioned by Nakajima-san, especially among older people. As implied by the term's foreign origin (*puraibashī*), privacy is often associated with Western modernity and concomitant alienation (e.g., Giddens 1991:151), and as foreign to the Japanese "sense of self," typically considered to be "group-oriented" and enmeshed with other members of one's group, who are inside (*uchi*), as opposed to those who are outside (*soto*). While this distinction is relevant, Inge Daniels points out that it is not absolute, but rather a difference in emphasis: "The stress is on us versus others instead of the individual versus society" (2010:75). The emphasis on the group rather than the individual need not mean that there is no distinction between private and public or that the distinction is irrelevant. What it may mean is that the privacy of individuals is less important than the privacy of the family-household in relation to the community, at least in this case. Undoubtedly, the visitors to the salon guard their privacy carefully, by keeping to themselves certain kinds of personal information, and not least by employing polite and formal forms of speech, thus maintaining a minimal distance from potentially intrusive others.

A good life, then, is one with rich social relationships, a multitude of links to others in the community on whom one can rely for support, but one in which the intrusive and constraining aspects of these relationships is minimized and the social burden that one feels toward others is kept manageable. It is about maintaining links to others without being fully absorbed into the thick social fabric through its excessive demands. Well-being in this context may be precisely about balancing sociality and a sense of freedom. Such a balancing act may be universal, even if its form is undoubtedly specific. The following statement, referring to the Kuranko of Sierra Leone, resonates with the concerns expressed by my interlocutors: "Well-being is . . . dependent on an adjustment or balance between our sense of what we owe others and what we owe ourselves" (Jackson 2011:195). While the Kuranko place their demands on others loudly and explicitly, in contrast to the more formalized interactions and internalized expectations experienced by the inhabitants of Shimoichi, they share the concern with finding a difficult yet valuable balance.

Chapter 4

Living Well Together

Many shopkeepers were still arranging the goods displayed in the front of their stores as Sato-san walked past, through the shopping arcade. Exchanging nods and smiles with most and a few words with some, she arrived in front of the salon just before 10 a.m. She unlocked the door and went straight to the kitchen to hang up her coat and boil water for the first customers, then wiped all the surfaces and swept the floors. The first customers arrived soon enough: Ikeda-san and Kato-san, the eighty-seven- and ninety-year-old sisters who frequented the salon daily. They were content to chat to each other while she made them tea. Sato-san later told me how relieved she was, as it was her first day volunteering on her own and she was rather nervous. Luckily, the two ladies and a few other customers who arrived during that morning shift seemed quite comfortable and used to the routine of the salon. A short, white-haired lady slowed down in front of the entrance and peered in curiously but hesitated to enter. Kato-san sprang to her feet and rushed toward the sliding door with a smile on her face. "Irrashai! Irrashai! [Welcome! Welcome!]," she exclaimed, using a less formal version of the phrase used by shopkeepers to greet their customers or invite in guests. Ikeda-san prepared a chair at the table at which she and her sister were sitting with Obāchan (Granny), an older lady in her nineties, and a quiet, dark-haired lady with glasses in her seventies. A man in a baseball cap was quietly sipping his coffee at the other table and flicking through a newspaper. Cheerfully talking over each other, the ladies made sure to explain how the system worked: one can order a hot drink: coffee, black tea, or green tea; one pays a hundred yen upon receiving it and one can request refills or even order a different hot drink without paying more. They inquired about the area in which the lady lived and deduced that they knew a tofu seller a street away from her house. Making sure that the newcomer participated in the conversation, the four ladies and one man chatted about a famous singer who (according to the news) was celebrating her eightieth birthday.

Lunchtime in the salon always causes a certain amount of commotion. Some customers leave to eat at home with their families, just like Obāchan did that day. Others strolled down the shopping arcade (*shōtengai*) and chose one of the boxed lunch options, such as *okonomiyaki, yakisoba* (fried noodles), boiled rice with vegetables, or sushi. Komatsu-san and Kuroki-san wandered down from the NPO office upstairs to heat up their lunch in the kitchen, joking and chatting with the customers, while Nakajima-san rushed away to a meeting in the city hall. Kato-san went to get some soba for herself and a couple of *onigiri* for her sister and came back to have it at the salon, saying to the ladies sitting around the table: "My sister was sick and now has many likes and dislikes [*suki kirai*]. She doesn't like soba, she prefers udon or rice. And some things are too greasy." Her sister explained somewhat apologetically that she had a stomach sickness and still has some problems. A conversation started about different tastes in food, with everyone volunteering information about their likes and dislikes. The conversation turned to restaurants in the area and how to get to them, with people offering recommendations and singling out places that were definitely not worth visiting. As we were chatting, we were joined at the table by Ueda-san—a tall, sturdy, bespectacled lady in her sixties, who sometimes volunteered in the salon and was always smiling. She had brought me a belt for the *yukata* she had heard I had recently received as a present. Kato-san, one of the two sisters coming to the salon on a daily basis, suggested: "This is good, you don't need to spend money. You could give this as a present to your friends when you go back home and you won't need to buy something for them. You don't earn any money here, but Ueda-san has her pension, she worked as a civil servant."

Feeling that this might be disrespectful to Ueda-san, I replied I would prefer to keep my present and explained that I do indeed have some income through fellowships. I knew that Kato-san was worried about me not being paid for my volunteer work in the salon. But Ueda-san retorted that it is not good to assume things about people. She did not in fact have a pension, she informed us, as she had stopped working for health reasons just a month before fulfilling the minimum employment requirement. After she recovered somewhat she found out that she would need to work for another year to compensate for that month, and felt that would be too difficult for her. She had

her husband's small pension and devoted her time instead to voluntary activities. Quietly but firmly, she insisted that one hears good and nice things
from people because they do not always mention difficulties, but that doesn't
mean that one can assume that their life is all set and easy. "This is a salon.
People come here to enjoy themselves and don't feel like talking about difficulties, or burdening others with their problems," Ueda-san concluded. The
sisters seemed quite surprised at her situation, and readily agreed with her
point, while another lady said: "That's exactly what I thought when I was talking to Sumiyoshi-san the other day. She complains a lot about her situation
and assumes that everybody else's life is easy. But people have hard times
[*kurō*] too." Ueda-san then concluded: "Everyone has hard times, even if they
don't mention it. If you're going to talk like that, you have to hear the other
side of the story. Even when people are all right, they have difficulties that
you may not know about. Other people's lives always have another side that
you need to ask about, if you're going to speak about that." Everyone seemed
to agree with Ueda-san and nodded approvingly.

A tall, handsome man in his late sixties known as Shachō (literally "company director"), who came regularly in the afternoons, pulled up a chair at
the busy table next to Kato-san and joined the chat. Now retired, Shachō had
once owned a company that made writing brushes, and the ladies rather enjoyed calling him a director. He was in turn always careful to pay compli-
ments to the ladies and to ask after those he hadn't seen in a while. Ikeda-san
ordered some more green tea for everyone, and when I brought it over she
poured it into cups with an elegant gesture. She couldn't quite reach all the
way across the large table, and another lady took over on that side. She poured
some for me, too, insisting (as she often did) that I sit down with them to chat
when I was finished serving at the other table. Our unspoken agreement was
that I would pour the first round of green tea for them when I was serving,
but that they would subsequently serve each other in the following rounds.
Then, with her usual whirlwind of greetings, Kobayashi-san entered and
joined the table. She had brought some seaweed crackers for everyone and
the chat took on a friendly and cheerful tone, with people from both tables
participating. The theme was local politics and the promises made ahead
of the local elections. Unlike the serious conversation that ensued in one of
the days to follow, this one was full of jokes and throwaway remarks. Someone then brought up the issue of a murder covered in the news. One of the
ladies remarked: "He was crazy, the murderer. He was young, in his thirties,
and lived all alone in a *manshon* flat. He didn't have any friends and spent all

his time alone. That would make one crazy." They all agreed it was important to talk to other people, and one of them replied: "One can also get senile [*boke*]. It's so important, talking to people every day." An elegant, silver-haired lady in her eighties wearing a pale blue dress with a lace collar nodded approvingly: "Yes, this is my talking practice [*hanashi no okeiko*]. I come here to have a chat and a laugh," she added with a cheerful smile. This caused a round of warm laughter and approving noises. Another lady exclaimed: "This is the source of our health [*wathashitachi no kenkō no moto*]!" Closing time was approaching, and after half an hour or so everyone started getting ready to leave. Some of the ladies helped me to collect the empty cups while the others said their goodbyes. Ueda-san and Kobayashi-san stayed behind to keep me company, chatting away while I tidied up and closed the salon.

Welcome, Welcome: The Salon as a Place to Belong

This chapter explores the dynamics of interactions in the salon, from greetings and seating patterns to informal alliances and sharing and avoidance relations, all of which one might discern in the above description of a typical day. The salon is seen by some as a place to drop in occasionally and by others as a place to spend time on a daily basis, but always as an opportunity to meet others and socialize. For most visitors, it is their "place" (*ibashō*), somewhere they feel a sense of comfort or belonging—a theme explored further in this section. Subsequent sections explore the nature of conversations and a variety of issues related to living well, such as food and sociality, the importance of looks, local geographies and the relevance of place, health and aging, form and manners. With respect to the latter point in particular, I argue that underlying many of the issues mentioned is a preoccupation with politeness and above all with "doing things properly" (*chanto suru*). These are part of an abiding concern with "form" that has important implications for well-being and for ideas about *how* to live well. While the constraining aspects of formality have often been noted, my older interlocutors made it clear to me that doing things the way they should be done can induce calm, pleasant feelings of competence and satisfaction.

A visitor to the salon is usually met by a chorus of greetings from all corners of the room. Particularly in the afternoons, after lunch, a larger crowd gathers and the atmosphere is jovial. This is the time when greetings are numerous and cheerful, mixed with calls to sit in a particular spot, or questions about the length of or reason for one's absence, or just cheerful statements that so-and-so has arrived. Instead of just a plain hello (*konnichi wa* during the day, or *konban wa* in the evenings), people are sometimes told how nice it is of them to have come (*yō kite kuremashita, ne*; or more often in Osaka dialect, *yō kite kurehatta*). This cordial phrase has a subtle host overtone, and while it mostly reflected a warm, genuine feeling it also indicated that the addressee is more of a guest than the speaker, who is "at home." The more frequent customers have a good idea about who came when and pass on the information to each other, while some of the regulars who come less frequently inquire if someone was in recently and how they are doing, if they had not seen them of late. People in the salon frequently expressed their concern for others if they have not been in for an unusual amount of time—with those who come daily this could be a day or two, while with those who come once or twice a week one week would suffice. Some would inquire with the shopkeepers or acquaintances and neighbors, or less frequently, they would drop in to check on them. This appeared to be a spontaneous extension of neighborly behavior, even though some of the visitors lived considerably farther away and arrived by bus or by bicycle. The expression of concern was rather casual and would rarely lead to a full conversation about someone who was absent. Most visitors were nevertheless aware of their links to the group of people who came to the salon on a regular basis, so they made an effort to poke their head in on their way somewhere just to say hello or let others know what they're up to.

One afternoon in late March, Okuma-san came in after a longish absence of two weeks. She had short white hair and was sporting a polo shirt and sneakers. Upon greeting everyone she apologized for her long absence and explained that she had been very busy for the past few weeks, during the cherry blossom viewing season. She had a couple of house guests and complained how exhausted she was from all the cooking and serving of elaborate Japanese-style meals, though she had also had a lot of fun, going to interesting places while showing her guests around. Her story attracted the attention of most people gathered around the table, and they listened attentively. Three ladies and Shachō were very happy to hear she was well, because they had been getting worried about her and thought she might have fallen ill. Kato-san had even walked to her place but was baffled at what to do, as Okuma-san lived in a massive apartment block (*manshon*) with hundreds of apartments and a securely locked front door. She realized she couldn't just knock and check on her so she left. Okuma-san thanked her for her concern and took out a big box of biscuits from Nara, which she had brought as an *omiyage* (a present from a trip, a souvenir) from a trip she had made with her friends during their stay, and offered them to everyone. This little episode highlights the expressions of concern for others, or a particular mode of care, among the frequent visitors to the salon.

Concern or care seems to color the common phrase used when someone leaves the salon and which follows a farewell: "Take care" (*ki wo tsukete ne*). The expression used in this context is of course formulaic and usually does not reflect an interest in personal particulars, but rather refers to a general sense of keeping safe and looking after oneself: walking without tripping, being safe in traffic and in the street, looking after one's health. On particularly cold or hot days, or if the salon visitors noted that someone's health is somewhat diminished, farewells might be followed by *karada wo daiji ni*, a slightly less formal expression translating roughly as "look after your body/ health." The person leaving might also exchange a few words with other visitors about when they will next be in the salon and when they might meet again, or mention their plans for the coming days, all of which helps others to notice if someone is absent for a longer period of time than expected without a known reason. The concern expressed in statements or acts such as these could easily pass unnoticed by an external observer. Unlike the very tightly knit network of a small community such as a village, or some urban neighborhoods where everyone's movements and actions are closely observed and monitored, the "neighborly" relationships of the elderly salon goers are somewhat looser. Older people of the salon spoke fondly of their sense of (sometimes newfound) freedom and took care to protect their privacy. Nevertheless, the concern they express for others is personal, founded on their knowledge of the personal circumstances of their peers, even if such knowledge is partial or circumscribed. This type of concern reflects a broader characteristic of the relationships between the older people visiting the salon, which I would argue are personal but not intimate.

The relationships of the salon visitors in many ways resemble the neighborly networks of support and in some cases form an extension of these networks. The modes of interaction thus resemble neighborhood greetings, a superficial knowledge of other people's circumstances, including the rough whereabouts of their home, the exchange of small or "meaningless" gifts such as food, particularly redistributing a surplus or bringing delicacies such as any seasonal specialties (chestnuts in autumn, mandarins in winter, yuzu citrus tea in summer, and so on) that one managed to obtain. At the same time, the salon provides a space to meet other older people from the neighborhood to whom one might not otherwise have a personal connection, which is especially important for those whose acquaintances of similar age have passed away or become immobile. The salon also proved an extension of these networks in another important way, as it provides a space for people who seek the company of peers but do not live in the immediate vicinity. Many salon visitors—at least a third—arrived from neighborhoods farther away, by bicycle or public transport. Most important, according to both the volunteers and the visitors, the salon provides a place to be, a place to interact and meet. Entertaining at home can be tiring and perceived by the guests as a burden on the host, as Okuma-san made clear in the story above. Moreover, receiving less-well-acquainted visitors in one's home is perceived as dangerous, especially for older people living on their own. Thus, among all the salon visitors, entertaining at home was extremely rare. Finally, the salon provided more than just a place to spend time—it was perceived as a meaningful place (*ibashō*), where one feels comfortable and has a sense of belonging. On several occasions, I heard people mention in spontaneous conversations how good it was to have a place to be (*ibashō*), or that the salon was their source of health (*kenkō no moto*).

This sense of belonging to the salon as a place can be contrasted with the feeling of discomfort that newcomers experience when first entering. This feeling of the salon being in some ways "hard to enter" (*hairinikui*) at first was mentioned by almost all the salon visitors, especially those who came on their own for the first time. As one of the veteran visitors mentioned once: "This place is hard to enter [*hairinikui*]. When I first came here I was reluctant, because you don't exactly know what this place is. It doesn't look like an office or a shop, but it's somewhat different from a café, because you can see from the large window at the entrance that everyone's sitting at one of the two large tables. Also, there's no menu or price list out the front. I didn't know what to expect!" This feeling of being out of place in the salon is, paradoxically, linked to the feeling of it being a warm, welcoming, and cheerful place. The laughter and lively chats coming from the inside can be equally inviting and intimidating. The reason for this is a lack of clear information about how open or closed is the circle of people inside, which makes one feel like an outsider. In literature about Japan the twin concepts of inside (*uchi*) and outside (*soto*) is often mentioned as an important principle of classification: one either belongs to the group or is on the outside. This group may be a family, a company, or a class, and the social world comprises a number of such overlapping circles. A public place such as a café, by contrast, does not usually house a tightly knit group but rather an assemblage of strangers who do not communicate with each other, except with the person whom they arranged to meet: space is divided between strangers and friends. The salon aims to create a different kind of place, where one can talk to others who may not have been acquaintances but are not strangers either. Equally, one may come to meet a friend in the salon, but most would be reluctant to display particular closeness and intimacy with one person in particular in a way that isolates them from the overall conversation. Around a shared table, common courtesy demands that the conversation can be shared. Frequent visits and many familiar faces undoubtedly create a sense of belonging, especially when even one's short absence is noted by others, but the relationships between the salon goers could not be described as close or intimate.

The aim of the NPO management was to create a place where people could make acquaintances in the neighborhood and to keep it open for all newcomers. That is why polite notices state the rules and prices on every table, in place of a menu, and an information brochure with a description of the aims and upcoming events is placed on a stand near the entrance. The discomfort of newcomers is often eased either by a previous invitation from one of the regulars or by an impromptu invitation on the very threshold. Just like Kato-san sprang to her feet when she saw a lingering silhouette near the front door, most visitors would make sure to invite the reluctant newcomer in and make sure they feel comfortable even before the busy volunteer would have time to approach the table. Furthermore, the management organizes numerous events in the salon, such as workshops and concerts, which they advertise via leaflets and posters in the shopping arcade or advertisements in local council publications. Once one has visited the salon on one of these more formal and therefore public occasions, at least the place becomes familiar. An effort is made by all the staff and volunteers to serve hot drinks to all the visitors after these events, a task that is rather difficult with only one small water boiler and a very small filter coffee machine. On these occasions, visitors have a chance to converse informally with each other over a cup of tea, as well as to become acquainted with the way the salon operates. The system is very simple but quite different from a café or a teahouse, as only a few kinds of drinks are served and prices are kept very low. Coffee, green tea, and black tea are priced at 100 yen and additional servings are free, as is cold water.[1] No food is served, and one is encouraged to bring lunch, provided that one takes away all the rubbish. Smoking and the consumption of alcohol are forbidden. Some events and weekly workshops are free, but those that require a small fee are clearly marked on the printed schedules available near the door.

Chatting or Sitting Together: The Construction of Salon Sociality

While some visitors use the salon as a place to quietly enjoy an inexpensive hot drink, and the occasional person comes in order to meet up with a friend as in a café, a large majority comes to enjoy other people's company: whether quietly listening to a conversation and nodding occasionally, having a quiet chat with one or two others during a lull, or participating in a loud and cheerful exchange within a larger group. Conversation lies at the core of salon sociality, and for those living alone or with a working family, a visit may offer a valuable opportunity to talk. This point was made on several occasion by the elegant, slim, silver-haired lady who mentioned that she likes to laugh and chat and would call the salon her "talking practice" (*ohanashi no okeiko*), choosing an old-fashioned term for artistic practice, *okeiko*, usually used in the context of self-development. Conversations in the salon covered a wide array of topics, including food, local geographies, politics, self-development, appearance, aging and health, death, family, leisure, and old times. Recent work in gerontology shows the importance of communication for "successful aging" (see Nussbaum and Fisher 2011), but I would argue that as a mode of sociality, communication is directly linked to a sense of well-being and a meaningful life.

Mornings in the salon are usually quieter and the conversations more subdued, taking place between just two or three people. On the quiet days, when it is unusually empty, some private and more personal conversations take place. Sometimes people grocery shopping in the arcade would stop by and have a quick coffee before rushing home in time to make lunch. During lunch hours (between noon and one o'clock), some people leave, but others may stay or even come to eat their lunch and enjoy a cup of coffee after their meal. During this time people usually conversed in a low-key manner about everyday matters. Afterward, some would return home to rest, and few guests would enter, as they also might be enjoying a nap at home. A peak time was around three in the afternoon, when the largest crowd usually gathered and the mood was particularly cheerful and loud. Conversation topics ranged from politics to olden times, often involving some banter and jokes. This was the time that regular customers who did not come on a daily basis but less frequently, perhaps twice a week, would choose for their visits, as well as some volunteers who lived in the neighborhood. Many such regular visitors were men: Shachō, the handsome, retired company head; Harada-san, a stocky man who particularly enjoyed learning unusual kanji characters; or a loud, thin man wearing a baseball hat and large wooden bead necklace over his sports top.

It may be useful at this point to make a few remarks on gender. Overall, there were fewer male then female visitors to the salon, perhaps making up around a third of the customers during the day. Several of the salon goers explained that men were perhaps playing Go and preferred not to sit and chat. Murata-san, a male salon volunteer who used to work as a helper in a day care center where there were even fewer men, commented that many men have no social skills (*shakōsei ga nai*) and felt uncomfortable having conversations with unknown people, a statement that sounded like much of the popular discourse of the time. A couple of regular morning visitors seemed to conform to that description entirely. One, in his late sixties, arrived early, ordered a coffee and sat in silence at an empty end of one of the tables and left as soon as he finished his drink, no more than half an hour after arrival. Another, in his seventies, also chose an empty part of a table and read his newspaper without a word, constantly ordering refills of coffee and leaving a couple of hours later. In contrast, the three men mentioned above appeared to be at the very heart of the social life, arriving at busy times and drawing their chairs up to the most crowded part of the table to enjoy a lively chat. The ladies responded in kind and often made quite a fuss when they arrived, making sure their drinks were ordered promptly and calling them and making space at the table. If the first group of male salon goers seems to support the stereotype of poor social skills, the second group are positively at the heart of salon social life and challenge the image of the impolite, stern, and demanding older man with the sense of entitlement known as *oyaji* (Bardsley 2011). In general, the modes of sociality, behaviors, and conversations in the salon often challenged stereotyped images of older Japanese.[2]

Sharing: Food, News, and Information

Ono-san always comes to the salon on Thursday mornings to enjoy a cup of black coffee and some dark chocolate that the volunteer lady would happily keep in the refrigerator for him until the next week. This man in his late sixties runs a shop with pictures and decorations he makes himself from wood. After a stroke his command over the right side of his body is weakened, and he has difficulties walking longer distances but gets by on a bicycle. "I like Thursdays, it's my rehabilitation day"—Ono-san has a free day on Thursdays, when he gets to rest from the woodwork in his shop, which he finds increasingly exhausting with his weak right hand. He finds it difficult to admit it to his wife and goes to work daily so as not to disappoint her, as he admitted quietly to the volunteer lady on one occasion. After having finished vocational school, Ono-san worked in a large publishing house as a designer, and some years ago, after he retired, he designed the first logo for the NPO. Ono-san was convinced that years of a stressful lifestyle and long hours, made even longer by extended work-related drinking sessions, had cost him his health and eventually led to his stroke, so he always complained, in a good-humored manner, that work and drinking made his head weak, and continued his conversations with the ladies in the salon, offering them chocolates he brought. Some accepted but most declined, saying that they avoid sweet things and prefer simple food, especially light Japanese dishes.

As a topic of conversation, food deserves attention as it was probably most often mentioned and discussed with much relish among the salon goers. Furthermore, the salon is a place where people occasionally have a meal or a snack. Not a day would pass without someone bringing a small snack to share, just like Kobayashi-san in the opening story, usually packaged food that they had received as gifts and wanted to share with others. Those who had traveled somewhere, for instance to visit their family or to a hot spring (*onsen*), would always bring packets of food to share as souvenirs (*omiyage*). These beautifully wrapped boxes of biscuits, traditional sweets, or other foods, all portioned and individually wrapped inside the box, are usually presented as a local specialty. Others brought local specialties that their families sent them from their native village or town (*furusato*), most commonly fruits such as mandarins, pears, or persimmons. All of these gifts were consumed together; only if there were a few extra pieces, the person who brought it, or one of the more assertive older ladies such as Kato-san, would encourage others to take one home. The importance of sharing food and eating together for the construction of sociality or relatedness is widely recognized in the anthropological literature, and eating patterns in the salon are somewhat indicative of the types of relationships created among the loose group of salon goers.

While the snacks brought to the salon were always promptly and efficiently shared with the help of several regulars, not all food is expected to be shared. Lunches, brought in individual portions, were not meant to be shared, and there was no pressure to offer food brought as lunch. However, people would offer to go and buy something for others if they were going to the shop and were given the right amount of money upon their return, which they were not reluctant to take. As paying for other people's food, or treating them to a meal, may indicate a higher status, the attention to paying back the money spent created an atmosphere of equality. This was further maintained by careful attempts not to single out anyone in particular when bringing gifts of food and by keeping extras for those who might come in later. One day, Shachō came in late in the afternoon and was offered a cracker by Ikeda-san but seemed reluctant to take it, until others confirmed that they had already received one and that it was an *omiyage* from Murata-san's recent hiking trip, which he had brought for everyone earlier in the day. Similarly, if a group of a few ladies wanted to go to have dinner in a restaurant, or eat cake together without inviting everyone present, the arrangements were made very discreetly, usually over the telephone before arriving at the salon, as Kato-san and Ueda-san explained to me on separate occasions. If salon goers knew each other well and spent some time going places together outside the salon, what they did was not discussed in front of others, lest they felt left out. In short, food sharing in the salon is an important part of everyday sociality and the creation of a warm atmosphere, but it was limited to the occasional sharing of snacks. It did not extend to sharing meals, which could be seen as creating an overly close and familial atmosphere considered by many to be intrusive or burdensome to others.

Despite the fact that they do not often eat in restaurants (roughly a third of salon goers never go to a restaurant, and the majority go to restaurants once or twice a month) salon visitors happily discussed the types and quality of new restaurants open in the area, or the places they particularly like for certain specialties. Murata-san, a man in his sixties who lives on his own, explained that he eats in restaurants a couple of times a month and enjoys eating those dishes he cannot make at home for himself, either because they are complicated or not the kind of food one would prepare for one person. Murata-san on several occasions pointed out that he looks after his health and his body by carefully choosing what he eats—mostly cooked food with lots of vegetables and fish—and limiting the consumption of alcoholic drinks, making sure that he doesn't have any alcohol at least one day a week. Most women visiting the salon claimed that they were not able to drink more than half a glass of beer and drank rarely, only on social occasions. The importance of healthy food was often discussed, and some of the salon guests were very proud of their health, seeing it somewhat as their own achievement.

Kondo-san is a good example: she grows her own vegetables and cooks her own meals with little salt or seasoning—*usukuchi* (lightly flavored). She was proud that she did not need any medicine and her physician praised her good health. In contrast, a lot of meals that could be bought, such as boxed lunches, were considered to be much less healthy. Okuma-san told us of a time when she was in the hospital, and after her return home she was too weak to cook. During her recovery period of several months she ordered boxed lunches, and when she visited her physician she was told she had high blood pressure and heightened cholesterol in her blood. Instead of taking the medicines she was prescribed, she started eating only *usukuchi* meals, and after a couple of months her readings went back to normal. She was convinced that the meat and fried foods in the boxed meals were one of the main things that harmed her health.

Usukuchi or lightly flavored food, without much added salt or soy sauce, was generally considered to be key to healthy nutrition, mostly comprising vegetables and rice, a little fish, and very little meat. Restaurant food and more extravagant meals, sweets, and seasonal treats were considered to be much less healthy and as something to be consumed only on occasion, but not necessarily something craved and desired. Kondo-san and others did not deny themselves these pleasures, but many found that they were happiest when they were eating lighter food. A petite, grey-haired lady who always left before lunchtime to cook for her brother and came back in the afternoon often commented that she enjoys cooking but would not cook much for herself if she lived on her own, as she would be quite content with *chazuke* (a simple meal made of rice with tea poured over it) almost every day. Simple and humble meals were mentioned by many as a source of contentment. The wholesome foods that were of particularly high quality in particular areas were sometimes a topic that sparked a conversation about the food available a long time ago or something that people used to eat in their hometown. Many of the salon visitors (probably close to half) were not originally from Osaka, much less the neighborhood; most had moved to Osaka as a regional center in their youth. Conversations about food could therefore often lead to stories about the past and childhood, mostly fond recollections of cheerful times and special events and holidays, such as New Year, and rarely melancholy.

On most days, however, the conversations about food revolved about more everyday matters, such as grocery shopping. Salon visitors, especially women, exchanged information about certain grocery stalls in the shopping arcade and other nearby arcades, commenting on the prices but especially on the quality of goods and their freshness. This exchange of information extended to other topics, such as services for the elderly, municipal services such as transport, news, and interesting events such as free concerts. Kondo-san was particularly well informed about food service for the elderly in the area and happily recommended particular ones to her interlocutors: the one on Wednesdays in A-chō (neighbourhood A) has the best menu, as they serve miso soup for free with every meal, whereas the one in D-chō (neighbourhood D) on the first Thursday in every month has the most interesting music program after the food is served. The one in B-chō is very strict, as they read out the names of all older people registered and check attendance, which she finds rather annoying, but the one in C-chō is really friendly and one gets a little gift and a photo taken for one's birthday. The amount of information on various services, including health and welfare schemes and cultural events run by the municipal authorities and voluntary associations, is extremely large and one could easily become lost. Some of the information was available through newsletters that were delivered to all the inhabitant's houses, some was circulated through the leaflets in the salon and town hall, a lot was available through the internet, but all of these were not equally accessible to everyone (not to mention difficult to use and find), and the sheer abundance made it difficult to follow. Recommendations by acquaintances were considered by most salon goers as the most convenient and reliable source of relevant information. This made the salon a valuable resource for older people who might have otherwise lacked a wide network of acquaintances of the same age group or similar interests. Sharing information one had acquired with the others can also be understood as a form of expressing concern and care.

Public Faces: Politics and News

Kobayashi-san's passage through the shopping arcade could be noticed by an onlooker from a distance by her sheer intensity and the number of greetings she exchanged on the way. Everyone seemed to know her. With a broad smile on her bespectacled face, Kobayashi-san asked about the newsagent's daughter's entrance exams, the butcher's wife's health, the florist's visit to the dentist. A thin, slightly stooped woman in her sixties who has survived a serious disease, she has an air of determination and positive energy around her. Her laughter and smiles immediately fill the room with energy whenever she enters the salon, often bringing treats for everyone present. Somewhat younger than other salon visitors, who call her Kobayashi-chan (a diminutive form usually used for young women or girls), Kobayashi-san often expressed delight at having a chance to meet people in the salon and shouted from the door, "All my favorite people in one place!" On one occasion when we walked together, I expressed amazement at how many people she knew and helped, to which she replied pragmatically that she has no close family other than her brother and her twenty-five-year-old niece, who lives abroad, so she needs to make an effort to help people and support her friends as much as she can, so that she can get support and care when she needs it. One day, after a longer absence, Kobayashi-san arrived in the salon even later than usual, just half an hour before closing time. Some of the regular salon goers knew through acquaintances that she was involved in a political campaign, so we were all curious to hear how that was going. Kobayashi-san explained that she is helping in the election campaign of the local representative of one of the two major political parties, and her role was to educate young campaigners who were visiting the people in the neighborhood that was their constituency. She fondly recalled the days when she herself did this job and even made speeches through a loudspeaker on a truck that cruised the streets as a part of the campaign. Kobayashi-san was interested in getting to know as many people in the neighborhood as possible, and the campaign was a real social event for her. On several occasions, though, she expressed a genuine worry about the future for young people and a diminishing sense of hope: "We lived in times when every year our salaries would gradually increase. Young people today can't even count on a stable job. There is no hope [kibō ga nai], everyone feels a lack of hope."

Far from being uninterested in matters of national and local politics, the salon goers kept abreast with daily news through the media, mostly national television and major radio stations, but also through the newspaper and local newsletters. Local politics and daily news occupied a large part of conversations in the salon, mostly revolving around matters mentioned in the morning news or the news of the day before. Given that the news was available to everyone and thus an inclusive theme for conversation, it is unsurprising that it was a very popular topic in the afternoons, when larger groups gathered and chatted together rather than the two or three smaller groups that often formed when the salon was emptier in the mornings. While the conversations usually took the form of a lively discussion, often interwoven with jokes, the opinions expressed were restricted to worries about the competence of the Japanese government, or the way a particular statement was formulated, or about the trustworthiness of a particular politician—general themes that everyone shared an opinion about. Open views about certain political matters were almost never expressed, and while the conversation was rather loud, it rarely took a form where anyone could disagree much with anything that was being said. These conversations appeared heated and seemed genuine, with no veiled sentiments being expressed afterward on the side or concealed with difficulty. In relation to this issue it might be useful to look at the Japanese concepts of *tatemae* and *honne*, which have attracted much attention among anthropologists, the former denoting the way one is expected to behave and the latter one's true feelings and the way one would like to act with one's own interest in mind. In other words, *tatemae* is associated with an external, rule-bound social persona, while *honne* is supposed to be an expression of one's true self (e.g., Sugimoto 2003:28). It could, therefore, be concluded that what was expressed in these conversations was simply *tatemae*, while true feelings were kept to oneself. This view, then, might assume that the views expressed were insincere and less than fully true, but rather a façade in a public situation, a necessity to maintain harmonious relationships in the group. However, the conversations in the salon, combined with a number of private conversations conducted with some of the salon goers with whom I developed a closer relationship, complicate this picture based on a duality between private and public spheres.

First, different themes, as will gradually become clear throughout the remainder of this chapter, were treated in different ways and taken up in different social settings within the salon: in smaller or larger groups, with a more or less personal attitude. Second, the heated discussion about politics was genuine and the opinions expressed were most likely really held by the participants. The level of discussion was limited and certain lines were not often crossed, so that the kinds of opinion offered could not really be expressed in antagonistic or irreconcilable ways. In other words, what was said was sincere, if somewhat circumscribed. The variety of themes taken up in the salon coincide with different modes of sociality, which taken together might provide insight into the balance between public and private spheres, while revealing something of the nature of relationships more broadly.

No Idle Pastime: Self-Development and "Study at Sixty"

Harada-san is a tall, sturdy man with heavy, dark-rimmed glasses and a golf hat, who visits the salon regularly two or three times a week. He could most often be seen in the afternoons, enjoying a lively chat with Shachō and the ladies. A retired shopkeeper in his early seventies, Harada-san amused the company with his knowledge of unusual kanji characters or wordplay based on them. He once told us that the study of kanji and calligraphy had been his favorite pastimes for a long time, but that after retirement he had more time to pursue them. Similarly, Murata-san, a youthful looking man in his sixties who often volunteered in the salon, often told all present about his hiking trips and brought albums of photographs he took in the mountains. The ladies present were always very curious and happy to have a chance to see the photographs he took of breath-taking views or rare wildflowers, about which conversation could continue for a long time. Murata-san was grateful that he had more time since retirement to go hiking with a group of companions, men of a similar age. With more time on their hands, they could go away for longer, and this allowed them to reach places that were considerably more remote. This required planning and preparation, as they climbed for longer stretches of time, and he often spoke of the next challenge they planned. While Harada-san and Murata-san both continued their hobbies from long before their retirement, they both spoke of the challenge and the need to make progress: to learn more or to climb higher. Other salon visitors set themselves different challenges: rather than improving a skill they already had, they decided to embark on a new hobby. Okada-san, a very vigorous lady in her sixties, took up weaving and attended weaving workshops held in the salon twice a week. The fruits of her labor were clearly visible, as both she and her husband wore colorful handwoven vests on cold mornings. Like her husband, who had taken up carpentry in the past few years since retirement, Okada-san liked the idea of learning something new, a skill she did not have before.

This tendency to take up a new hobby and focus on developing a skill in later life is sometimes termed *rokujū no tenarai*, or study in one's sixties. Another man in his late sixties whom I met in Awara salon (my secondary field site) told me about his own new hobbies and those of his friends: he started a drawing course and joined a choir, while his wife attended a hula dancing class with her friends, and his neighbor enjoyed photography classes. I spoke to all of them and they explained that they enjoyed the group learning as it gave them an opportunity to make new acquaintances, other than their work colleagues or neighbors. They explained that the sixties were an ideal time for studying something new, as one was finally free of many obligations, one's children having grown up, and after retirement one finally had more free time. They also spoke of the fear of becoming too dependent on the routine that their work (or care for the family and housework) provided, so learning something new was a way for them to move away from their earlier roles. Those attending the Fureai salon, in contrast to the somewhat younger and more dynamic elderly people in Awara salon, rarely mentioned their pastimes as hobbies or the pursuit of *ikigai*. They talked less in terms of pastimes and more in terms of practice, or the importance of being in the moment and becoming immersed in the task (*muchū ni naru*). They emphasized the importance of dedication for doing things properly, but also for feeling a sense of achievement and relaxing by not thinking about anything else. Pastimes and daily activities, whether artistic or mundane, were often guided by the principle of "doing things properly" (*chanto suru*), the way they should be done and not sloppily. While this principle may seem constraining in its formality—especially in its more mundane forms, such as being aware of the proper way to serve coffee to customers—knowledge of the rules and mastery of the pleasing form of an action may bring genuine pleasure, as explained by Murata-san on one occasion. Doing things properly need not be restricted to mastering new skills, but when it is, it can further be linked to a notion of self-development or self-cultivation.

This striving for self-development should nevertheless not be understood as a merely individualistic pursuit aimed at one's own pleasure. Conversely, self-cultivation can be understood as equally important for the advancement of the community, and indeed may even be presented as an obligation to a group. The notion that self-cultivation is at the basis of community development has a long history. In her book about ritual and religious practices in nineteenth-century Japan, Janine Sawada attempts to explore the interplay between different coexisting groups engaged, for example, in divination, Shinto purification rituals, and Zen practice, out of which emerged a common concern with "personal cultivation" (*mi o osameru; shūshin*) or "learning" (*gakumon*)—that is, the moral, ritual, physiological, and/or educational process by which individuals were believed to attain well-being (Sawada 2004:3).

A noteworthy contribution to the discussion of self-development that elucidates some of these issues of individual-society dynamics can be found in the work of John Traphagan (2004), concerned primarily with well-being and aging in contemporary rural Japan. Here he expands on his previous work (Traphagan 2000) in which he argued that senility in Japan should be understood less as a biomedical category and more in relation to ideas about the "good person," defined in terms of activity (Traphagan 2004:9). He makes a connection between the notion of the "good person" and well-being, which "is closely related to physical and mental health, but also includes broader ideas of success and avoidance of calamity, is interwoven with values of family, self-discipline, and control that are constructed not only in terms of biomedicine, but in terms of social interactions" (Traphagan 2004:21). Thus, well-being should be understood as pertaining both to the individual and to the group or community. Furthermore, Traphagan argues that well-being and health in the Japanese context can be thought of as a type of embodied social capital representing individual and collective abilities, a capital accumulated by investing in self-improvement (Traphagan 2004:58). The very engagement in hobbies or pastimes indicates an individual's focus on self-cultivation and discipline, which as such benefits the community, and which in the case of elderly people means showing an effort to maintain mental and physical health in order to avoid burdening the family and community (Traphagan 2004:74).[3] The well-being of group and individual are, therefore, conceived as closely linked through the idea of the "good person."

Another important aspect of "study at sixty" is the age itself. While one of the meanings of this phrase is a sentiment that it is never too late to learn, the age of those of my interlocutors who took up new hobbies and dedicated their time to self-development was indeed the sixties, and less frequently the early seventies. Some of my older interlocutors explicitly expressed a lack of interest in learning something new or taking up a hobby, dismissing it as something fanciful or frivolous. This need not mean that this generation, now in their nineties, has no interest in pastimes, but usually they cultivate those they were already involved in, such as origami or growing vegetables. While they happily participated in singing classes organized in the salon, where they sang traditional or old popular songs, several of the ladies in their nineties and late eighties flatly refused invitations to participate in workshops that involved mastering new skills such as weaving. When Kato-san was presented with a leaflet advertising "fun classes" designed to improve mental ability, she just giggled and waved her hand saying she does not need such things (*sonna koto iranai ne*). The reason for this was not that she thought of herself as mentally agile enough, but that she did not feel a need to maintain her abilities for a future far ahead. In another conversation this sentiment was made even clearer. When one of the ladies in her late eighties expressed concern about her memory and the need to socialize and talk to other people as a form of mental practice, the reaction was positive and encouraging. Ikeda-san and other ladies in their eighties and nineties confirmed the importance of conversations and keeping active, but they also agreed with Kato-san, who suggested that if you get to the age of ninety or thereabouts without becoming senile (*boke*), there was really no more reason for concern, as one is most likely to stay bright enough until the end of one's life.

Family

Kondo-san is a calm, broad-faced lady with a dark complexion who spends a lot of time outdoors. She grows her own vegetables in pots in neat rows in front of her house and checks them every morning as soon as she combs her hair, even before breakfast. On several occasions she spoke of growing vegetables with passion and was asked for advice by others who enjoyed gardening in the narrow streets, with barely enough space for narrow Japanese cars to drive through. Having read quite a bit about gardening, Kondo-san has both theoretical and practical knowledge, which has earned her a nickname: "a vegetable expert" (*yasai no hakase*). Kondo-san is in good health and seems no older than sixty-five, so everyone was surprised to hear she is in fact seventy-six, something she put down to a healthy diet. Kondo-san lives on her own, a situation that she described as very comfortable: "This is heaven [*gokuraku*]! I had many hard times in life and now I'm finally free, everything is so easy, I don't have to look after anybody." Her son had invited her to live with him and his family in another prefecture, but she didn't get along with her daughter-in-law, who demanded that she move away. Kondo-san then moved in with her daughter but realized that to live harmoniously with her daughter's family she had to be the one to adapt, and she had a feeling that in order not to be a burden she had to endure many things, mostly small annoyances. She then decided to make do on her own and now takes pride in living independently with her very limited means. Kondo-san was not the only happy person who lived alone and was comfortable with her living arrangements. Perhaps around half of the salon goers lived alone, and most of them spoke of a sense of freedom and their comfortable way of life.

Like Kondo-san, many salon guests happily discussed their family relationships and complained about their daughters or daughters-in-law. They mostly discussed these issues quietly in smaller groups, especially if they voiced concerns or worries, or wanted to complain about a difficult or unfair situation. These conversations were much more likely to occur among women; I have only witnessed three occasions when men spoke of their family problems. In all three cases men were speaking quietly with an older woman whom they knew fairly well. These concerns were often voiced in a jocular or comical manner. In her work with older Japanese women, Yoshiko Matsumoto (2011) similarly found that painful self-disclosure was often comical or humorous. I suggest that the need to share one's worries is accompanied by a sense that in order not to make the atmosphere overly grim and so as not to burden others—much as Ueda-san argued in the opening episode— one must maintain some humorous distance.

Conflict and Tension

While the salon is perceived as a place to relax and enjoy company, and efforts were made to maintain a good atmosphere and harmonious relationships, this does not mean that there was no conflict or tension. Not all the conversations made friends—some alienated people or caused strain. One such occasion with heightened tension occurred one warm morning in early May, when not many people were present in the salon. Ikeda-san, the younger of the two sisters frequently coming to the salon, came in for a cup of coffee and noticed Abe-san, a short, round-faced lady in her late seventies, sitting at the table closer to the entrance, diagonally from a quiet man reading a newspaper. They exchanged greetings and Ikeda-san made her way directly to the farthest corner of the other table. The atmosphere grew tense, until another couple of ladies came in and joined Ikeda-san's table. After Abe-san had left, Ikeda-san hissed nervously to the lady sitting on her left that Abe-san had brought her friend to the salon the day before. Ikeda-san had got along well with her and they had an interesting conversation about an old film; they broke into a song together, one of the famous songs from the film. Later, Abe-san accused Ikeda-san of stealing her friend, and now they were both too upset to speak to each other. Even though these remarks were made quietly and somehow on the margins of the conversation, the tension in the room was palpable. A public display of tension and conflict, something that this event came close to, was uncommon. More often, small annoyances were kept to oneself, and a careful choice of seat and timing of one's arrival was used to avoid people with whom one had a disagreement.

Salon goers usually strove for a pleasant atmosphere and avoided confrontation or visible tension. One might assume that this rule of cheerfulness and conviviality was somewhat constraining, but on several occasions my interlocutors explained that they would rather leave some problem in peace or just somehow avoid the person with whom they had a disagreement than lose the opportunity to enjoy themselves and have fun (*tanoshimi*). This echoes the statement of Ueda-san in the opening episode: the salon is a place where people come to enjoy themselves. They don't often feel like talking about unpleasant things, nor do they want to burden others with problems. Yet, as some of the above examples show, this does not mean that the conversations were shallow or insincere.[4]

Doing Things Properly: Emotion and Form

A long and heated conversation arose in the salon one afternoon when Mori-san, after ordering a cup of coffee, told us about an experience in a printing equipment shop earlier that day.[5] Wanting to print out some photos that he took of some of us at a local festival to exhibit in the salon, Mori-san went out to buy some ink for his printer. But the shop owner had run out of ink cartridges for that particular model of printer and refused to help. Mori-san got infuriated and walked an hour to the next closest shop stocking the ink. He was adamant that he would never return to the local shop again. The conversation now focused on what the actual problem was, and soon it transpired that Mori-san did not expect a different service in terms of actions taken, such as taking an order, but was much more concerned about the form in which this lack of ability to be helpful was conveyed. Instead of just stating plainly that they have none, the shopkeeper could have offered an apology or an explanation. This sentiment, that the way the shopkeeper spoke was inadequate, was soon confirmed and restated by everyone in the group and numerous examples of similar behavior listed. On other occasions, more closely related to the interactions within the salon, the sentiment was not that something should not have occurred, but rather that the message was to be conveyed in a particular way. This focus on a particular way things should be done seemed to be present in many other situations—tea should be served properly, guests at salon events should be greeted properly: in Japanese, *chanto suru*.

These examples indicate that when people express displeasure about the words or actions of another, this generally relates to how they behaved or expressed themselves rather than to what was said. The intentions of the speaker seemed less important than the forms used. Conversely, the feeling often present in the West, that a polite or pleasantly worded utterance might have been insincere and fake—stressing the importance of expressing one's "real" feelings—was conspicuously absent. It would appear that while Western discourses of intimacy assume the truthfulness of the essence, or content, such that the intentions of the speaker may be concealed by the words themselves, this may be quite different in Japan. Enquiring into how form may be considered more or less revealing of intentions than "essence" could help shed light on particular epistemologies or local ideologies of knowledge. In her book about gifts in Japan, Joy Hendry (1995) proposes that in the Japanese context, wrapping might be at least as important as the content of the gift, if not more so. In fact, in case of a prestation (or a gift, which is always linked to a sense of obligation), it is impossible to separate the content and the wrapping. Extending this idea to language as a form of wrapping, especially polite language, one could infer that form and content change places in terms of priority. Yet rather than investigating this simply in terms of essence and form, it might be more productive to consider the issue with reference to theories of language ideology, formalization in language, and politeness.

In linguistic theories of politeness a dominant concept is that of "face work," based on Erving Goffman's concept of face: actors manage their face, avoid losing face, and so on. A criticism of some of the most prevalent theories and a new model has recently been offered by Richard Watts (2003:1): "Some people feel that polite behaviour is equivalent to socially 'correct' or appropriate behaviour; others consider it to be the hallmark of the cultivated man or woman. Some might characterize a polite person as always being considerate towards other people; others might suggest that a polite person is self-effacing. There are even people who classify polite behaviour negatively, characterizing it with such terms as 'standoffish,' 'haughty,' 'insincere,' etc." In order to understand these differences, Watts introduces a social model of politeness based on the idea that individuals use language as a symbolic resource to manage their "face," their public persona. "Face work" is used here to refer to the management of these appearances to the others, to avoid losing "face" or being sensitive about the "face" of others. When linked to specific threats, face work can be evaluated negatively by the listener, since it doesn't do much more than emphasize the threat itself (Watts 2003:247). In those cases the speaker's intentions are obscure, and politeness can be read as a lack of sincerity (Watts 2003:253), an issue to which I will shortly return.

In his introduction to a volume about political language and oratory, Maurice Bloch (1975) points to a continuum of speech forms ranging from everyday forms of speech to formalized ones such as political speeches. While

I am interested in everyday speech acts in the salon and other daily situations, as described by my interlocutors, these speech acts, especially when problematic, were not formal enough or did not satisfy the polite form. Polite behavior on occasions such as serving tea, receiving and requesting favors, or greetings, which formed a large part of interactions in the salon and a connective tissue of many relationships in the community, were similarly guided by this principle that things should be done properly, or that there is a specific way things should be done. It is therefore reasonable to think of these speech acts as somewhere on Bloch's continuum of speech acts between informal everyday speech and fully formalized speech. According to Bloch, formalizing speech removes it from the particular toward the "eternal," thus ruling out disagreement, since it is harder to disagree with the "right order," and the speaker seems to speak less for himself and more for his social role (Bloch 1975:16). This seems important since polite language, as a form of formalization, is used in non-intimate situations, and social roles may be important.

In his work about the efforts of early Dutch Protestant missionaries to convert the inhabitants of Sumba in eastern Indonesia, Webb Keane elaborates the concept of language ideology or "people's assumptions about language" (2002:66), local ideas about how language works. He argues that Sumbanese and missionaries had very different language ideologies, leading to disagreements over the nature and efficacy of prayer, among other things. While Sumbanese felt that the words used in prayer should come from a repertoire given and approved by ancestors, Protestant missionaries stressed that in order to be sincere, the prayer must come "from the inside." The efficacy of words and language is judged in opposite ways: as coming from the inside or from the outside (of the self). The missionaries thought that if the words coming from an external source were used in prayer, this implied a lack of autonomy and responsibility. Keane links this to modernity and the processes of purification: "The subject, to the extent it aspires to modernity . . . seeks to act as the source of its own authority" (2002:74). The idea of sincerity, as implied in this kind of language ideology, is based on an assumption of a specific relationship between the language and thought, and interior states: "[the] sincere speaker makes that interior state transparent" (Keane 2002:74). Keane's argument ties different language ideologies directly to issues of modernity and self, posing a connection between interiority and truth.

An interesting point on a similar matter is made by Richard Sennett (2002 [1974]) in his historical sociology of the changing notions of private and public from the eighteenth century onward, in which he traces the emergence of a notion of authenticity based on the character of the actors, their internal qualities, rather than the actions they perform. As the presentation of emotions by men as actors was gradually replaced by the expression of "authentic" emotions, the fears of involuntarily expressing inappropriate emotions in the public realm rose and led to a withdrawal into a private sphere. At the same time, formalized behaviors in the public sphere were seen to be insincere and inauthentic. This led to the need to mimick the intimate relationships of the private sphere in the public sphere, and thus the public sphere became eroded: "Playacting in the form of manners, conventions and ritual gestures is the very stuff out of which public relations are formed, and from which public relations derive their emotional meaning. The more social conditions erode the public forum, the more people are routinely inhibited from exercising the capacity to playact" (Sennett 2002:29). Sennett illustrates this change in the understanding of formality and roles as "empty" and damaging to a meaningful public sphere, as individual character becomes a key to social relationships, even in the public sphere. For example, in community groups people may feel the compulsion to get to know each other in order to have meaningful relationships, but in the process of getting to know each other they become focused on each other's characters and lose sight of their communal action (Sennett 2002: 11). Sennett shows that the idea of sincerity and authenticity based on interiority is peculiar to a particular historical period, bound up with processes associated with modernity. Having analyzed the trends toward intimacy in the public sphere and some of its consequences, Sennett argues that a healthy public sphere requires a certain level of formality and role-play as a form of protection that allows communication and thus joint action, making a point that "boundaries around the self are not isolating, but can actually encourage communication with others" (Sennett 2002: 10).

Both Keane's work on sincerity and Sennett's work on private and public spheres provide a backdrop for understanding the importance of form and manners in the salon and their relevance for morality. In the case of older Japanese, it could be argued that formality serves as an enabling device for creating new relationships (like those in the salon) and maintaining sociality while protecting oneself and others from the burden of emotion.

Chapter 5

A Life in a Story

A man is never an individual; it would be more fitting to call him a
singular universal.
   —Jean-Paul Sartre, *The Family Idiot: Gustave Flaubert, 1821–1857*

In more ways than one, no one's life story is just their own. To a greater or
lesser degree our lives are entwined with those of others, and the stories of
our lives are crafted from a range of available narratives that provide meaning to our actions and more or less directly inform our ideas about the options available to us. In his well-known work on aging in Japan, David Plath
puts forward the idea of the "convoy," or a group of "consociates" with whom
one shares one's life over a long period of time. This concept is based on a
recognition of the importance of our interactions with others for affirmation
and support (not unlike the idea of "significant others") but with an added
element of temporal depth, as prolonged engagement with others allows for
a layered, nuanced interaction in more than one role (Plath 1980:227). While
the impact on our lives of others with whom we are in direct interpersonal
contact is readily apparent, the influence on our life choices and life story of
those with whom we are not in close contact—some of whom we do not know
in person at all—is more difficult to capture. One way it may be described
draws on the idea of narrative identity, in which one's life is viewed as a story
one lives out, a story that can only exist in relation to the others available in
one's culture or which circulate in society. Such stories provide examples of
how to live: "We learn through stories not only which identities are available;
more fundamentally, we learn what an identity is" (Frank 2010:199). Stories
of this kind can present themselves to us in any number of forms: told to
us by people we know, enacted in films or theater plays, or referred to in

newspapers or on television, among countless other possibilities. For the postwar generation to which my interlocutors belonged, one such story with which they were all extremely familiar, and that structured many of their expectations in life, concerned the complementary ideal lives of the salaryman and housewife.

Model Lives: Salaryman and Housewife

> They become successful, but not too successful, middle-class,
> white-collar workers. They are married, have one or two children.
> Their homes are in the suburbs. They commute long distances to the
> offices where, after working long hours, they go out drinking with
> their fellow workers.
>
> —John L. McCreery, *Japanese Consumer Behavior*

During the period of growth and expansion that marked the 1960s, Japan witnessed the creation of "mass culture": the formation of "uniform and standardized taste groupings," differentiated more along lines of gender and age than region or class, which led the majority of Japanese people to identify themselves as being in the "middle" or as "middle class" (Ivy 1993:241). William Kelly (1993) traces the rise in identification with "mainstream consciousness" (*chūryū ishiki*) to the expansion of white-collar occupations during the 1960s, at the same time noting that these never reached the point of forming the majority of the working population.[1] Nevertheless, he writes, "it was in the 1960s that certain key elements of middle-class life and location became nationalized into a model of 'mainstream' life that has since powerfully represented designs for living" (Kelly 1993:236). This orientation toward the mainstream definition of aspirations and ways of life was so powerful due to its embeddedness in public discourse and the institutional fields of work, family, and education. Thus work was idealized in the form of the Japanese company, based on lifetime employment, salary, and a seniority system based on years of service, but that at the same time relied on the existence of smaller firms and irregular employment. The system was described as meritocratic, based on twelve years of formal education, mostly in public schools and structured by a uniform curriculum. The prevalent and widely promoted form of the Japanese family was the nuclear household, consisting of a conjugal couple—a working husband and a caregiving wife—with children. This family model developed through an interaction of legal reforms, demographic shifts, and economic changes and was conceived as an extension of institutions such as schools and workplaces, rather than as a refuge from the outside world. These institutions shaped a mainstream ideal but did not unify or homogenize the population—it created new differentiations while providing a unifying frame for people's experience (Kelly 1993:241).

The dominant or mainstream life model therefore consists of a working husband—a "salaryman" (*sararīman*)—and a housewife in charge of the household and the children's education. In his book about the new Japanese middle class, Ezra Vogel (1971 [1963]) refers to the salaryman as a man with a stable salary, usually a white-collar worker, and describes the appeal of becoming a salaryman (or of marrying one, instead of, say, a farmer or a merchant) in terms of stability (of salary and working conditions) and the appeal of a "bright new life" (*akarui seikatsu*) bound by fewer formalities and facilitated by electrical goods. This model has been somewhat transformed and extended, sometimes even to include all men receiving salaries (Robertson and Suzuki 2003:7). Masculine identity in this model is linked to the position of household head and breadwinner, an identity bound to work and "the outside," separated from matters "inside" the home, which is the wife's realm.[2] This distinction of labor and responsibilities was not always so clear-cut, and it often remains more blurred and cooperative, as in the case of blue-collar workers or farmers, for example (Allison 1994:91), and on the other side of the social spectrum, among influential business families for whom women's contacts were essential for successfully conducting business (Hamabata 1991:29–30).

The image of the salaryman as an ideal type is not complete without his female partner, the housewife. As mentioned above, the salaryman life model is based on the strong division between a domestic and a working role. While women may work, their role as a wife and mother, caring for and nurturing their family, remains primary. Anne Imamura (1987), in her classic ethnography *Urban Japanese Housewives*, emphasizes that new Japanese housewives do expect to have a right to engage in some activity of their own, unrelated to their homemaking role, yet are still expected to prioritize their family and the educational results of their children, for which they are held directly responsible: "Children's education is based on the premise that a mother will be free to devote a lot of time to helping the child—not only with the homework and at the examination time but making nutritious and varied lunches, seeing that a child does not forget to bring items to school" (Imamura 1987:19). Interestingly, Imamura devotes space to the type of housing in which women

live: detached family houses, social apartments (*danchi*), or company housing (*shataku*). All have significant influence on women's lifestyles. Company
housing places a great deal of pressure on a woman surrounded by the wives
of her husband's work colleagues, where she needs to observe the strict hierarchy related to their positions in the company (Imamura 1987:4). The *danchi* women do not participate much in the life of the community except via
their children, through school meetings and the Parent-Teacher Association
(PTA). Some of Imamura's interlocutors living in apartments admitted that
they enjoyed freedom from "sticky social relations"—from close community
ties and obligations toward parents-in-law—but also that they do get lonely
more often (Imamura 1987:56).

The dominant model of family, like that of work, does not remain unprob-
lematized by those who live by it. An excellent example is given by Amy Borovoy (2005) in her book about women attending a support group for wives of
alcoholics or mothers of drug abusers. Through discussions of their personal
stories, women often came to problematize the dominant construction of
family and the female role within it, focused on prioritizing the family's needs
and nurturing family members. In their case this led to "codependency"—the
unconditional support they were providing to their husband or child had
enabled the latter to continue with their addiction. But, as Borovoy stresses,
these women "do not explicitly position themselves outside or in the opposition to dominant cultural ideologies; nor do they set out to criticize the
system in which they live. They are largely middle-aged, middle-class housewives who conceptualize themselves within the mainstream; yet, owing to
unfortunate family problems, they confront a fundamental barrier to continuing to make dominant cultural assumptions work" (Borovoy 2005:31).

It was mentioned above that the salaryman life model should be situated
historically, economically, and politically. Thus, while the normativity of the
housewife life model is so strong that it almost came to be equated with womanhood, it should also be understood in a historical perspective, as Emiko
Ochiai (1997) notes in her book about the transformation of the Japanese
family system. She reminds readers that the variety of images of womanhood—
a young bride in the farmer's families, a wife in the merchant family taking
an active part in family business, among others—came to be replaced by the
standardizing image of housewife (*okusan*) in the postwar period. This was
followed by a similar standardization of the size of the family, with two or
three children (Ochiai 1997:43). Furthermore, the image of the family as a
nuclear one, formed around the conjugal couple, was becoming dominant,

and the ratio of nuclear families rose, mostly due to the demographic boom. While the oldest son was usually expected to stay with his parents, younger siblings were expected to move away and to form households of their own. Therefore, at the time this did not mean that the number of three-generational households was decreasing (Ochiai 1997:61). Harald Fuess summed it up, in line with Ochiai's argument: "From the 1960s on, fewer couples lived with their in-laws. The main reason for this was less a rejection of older ideals of cohabitation, mutual assistance, and obligation than the result of a sheer surplus of children reaching adulthood who had been born in the demographic transition decades of high fertility and low mortality. Contrary to the popular perception, the absolute number of three-generation households remained stable until the end of the century; it was the number of nuclear families—households consisting only of parents and children—that increased" (Fuess 2004:153).

The dominant life model of salaryman and housewife has recently been undermined by various practices, but no other dominant unitary concept has replaced it (Mathews and White 2004). While alternative lifestyles have proliferated in recent years, the dominant life model still often serves as a point of reference, implicitly or explicitly. The story of a salaryman and a housewife, here reconstructed from works of ethnographers and social scientists, is well known in some form to all my interlocutors. They have seen it represented on TV (for example in serial dramas such as *Sazae-san*), from literature and comic books, and they all know a "Mr. and Mrs. Jones," or a "Sato-san," in the form of their neighbor, their relative, their work colleague, or even themselves, who fits this broad description. Once they are aware of this story, they might conform to it, aspire to it, resist it, or attempt to ignore it—but they cannot pretend that they have not heard it.

Stories and Lives

In her work on death and dying in Japan, Susan Long (2004) explores different end-of-life choices, building on sociologist Clive Seale's (1998) concept of "cultural scripts" for dying: narratives available in a particular culture that contain representations of death. These scripts are available as a framework for making sense of events surrounding dying, outlining a potential course of events and providing guidance for making choices. People can draw on multiple scripts both simultaneously and consecutively (Long 2004:914). Similarly, people in any culture may draw on a number of different stories available to them in order to make sense of their lives at any life stage. In this context, I suggest that the notion of "story" might even be more appropriate than "script," since it implies a degree of elasticity: stories can accomodate various life circumstances, which allows different people to find their place in the plot (Frank 2010:39). Moreover, the notion of story implies a degree of ambiguity or even uncertainty that allows for multiple interpretations, a feature that may be particularly well suited to the transmission of complex moral messages. Arthur Frank draws out this point: "Stories are good at being several things at once, and they are good at equipping humans to live in a world that not only is open to multiple intepretive understandings but requires understandings in the plural" (Frank 2010:34). Stories have a capacity to make a particular point of view particularly compelling, which can help us understand someone else's predicament (thus people feel a need to hear someone's story or to tell their own story) and develop our understanding and empathy for a different point of view. Yet this quality of stories may also make one perspective particularly prominent and overly compelling, to the point of becoming constraining, prescribing the right way to do things. In contemporary Japan, the stories of salaryman and housewife that make up the dominant life model may provide guidance in making life decisions but may equally cause distress because of the constraints they impose. It is virtually impossible to be unaware of this story as one rather prescriptive model for leading one's life.

In exploring these issues, this chapter presents the life story of Kawasaki-san, a slim, bespectacled man in his sixties who in some respects aspired to this dominant story and in other respects resisted it, as well as a brief outline of the story of Kato-san, a lady in her early nineties who in many ways lived her life in alignment to the story. Kawasaki-san's story and the other life stories were told to me in the form of an uninterrupted flow. This allowed the speakers to give voice to their stories in the order of their choosing and with an emphasis on those events and aspects of their lives they thought appropriate. As I discuss in more detail below, the framework of narrative form can potentially reveal interesting themes when dealing with life stories. For this reason, I retell the stories here more or less in the form I received them— thus with occasional repetitions and omissions, or events sometimes not in chronological order but rather in the order in which they were told to me, with minimal editing to make the story easier to follow for the reader. Because of this light editing, I have elected to recount the stories in third person, to avoid giving the impression that a statement is verbatim, with only occasional direct quotes when the phrasing was particularly interesting. I have also removed stutters and pauses, as I do not attempt here a linguistic or discourse analysis. Nevertheless, I have made every effort to keep the phrasing as close as possible to the original. Of course, the very fact that these stories were solicited by me—a young female foreign researcher—doubtless had some impact on their form, and I doubt that either of my conversation partners—or indeed any of my interlocutors—had given an account of their life as a whole before. That is not to say that storytelling or narration were foreign to them, however. On the contrary, most of them quite frequently told stories of events to those gathered in the salon, and sometimes told stories from their lives.

Kawasaki-san

Kawasaki-san has an interest in photography, and on several occasions he proudly opened large albums to show me his recent work. It seemed mostly to depict landscapes and seasonal plants and flowers in bloom, some of them captured close-up, in minute detail. These seemed to be quite like the photos taken by other retired people, mostly men, who could often be seen taking photographs in the local park with a pond. They could be seen alone but were most often in small or large groups, gathered around some often small or insignificant-seeming object. But unlike many other retired men in Japan, Kawasaki-san does not like taking photos in a group or with a club. As he once told me, they usually just have one model and all have the same view, and time constraints, but he doesn't like that. Instead he goes out on his own, when and where he likes—he laughed and said he was a bit selfish (*wagamama*).

Before we started with the interview, Kawasaki-san put the kettle on and started preparing the coffee. He was wondering what to tell me about his life and where to begin. He worked in a fire insurance company. His job at the time was not restricted to office work, but he also had to go and speak to people from all walks of life, from the top to the bottom of society. He got up and poured hot water over the freshly ground coffee and turned a small cooking timer on. Kawasaki-san prides himself on his meticulously brewed coffee and serves it with small dark chocolates. He had many enjoyable experiences in that job, he said, and sometimes dangerous, with *yakuza* (members of criminal organizations). He had to interact with people ranging from "high society," such as a judge, to people living in slums in the Nishinari area of Osaka (famous for day laborers and homelessness). People there sometimes rebel. He went to such places, spoke to such people, had various life experiences and learned a lot, and really likes having conversations. "Would such a story be all right?" Kawasaki-san asked. I nodded and sipped my coffee, trying to interrupt him as little as possible. That is why, he opined, he had experienced things that other people hadn't, through that job. In that sense, that was really good.

Glancing at my recorder, he paused to gather his thoughts and proclaimed he will start from the beginning. For ten years, he worked in a fire insurance company in a section that involved talking to various people, ranging from the high society to the people living at the very bottom. Of, course, he interacted with the people in the middle, too, but he often had to interact with the kind of people one otherwise might not have a chance to meet. In his job he had to interact with them. One of the more unusual things was talking with yakuza, right-wing people (*uyoku*), who easily explode, but also with university professors, lawyers, and judges. Not only people from Japan were his clients but also people from abroad. There weren't many Europeans, but there were Americans, Chinese, Koreans, and Taiwanese who came to Japan. One of the more interesting people was a Peruvian man who ran a Peruvian restaurant in Kobe and seemed to be an important person back in Peru, he even had a photo taken with the Peruvian president. During the Hanshin-Awaji earthquake that Peruvian man helped a lot; his volunteering efforts were even noted in a newspaper. Kawasaki-san spent a lot of time talking to him about Peru. Kawasaki-san believes that through his job he spoke with many different people and he achieved a certain balance in his life (*baransu ni natta*).

During his lifetime, Kawasaki-san also experienced quite dangerous situations, especially while talking to yakuza. But then, he was sometimes deeply moved by a conversation. Having been exposed to such different worlds, what most strongly stays with him is the overwhelming impression that rather than people with lots of money, it was the people from the lower sections of society who were amazing, good people. After pausing for a moment, Kawasaki-san said in a low voice that he had learned a lot, through his job, through successes and failures. He felt very strongly that one must learn new things, no matter how old one is.

What else could he tell me? He worked in that section for ten years; he started his job there in 1989. Before that he had a job as a teacher, but he changed jobs halfway. Before working in the insurance company he taught children. It wasn't a usual primary school, but one could say it was a school, not a cram school. But he didn't like that job. It had nice moments, but he often asked himself if that was the right thing to do, and so he decided to change occupations. It didn't have particular ups and downs, it was an ordinary job. A kind in which one feels like one could just continue it until retirement without thinking. Kawasaki-san missed some motivation, he always liked challenges. Admittedly, he never liked ordinary, mediocre things and always looks for stimuli. He is that type of human being, that makes it his *ikigai*. Therefore, he thought, to continue this life that he knew so well, just as it is, until his death—he couldn't bear that. So he changed his job to something less ordinary. In his new job, he had to talk to different people, and talking to them in the same way, using the same pattern, just wouldn't do. One has to think how to phrase things, which phrases to avoid. In that sense, his job was a challenge every day. And those ten years in that job were lots of fun, he thinks the world of those times. Sometimes, in an average household, the conversations would gradually move away from work, and they would decide to call it a day and continue their chat. Getting along like a house on fire. "We'd have conversations about hobbies until late at night." Those were the times when he was really glad he had a job like that. "What else shall I tell you," he wondered. After a while I asked if he had left that job. Kawasaki-san replied he had retired at the age of sixty-three. After retirement he decided to dedicate his time to his hobbies: listening to music; taking photos; that is what he does these days.

A silence followed and it lasted for a long time. I remembered the day when Kawasaki-san came to introduce himself formally as our new next-door neighbor, bringing a box of washing powder. Rather than being surprised, I actually felt relieved, since I was quite unsure if the old-fashioned custom of bringing small token gifts to one's new neighbors was still practiced—though I had done precisely that myself a few months earlier. Some of our other young Japanese friends had laughed at my partner and I for being so old-fashioned, but given the nature of our old *danchi*, built in 1955, we figured it would probably still be a good idea. And here, finally, was proof that the custom was still alive: a neighbor at our door, a tall, slightly tanned man with greying hair and a beard, with a friendly smile. I asked Kawasaki-san, who was now nervously looking around his house, as if not being able to find anything worth telling, while smiling quietly, where he lived before he moved to Osaka.

Kawasaki-san replied very briefly—he lived in Aichi-ken for six years before moving back to Osaka after his retirement. "Did you move to Aichi

Prefecture straight after your retirement?" I asked. "Well, not quite straight after, in two years' time." After his retirement from the insurance company he heard about another job. That was an ordinary job, more like a part-time job (*arubaito*), which he did until he was sixty-five, and then in one or two years he moved to Aichi Prefecture, where his wife is from. Her father is ninety-five and needs care—he is bedridden and cannot speak any more, he is in such a condition. But Kawasaki-san missed Osaka. He had lived in Osaka for a long time and he started to feel that Osaka was indeed his hometown. So he told his wife he decided to return to Osaka and this year he came back—Osaka is a good place. I asked where he was originally from. From Shikoku, from Ehime Prefecture, he replied, looking out of the window. It is a place full of hot springs (*onsen*), famous spas. It is on the coast of the Sea of Japan (or the East China Sea) and the climate is warm, so the people who live there aren't stressed, they are rather reckless, Kawasaki-san mused. That is the place where he is from, but he left when he was eighteen and since then he moved around, through company transfers and changing jobs. For a long time, though, he didn't much like Osaka as a city. Osakans, especially middle-aged women, can be quite cold. Before he got to know Osaka well, he had such an image of it and didn't think it was a good place at all. He moved to Osaka for work and during that time, he saw other faces of the place and grew fond of it. Now he thinks that people living in Osaka are rather warm and kind. In Aichi Prefecture people are a bit wary of outsiders, and Osaka is good in that respect, Kawasaki-san understood over time. He would dislike moving any-where again.

After a long moment of silence he asked what else he could say. The silence continued for a while longer, so I decided to ask him how he met his wife. They met at work, he said. She was the secretary of the company president. He had to take documents to her office every day, and one day while she was preparing tea he said "good morning." He surprised her and she re-plied in a shaky voice. He thought she had an unusual voice, and that was the beginning.

Back in her natal home, he wasn't getting along with her family, Kawasaki-san continued without much of a pause. Somehow, no matter what, they just couldn't get along. For six years they lived relatively close to each other and whatever he did . . . there just wasn't a way. This continued for a while and Kawasaki-san couldn't take it anymore. One day he said to his wife, with an apology, that he will go back to Osaka ahead of her. And so he moved to Osaka. "Human beings are difficult, aren't they?"—he asked and looked at me with a troubled smile on his face. During his working days he met many people, had many different conversations, and realized that there are many different kinds of people. If they (his wife's family) were similar to some of those people he had met, he could live next to them, he thought then. But with people of opposite character, somehow, it seems, they just couldn't get to accept each other (*otagai ni ukeireru koto ga dekinai*). There are such types, of course, there are many kinds of people, and somehow, whatever he did, things just wouldn't work out between them. Kawasaki-san's face grew darker as he spoke of this and he asked that we change the topic.

I recalled that he said that there were dangerous times at his work and wondered if he could tell me more. He replied in an invigorated manner that at those times, the conversation just couldn't continue. If he realized, while he was having a conversation he realized, oh, the atmosphere is getting loaded and dangerous, well, he would stop the talk. If the conversation is going in this direction, there is nothing to be done , one can only propose to talk through the lawyers then, if that is the shape it took. Don't poke your nose into our matters, would be the implication. When it comes to yakuza, common sense would sometimes not get through to them. They can get upset very suddenly, at times when they feel pressured, when you suggest you need to take a closer look at the accounts, or for that matter, while having a perfectly normal conversation. One had to recognize signs from the very beginning, know how to look for them. Because, when things start going strangely, there is not much that one can do; one can only communicate through a lawyer. When he said that, some of those people got flustered, embarrassed, since they are not good with lawyers, so they say: "wait a minute, I hear what you're saying." That would happen quite often. At such times it is important to follow the atmosphere, the flow of the conversation.

I wondered aloud how one recognizes the warning signs or, for that matter, knows if someone is related to the underground world of yakuza. Kawasaki-san launched with panache and more than a little pride into a detailed explanation. First, there are people who tell you themselves that they are a part of such and such *gumi* (criminal organization). Furthermore, you could be warned in advance—for instance in Kawasaki-san's company there was a section that deals with that kind of information. Also, there are times when you find out for yourself—for example, if they have a *gumi* emblem on the wall. But most easily one can tell something about what people are like by the expression in their eyes. Doing that kind of job, one's sensitivity to such matters increases and one can pretty soon tell, regardless of what job they do, what kind of person you are talking to, what is their way of thinking. But people who work in offices, at their desk, they mostly cannot tell, I think, said Kawasaki-san. While actually having a conversation, through such experiences, it comes naturally. Of course, there are ones that you straight away think—this is yakuza or a right-wing guy (*uyoku*), judging entirely by appearance, the surface. On one occasion Kawasaki-san suspected that one of his clients might have ties to criminal organizations, and soon after, when he visited his office, he noticed an emblem on his wall, indicating membership. Then the client himself said, "Kawasaki-san, I think you have already noticed, but I am right-wing [*uyoku*]."[3] So there are some people who tell you. But mostly, it would be during a conversation, one would realize, this person thinks in a particular way. That said, not all of these people are involved directly in criminal activities as such. Many of the lower-grade members of these organizations (*soshiki*) work, for instance, in street stalls selling things like *yakisoba* during festivals. In Japanese, this is termed *tekiya*—translated variously as a faker, charlatan, racketeer, or stallholder, usually run by lower-ranked yakuza. But they also surprise people and cheat them out of their money. They also run gambling enterprises and are generally up to no good.

"One time in Nishinari, doing my job, I really got a fright," Kawasaki-san told me with a smile. He had already been there many times, and that time he had to go to talk to a client in their office. It was just a regular company. While he was there, his client turned his attention to a large gathering outside the window. They were on the second or third floor of a low building, and below there was a small garden in which many people were assembled, perhaps ten of them, creating a lot of commotion and noise. Their intentions seemed hostile and if they climbed the telephone pole they could easily break in. That was the time he was most scared. He then suggested I take a look at Nishinari before I leave, but warned me that a woman should not walk around there. There are no ordinary people, wearing suits or such, walking around there. But there are many people working as day laborers. The whole town has an oppressive atmosphere and the streets are lined with slum quarters.

After a silence, Kawasaki-san's tone changed a little: "People are interesting, aren't they? Many are forward-looking, regardless of what is going on. Even though they may be in a difficult position they have a proactive way of thinking (*maemuki na kangaekata*). There are people who are thinking about how they can pull themselves out of these circumstances. Even if they are struggling financially, eventually, they believe, things will pan out. Those people seem like they should be desperate. I really just think, please hang in there, do your best. Living in the world isn't just about money; these people are down to earth, they support the world. One wants to see something beautiful, worthwhile." Kawasaki-san was really grateful that his job was a chance to learn about people. For instance, some people put a lot of importance on their titles. His acquaintance, whom he mentioned earlier, phoned him and told him that he had become a judge, with not much by way of an introduction. That sets up a conversation in a certain way, commanding attention, starting with a sort of calculation. It is as if he was letting you know that he is now speaking to you as a lawyer and wants you to respond appropriately. . . . Kawasaki-san concluded that he is always on the side of the people who are struggling. He hopes they try hard and will do well.

What's in a Story?

Kawasaki-san started his story with a preface, what one might call a summary of his biography. This abstract of sorts singled out a part of his life related to work, rather than family, for example. But instead of a conventional achievement in terms of status within the workplace, Kawasaki-san chose to mention that aspect of his work that brought him into close contact with people and occasionally into dangerous encounters. His overall feeling was that that particular job, with the insurance company, was very good for him: through his interactions with various kinds of people he learned a lot. His previous job as a teacher quickly became routinized and almost went unmentioned in his account. Kawasaki-san felt that his work in school was utterly ordinary and unchallenging, and he felt he couldn't bear to think that he would spend the rest of his time in such a way. He is a human being who needs stimuli: "That is my *ikigai*." It seems that Kawasaki-san sees himself as a person who likes a challenge and dislikes routine, who replaced the security of this mild employment with the challenging and often dangerous environment of his insurance company work.

It is interesting to note that Kawasaki-san dedicated much more space to some parts of his life than to others. The reasons for this might be numerous, and not least because of my presence: certain topics might be more appropriate than others in a conversation with a younger female researcher; but both the repetitions and the omissions in the narrative reflect the placement of stress and focus. Just like his other employment, before and after the insurance company work, the period of his life outside Osaka received little attention, indicating that Osaka and that job carried most relevance for Kawasaki-san and his sense of identity. His affection for Osaka grew over time and the true appreciation of its openness came after living in Aichi-ken, where his wife's family was from. In this particular narrative, Kawasaki-san spoke of that period of his life so little that he even left out details that he mentioned in previous conversations, for instance that he ran a café there. Such omissions are revealing: one forms a certain idea of oneself, and any narrative of oneself will reveal aspects of this self-image. In conscious and unconscious ways, one reveals elements of one's self perceptions, of what one thinks one is like (Watson and Watson-Franke 1985:63).

A narrator of a life story also wishes to control their created self-image and the way it is represented. Kawasaki-san was well aware that his story was being recorded and did not hide the wish to control its contents. The interview situation is slightly threatening in its boundedness and finality; a person in such a situation may feel as though as he or she has only a single opportunity to present his or her account. Both the problem of power imbalance created by an interview situation and its time limitations were less pronounced in this case: as a young woman with a junior status as a student, I was hardly imposing or threatening as an interviewer.[4] Yet literature dealing with narrative as a form has argued that the conventionality of the narrative form exerts certain limitations on the tellers, thereby limiting their ability to manipulate the presentation:

> One of the singular aspects of biographical narrative is that the genre, once the speaker agrees to "do narrative," has certain compelling effect of its own upon the verbal flow of the speaker. . . . the attempts by the interviewee to avoid the compulsions of narrative—sometimes by a simple refusal to narrate, sometimes by inadequate detailing or peculiarities of "drawing the moral of the story," sometimes by interrupting the story-telling by digressions into other sorts of speech-activity and in other ways—provide the researcher with as many clues to personal and cultural reality as does the explicit narrative content itself. (Wengraf 2001:117–18).

Omissions in the narrative, silences, and diversions all therefore form a part of the story. At least on one level, Kawasaki-san thinks of himself as an independent man who seeks out challenge and new experiences, and that is part of his self-presentation. The omissions and disruptions in his narrative were no less interesting; for instance, when talking about how he met his wife, he cut the story short and said nothing about his life with her but instantly switched to an account of their present situation, in which they are effectively separated. Another disjuncture occurred when Kawasaki-san told me about the most threatening experience on his job: when he was in the neighborhood with lots of slums and a group of people acted in a rowdy manner in a park below. Rather than explaining what happened and how he felt, or what his reasons were for feeling afraid, he changed the topic and suggested that I should visit that part of town if I get a chance.

In a similar vein, it is possible to infer that it is relevant that certain issues were brought up a number of times, albeit not always in a straightforward way. Kawasaki-san returned to the issue of being unable to live with his wife on several occasions. While embarrassing and difficult, this was obviously an issue that weighed on his mind. He felt he was doing her an injustice by leaving her alone to care for her increasingly dependent father, but still felt compelled to move away. He felt he couldn't get along with his wife's family but did not place all the blame with them. He also felt that people in rural areas were not open to newcomers, even after a long period of stay, which made his life there difficult. In his later years, Kawasaki-san made a decision to live alone and independently.

Reading a Life Story

A life story does not simply tell us what our storyteller thinks she is like and how she wants to present herself. It also reveals something about the ideas of the person in the given society and about internalized cultural expectations (Watson and Watson-Franke 1985:63). The interplay between these ideas and personal choices is not straightforward but can be gauged against the backdrop of cultural context, which will be explored in more detail in the following section. Narrative also has a more direct link to personhood and self, since it is closely related to self-understanding and the creation of meaning. Narrative, or story—I use the terms interchangeably—is a specific sequencing where events build on each other, or as Frank put it, in which "one thing happens as a consequence of another" (2010:25).[5] In some cases, it can be understood in relation to the concept of "emplotment," which refers to "making a configuration in time, creating a whole out of a succession of events" (Mattingly 1994:812). This characteristic of the narrative allows us to create order out of a sequence of events that would otherwise just appear as a succession: one thing following after another rather than one thing following from another, or events building on each other.

The telling of a story allows the narrator to impose order on consecutive events and to create a link between past, present, and imagined worlds and selves, providing both the teller and the audience with an opportunity for self-understanding, albeit only partial (Ochs and Capps 1996:19). By recasting events within the narrative framework, we situate them among other events and create a meaningful whole with a beginning, middle, and end. Through emplacement within this framework, as a contribution to the plot, the event is given meaning (Mattingly 1994:813).[6] As not all endings are equally desirable, and some are even feared, the story is often structured as a striving toward a preferred outcome. Lying at an intersection between past, present, and imagined, the story is focused on what is expected and what actually occurred (Ochs and Capps 1996). But to be able to avoid or wish for certain outcomes and endings we have to be able to imagine them. Certain stories form our own personal repository, which shapes our imagination of events and influences our actions. This repository is sometimes associated with what is referred to as narrative identity: "We learn through stories not only which identities are available; more fundamentally, we learn what an identity is. . . . Narrative identity is as collective as it is personal" (Frank 2010:199). The concept of narrative identity points to the link between the social and the individual, and to cultural resources for identity formation. I would argue that the dominant life model is one such resource and can be usefully viewed as a story. In practice it consists of a number of smaller everyday stories concerning people we know and people we hear about in other ways, in the media and elsewhere. The dominant life model figures as a point of reference, whether it influences one's expectations in more or less direct ways.

The Storyline

> Narrative activity attempts to resolve the discrepancy between what is expected and what has transpired.
>
> —Elinor Ochs and Lisa Capps, "Narrating the Self"

Kawasaki-san's life story as presented above is just one of many possible narrative accounts of his life that he could potentially give; it is the one given to me when I asked for it. Like the other possible accounts, it is therefore only partial. Yet it nevertheless provides a (partial) insight into issues of self, self-representation, identity, and choice. In his account, Kawasaki-san focuses on his job, which in itself is not a surprising choice given the dominant Japanese life model, in which the prevailing focus for men is their work. Yet Kawasaki-san places his job somewhat in contrast to the expected career path when he refers to his decision to change occupations: he describes the change as happening "halfway" or "midway" (*tochū*) through his career. This implies that this discontinuity was in contrast to the expectations (of the listener), such as the model of lifetime employment. Kawasaki-san provided a detailed explanation of dissatisfaction with the job that he described as routinized, unchallenging, and generally mediocre. This part of the narrative is recognizable as what is sometimes referred to as a "problem" or "complicating event" that the plot is driven to resolve.

In this case, the resolution is preempted, since we already know that Kawasaki-san found a rewarding job, a challenging activity that provided him with opportunities for learning. In the process, he reveals that his *ikigai*, his aim in life (or that which makes life worth living), as he told me, is challenge and stimulus. He stressed that he "achieved a certain balance in life" in social terms, as he was in contact with people of different social backgrounds and status. This is a central point in the narrative: the value of getting to know many kinds of people and coming to a realization that certain underprivileged people are in many ways more impressive than people with a higher status. In some ways, it can be read as a moral of the story. This creates the core of the main narrative frame: a life story that is about challenge and learning through getting to know various kinds of people. Another complicating event emerges repeatedly, surfacing from within this outer frame: a story of the problem with his wife and his inability to get along with her family. The resolution to this problem is reached to an extent when he decided to move back to Osaka on his own, though he percieves this as problematic for his wife. This ties into his perception of himself as independent and "a bit selfish" (*wagamama*). The second narrative strand is absorbed back into the first by linking it with the idea that there are different kinds of people, and if only his wife's family were more like some of the people he met through his work, things might have worked out better between them. The disjuncture remains, and the issue that bothers him is not wholly subsumed within the larger coherent narrative. The life story in this sense can provide an opportunity for recasting one's life in a meaningful form, but can also point to issues of existential importance.

A Life Fulfilled—Kato-san

I spoke to Kato-san in her house, just around the corner from the salon, when I paid her and her sister Ikeda-san a visit one day, as she suggested I do. A slim lady whose calm and cheerful disposition and ability to laugh off troubles made her a favorite presence in the salon, Kato-san greeted me cheerfully and invited me in. Her sister was feeling a bit cold and weak that day so they decided to stay in and sip tea and watch television. Kato-san agreed to tell me her story and wondered where to begin—when she was young she worked as a shopgirl, should she start there? As I reassured her that she could begin wherever she would like, she wondered if that would be too long. She then started by telling me that after working in a shop she was married at the age of twenty-one, and her husband was twenty-nine. Twenty days later, her husband was enlisted as a soldier and sent away for two years. After he returned they had two daughters, and when they were aged one and two he was sent away again, this time to China. Luckily, his job was base-bound so he did not participate in fighting, but he never said much to her about his time in the army. While he was away, during World War II, her house burned down and she had to run away with two small children, and she made her way to the countryside. She told me (on another occasion) that she had grabbed a curtain from the window, put in a couple of things to make a bundle, tied her baby onto her back, and ran with the other baby and the bundle in her arms while the fire was raging and bombs dropping all around her—a traumatic and life-changing episode she recounted many times. She then went to Hiroshima to live with her uncle, and her mother joined her to help out with the children. Later, her older brother and younger sister (Ikeda-san) found a house in Shimoichi (one of a few areas where not many houses burned down), where the brother was hoping to live with his lover. But when the parents found out they made him move, and made him give the house to Kato-san to live in with her children.

Sometime after the war ended, her husband returned from China and got a job at the city hall with the Board of Education, where he advised on designs for school uniforms, as he had a background in tailoring. They had two more babies soon thereafter, a boy and later a girl. They lived in Shimoichi, in the same house her brother had found and the very same one we were sitting in chatting. She stayed at home with the children, as her husband thought it would be bad for the children if she were to go out to work, so she stayed at home as a housewife. She spent most of her time making sure they all got healthy food, lots of fresh vegetables. She did not know many people in the area, and many were difficult to get along with and enjoyed gossip, so she kept to herself then, even though she found it quite hard to look after the family with no one nearby to lend her a hand or to ask for advice. She made sure not to argue with her husband, as that was not good for the children. She then said that some people say bad things about their husbands, but that she was very grateful to hers, as he supported five people and was always hardworking and kind. She then offered advice on living a long and happy life: you need to respect your husband's parents (and your parents) and be kind to them, to get along well with your husband, and then the children will grow up to be good, and that is most important, they will grow up to be caring and considerate. Her daughters, all three of them, are volunteering—"always working for others"—and luckily all have supportive husbands. This was clearly a source of pride for her, and she considered all her children to be very kind people. Of course, having a good relationship (*nakayoku*) with your husband is important, she said. For a woman, her husband is life (*inochi*), as even children get married and move away, and you can spend time with your husband until death. In order to maintain one's health one must think about small things in life, like being careful with what one eats and enjoy it, not snack between meals, and be grateful. Every night before falling asleep, she thinks how grateful she is to be this healthy, how lucky she is, and expresses gratitude to the ancestors.

Kato-san told me her story very briefly, even herself concluding that it may have been a little too short. She went back and expanded on the war years, recounting in more detail her memories of having her house burn down, but not expanding much on her daily life after the war—summing it up with a brief "and then it was all pretty much the same as now." Her children all grew up, moved away, married, and had children, and were themselves now in their mid-sixties, and had even become grandparents themselves, as she told me on another occasion, so clearly there was no lack of subsequent events. What Kato-san was implying, like several of my other interlocutors, was that there were no more unusual, extraordinary events. When things are no different from what is expected, there just is no story, which is not necessarily a bad thing, as exceptional elements may well be distressing or traumatic. The story of running from a burning house with her two children was singled out as an extraordinary event, and being one she survived and coped with, perhaps even a source of pride. On a number of other occasions in the salon, Kato-san told me about the joy of small, everyday things such as fresh food or a small flower in a vase, but also about the freedom she enjoyed from having fulfilled her duties. For instance, in a conversation about living alone, some ladies mentioned the feeling of freedom that they enjoyed living on their own, mentioning how easy things were for them now. One of them then said that living with her late husband was very difficult, he was very demanding. Kato-san then pointed out: "You have to think of the good things that your husband did, supporting you. Now that you don't have any more obligations, you can enjoy yourself." Kato-san agreed that being free from duties is enjoyable but thought that holding onto bad thoughts makes one unsettled. Since one has already endured things, she said (and fulfilled one's role), one can have fun. Kato-san's story, as she told it to me, but also as it transpired from numerous other conversations in the salon, was one lived out in quite close accordance with the dominant life model. Having accepted the story of "housewife" as her own, Kato-san achieved a certain contentment, finding meaning in her life from her sense of a role fulfilled.

Accompanied by Stories

> The power of stories is the problem with stories: they are far too
> good at doing what they do, which is being the source of all values.
> —Arthur Frank, *Letting Stories Breathe*

Kawasaki-san's story presents him as a loner, who goes his own way and spends his days on his own. Nevertheless, his story, like every other, does not exist in isolation; it is not his alone. In fact, he presents himself clearly in relation to the "model life" story. His own life diverges from this story line in certain crucial respects, and it is precisely those elements of divergence, or difference from expectations, that form the focus. His choice to leave his first job, as well as the content of his second job, are set against the expectation of lifetime employment and stability, which in his view verge on boredom. His second job offered challenges and opportunities for excitement, such as dealing with the yakuza, something he seemed to take considerable pride in, as well as in his abilities to communicate with people. In short, Kawasaki-san positions himself in relation to the model life and both compares himself to it (at times unfavorably, pointing out his own "selfishness") and resists it. The explanations surrounding such points of divergence from the model life story are crucial in more ways than one. They do not merely offer justifications to others but also allow for an explanation of his motives and achievements, which then allow for an interpretation of his life story as a meaningful whole. In contrast, while Kato-san contrasts her own life implicitly with the model life and initially only expanded on elements of divergence, much like Kawasaki-san, she ultimately represents her life story as one that very much followed the model sequence. In many ways Kato-san draws meaning in her life from the very convergence with the model, from the feeling of having fulfilled her role. These two cases show how the stories available to us provide us with material for making sense of our own lives, but also that the ways in which we position ourselves in relation to such stories can vary widely. In turn, the ways in which a sense of a meaningful existence, or a good life, is narratively constructed may differ significantly. We can make the most of full identification with one of the stories available to us, or alternatively attempt to make the points of divergence precisely that which makes our life meaningful.

Chapter 6

Intimacy and Independence

It was a particularly hot and sticky afternoon in August, and the heat was heavy, so I was not too surprised to find that the mood was not very lively in the lightly air-conditioned salon. The two large tables with six seats each were only half occupied. Abe-san, a white-haired lady in her late seventies, was sipping her green tea in her usual place near the door, while at the same table, Harada-san, a tall, sturdy man in his mid-seventies, was flicking through a newspaper. The two sisters, Kato-san and Ikeda-san, both well dressed as usual, sat at the other table, closer to the counter. The older sister was chatting quietly to the volunteer in charge before my shift, while the younger sister, in her early eighties, was reading a book. Even the stifling heat, only somewhat eased by the air-conditioning (as it was dangerous to lower the temperature too much in a place with so many comings and goings) could not account for this subdued atmosphere. The younger sister always enjoyed conversations and I had never seen her withdrawn like this, but it was not until Harada-san left that I found out what had happened. Apparently, a couple of days earlier, having seen the younger sister engaged in a cheerful conversation with Oku-san, a man in his late seventies, Harada-san got upset and demanded her attention. After that unpleasant incident she started avoiding Harada-san even though she previously always liked to spend time with this educated, well-informed man. Later in the afternoon, when a few more ladies, frequent customers, joined in, she told them what happened. One of them cried out in dismay, "Boyfriends are many; one can have many male friends. Lover is one, but boyfriends are many!" Using the English word for boyfriend, she implied that the silly, possessive, jealous behavior of Harada-san was unacceptable.

This anecdote reveals the variety of feelings and expectations related to friendship and closeness, as well as the multiple meanings of intimacy.

Generally speaking, "intimacy" refers to relationships that are personal and close (emotionally and/or physically), private, and caring or loving (Constable 2009:9). The term is somewhat ambiguous, as it may refer to the feeling of closeness but may also be a euphemism for sexual relations. Furthermore, its meaning in the Western context has changed over the course of the past couple of centuries, once referring to the very state of being a family, or being married, and as a result being closer than with outsiders. With the rise of discourses of intimacy, by the late twentieth century the term acquired a meaning of a special kind of closeness based on verbal openness, and therefore something to be achieved rather than assumed. This specific notion of intimacy is associated with the rise of capitalism and concomitant processes of alienation (Shumway 2003:25). In order to be useful in understanding various social circumstances and relationships in different cultural contexts, intimacy must be understood in a broader sense, perhaps as a quality of closeness and trust that can be found in an array of different relationships: with parents, siblings, close friends, spouses, children, or indeed, lovers.

In the case of the elderly in Japan, it is often noted that while the numbers of older people living with their families in three-generation households are still relatively high, concerns are growing over the rising proportion of older people living on their own. While the links of the elderly to their children and family members are often discussed in the academic literature, it would seem that nonfamilial relationships are becoming at least as important in many elderly people's lives. Indeed, while the attention given to the intergenerational ties of the elderly is laudable (Thang 2001), recent work with Japanese elderly points to the importance of intragenerational communication, that is, communication within the boundaries of one's own age-group. Yoshiko Matsumoto (2011) draws attention to a number of psychological studies indicating that in Japan (as well as in China and Hong Kong), intragenerational communication between older adults has primary impact on the psychological health of the elderly (Cai, Giles, and Noels 1998; Ota, Giles, and Gallois 2002; all cited in Matsumoto 2011). Based on ethnographic material presented in the chapters in her volume, Matsumoto concludes that "among peers and friends, older adults engage in verbal and nonverbal activities that may not fit with the images and standards held by younger people. The elderly may feel free to keep their 'old' values or talk about topics that the younger may not consider appropriate" (Matsumoto 2011:3).

This chapter focuses on the close relationships elderly people have built around them—with their friends, siblings, within the community, and with romantic partners. It explores the meaning of marriage and of intimacy within it, of the narratives of reconstructing their lives after loss, and friendship ties in later life, drawing on an analysis of the life stories of two women. The emerging themes of closeness, family relationships, friendship, and independence are all explored in more detail with reference to other ethnographic examples.

Both of the women whose life stories are presented here had lost their husbands, and in the salon there were many other women who had been widowed, albeit not all so early in life. Widowhood is differently represented by my interlocutors for men and women, especially in the later years. Whereas a woman widowed while her children are still dependent on their natal family for support might experience significant practical difficulties (like Takahashi-san, whose case I describe below), it was not unusual to hear that women enjoyed their freedom in widowhood. My interlocutors would sometimes hear of a case of an acquaintance whose wife had passed away, and wonder with a sense of concern how he would be able to take care of himself. In contrast, some of the elderly ladies who frequented the salon whose husbands had long since passed away often noted how comfortable and easy their life alone was, and occasionally pointed out how much fun they were having now. "I'm in heaven now, it's all so easy. I had a really difficult time during my life, I went through a lot of hardship [kurō]. I'm in heaven now," Kondo-san told me one afternoon, referring to her life alone. Tall and healthy at the age of seventy-three, she enjoys growing vegetables in pots in front of her house and coming to the salon every day to enjoy a chat with her friends, who call her a "vegetable expert" because of her abundant knowledge about planting and gardening. On one occasion, she told me of a singing class she was taking in the salon and how much she enjoyed it, but more surprisingly, how much better she was than she used to be: "Since I became single again, I can let my voice out, I can sing like I couldn't before." She feels healthier and stronger now, she said—and, I presume, more confident.

This perception that women can experience freedom in older age, after their husbands have passed away and they have fulfilled their duties, seems widespread, and some men in the salon commented on it on several occasions, often in a self-deprecating manner. One cold and damp afternoon, for example, Kondo-san was discussing health with two younger ladies in their mid-sixties who always arrived together, a grey-haired, bespectacled man in his late seventies, and a couple of others. Kondo-san said that the medicine her doctor had prescribed for her shoulder was much too strong and made her sleepy, but that she'd healed herself by regularly visiting the hot baths and hot springs. Another lady in her eighties replied that it was good that she managed to get better, as injuries and related problems take so much longer to heal after you reach seventy-five or so. The bespectacled man jokingly added that Japanese women seem suddenly to get healthy once their husbands are gone. One of the two women in their sixties, a widow, commented that it is very lonely when you become single, "*hitori ni naru*." Although many agreed, the conversation soon resumed a cheerful and bantering tone. "This is your chance!" said one of the ladies to the man, referring to the widow in question as everyone laughed.

Fukuda-san

With her hair cropped short and wearing pastel-colored clothing, Fukuda-san looks youthful. A smiling sixty-five-year-old Kyoto resident, whom I met in the women's discussion group, she has a surprisingly busy social schedule. Most mornings she goes to her local gym. After lunch she visits her mother, who lives with her brother, and in the evening she attends a karaoke group or a social dancing class. At first she did not like living on her own. She felt lonely, she said, but now enjoys her freedom and comfort. A cooked meal lasts her for a few days, and everything is very easy—"like heaven." But her life was not always easy, she confided to me on one occasion. That was when I asked her to tell me her life story, which she agreed to do on another day. Several days later we met in Kyoto, and she insisted on telling me her life story in front of one of the many Buddhist temples. The day was rainy and rather chilly, but we managed to find a quiet and dry spot under the overhanging roof on a porch of the temple, overlooking a large garden. At first, this seemed a bit impractical, but as her life story unfolded, I realized it was the way Fukuda-san took ownership of her life story, by providing a backdrop that meant something to her, and framing it, much like the worn wooden beams holding up the roof framed the tranquil view of the pebble-covered garden.

Fukuda-san's parents were from Niigata Prefecture but moved to Kyoto after they were married in the nineteenth year of Shōwa era (1944). During the war, as things became more difficult, they returned to Niigata, and soon her father was dispatched to China—something she does not know much about as he never spoke about it. After he luckily returned safely (*buji ni*—literally, without any events or problems) she was born in a small town in Niigata. When she was four or five they moved back to Kyoto, where she has lived ever since, thinking of herself as a Kyoto resident. They lived in the center of Kyoto until she was eighteen, in a house where her father ran a shop selling silk goods produced in his hometown by his relatives. Her mother took care (*osewa*) of his employees, preparing their meals and looking after their accommodation, and for all the years Fukuda-san was going to school her mother was working. She was a very shy child but liked looking after her younger brother. Growing up surrounded by all her father's shop staff, who paid attention to her and spoiled her, she felt she was treated like a princess (*ojōsama*). She was very sturdy and healthy and was even given an award for being the student who was the healthiest and had not missed any classes for six years, even though she did not excel at study. Being very tall for her age, five-foot three, she really stood out in elementary school. She started various *okeiko* (training in artistic pursuits often thought as crucial for a young woman to get married), like playing the piano. During middle school she enjoyed studying; as she was getting better at this she felt a sense of accomplishment (*tasseikan*) and started studying hard, particularly enjoying English. It was a very strict Catholic school, and students' behavior was strictly monitored—for instance walking on the streets on your own was not acceptable. Because it was one of those schools that had its own elementary school, and there were many girls who continued on from the lower grades, the groups were already formed and she felt like she couldn't fit in. She had friends but did not have much fun, there or in high school, so (she laughs) she had no other choice but to study.

After finishing high school, she enrolled in a four-year course at a university. After spending so much time before just studying and not having fun, she now started enjoying herself, she giggled. In fact she did not study at all after entering the university. She spent a lot of time with her walking society, rambling around Kyoto (something she loved since childhood and got into the habit of doing with her parents), and neglected her studies, and soon decided to transfer to a two-year degree. After graduating, she continued *okeiko*, study in fine arts, and waited to get married, not for a moment thinking she could do something else. She did not have a boyfriend at university, but did meet one young man. But at that time, she pointed out, it was not the kind of relationship where they would say to each other that they liked each other, or meet frequently, it was mostly through correspondence. But there were many difficulties. He had to go back to his natal home and was engaged to be married, but they continued their correspondence for seven years, until she got married at the age of twenty-three. She went to several *omiai* meetings to meet prospective husbands, and soon her parents found her a husband. Given that his parents were close friends of her parents she felt really safe and content with the choice.

At first they couldn't say they liked one another, but as they lived together they grew close: while living together one looks for that love (*isshō ni seikatsu shiteiru uchi ni sono aijō wo sagasu*). That was a frequent pattern in the past, she said. His father bought a tiny house in Kyoto. He was a salaryman and she was a housewife, and they got along together and had fun (*kekko nakayoku tanoshiku kurashiteta wa yo*), she assured me. Two years later, their son was born, and she had to spend some time in the hospital because of a hormonal imbalance. When her child was born, that was the time when she was the happiest in her life, that's what she thinks, she told me with a gentle smile on her face, as if recalling those moments. Her husband was soon transferred to Nagoya, and they moved there for three years. As she had just had a baby, she made friends with other mothers whose husbands were moved there, and had a lot of fun. But when they came back to Kyoto, her son was of kindergarten age, and she was still a housewife. There were many days when there was nothing to do. She started feeling a bit blue and worried if what she was doing, the way she was bringing up her son, was the right thing to do. She remembered worrying a lot in that period. But when he enrolled in school she felt somewhat better. During all that time the three of them got along well, and her husband was very gentle. Even if she got upset or kicked up a fuss, he would not get upset with her. He was a very kind and gentle person.

And then one day he suddenly died in an accident. It was so sudden that she could not cry when she heard the news. Her son was in the first grade of elementary school, and she was thirty-two. It was the biggest shock of her entire life, she told me. Her parents suggested she could work in the office of their silk shop, but she thought she would be a burden on them. Even with the loveliest parents, when you see them every day and depend on them, there are tensions, she said. She had always had a bit of an independent spirit, so she had the feeling that she would somehow be able to make a living. Luckily, they owned a house so her financial situation wasn't very bad, and she started working part-time as a receptionist in a dental clinic and marking English tests for schools at home. With those two part-time jobs, they somehow got by. Her son was doing well, but she often felt lonely. She felt a lot of stress and anxieties about the ways she was doing things, particularly with regard to bringing up a male child. Raising children is strewn with worries and things you don't know, she told me. She felt it was very difficult but did not have time to cry. There were many good times, and her parents frequently took her and her son out to restaurants or on little trips and holidays, so she felt really grateful to them.

After a while she felt it was difficult to live on her own and asked her friends if they knew anyone for her. She was introduced to a man named Fukuda, and for a while they saw each other, going to the theater or the cinema. It was fun, and they enjoyed each other's company. In the end, she decided that if she was going to marry, Fukuda would be a good man. Without consulting her son, who was now in middle school, she decided to marry again. Her father agreed to break the news to the boy. Now she regrets that, and she knows she had hurt her son very much by not talking to him then, but she knew he would disagree, and she was afraid she would stay unmarried for the rest of her life. She and Fukuda both sold their houses and moved into a larger house together. He did not have children so he did not know how to treat her son, who mostly just withdrew to his room to study. They never argued, but the atmosphere was often strained and she felt caught up in the middle, and her husband often criticized her. Even though they had had so much fun and lively conversations during the year when they were seeing each other, now she realized he was a difficult man. Soon he became ill and was diagnosed with cancer, and within two years of their marriage he was in and out of hospital. Four years later, at the age of forty-six, she was widowed once again.

Unexpectedly, at the age of fifty she became more outgoing. First she joined a gym with a friend and made some new friends there. She became slim and less shy, met various men, and had several boyfriends. Soon she met a nice man there who liked hiking, and they enjoyed traveling together around Japan and abroad. They spent five years together, but he was twelve years older and sometimes she could sense a "generation gap." This is why she broke up with him when she met her current boyfriend. He knows many things, she told me, and is an interesting conversation partner. He helped her learn social dancing, and they trained for hours at a time. They do many things together, such as study English or learn how to use e-mail, and for the first time she feels like she has met someone who she can grow with, which makes her very happy and excited.

A Story of Change

This is how Fukuda-san described her life to me, focusing on the relationships that meant most to her, and leaving out the details about her several jobs, for instance. She openly admitted that she was frequently anxious about how she should go about bringing up her son, and that she regrets she did not ask him for his opinion about getting married again, even though she felt like she had no choice. She is grateful to her son that he studied hard, and even though he was often sulking in his room, he successfully passed all the entrance exams and eventually graduated from university. But she is not close to him and sees him and his wife and child only once in a while. Interestingly, she almost never mentioned her grandchild, on that occasion or others. She is attached to her mother, whom she visits almost every day, and is grateful to her parents for their emotional support throughout the years and occasional treats. At least twice a year, they go together on a trip to her mother's favorite mountain spa. She has a number of female friends that she meets at least once a week at one of her regular activities, such as karaoke. The way she describes her life, though, focuses on her close relationships with her male partners, her husbands or boyfriends.

Her first marriage was arranged with the help of her parents, a decision she was very satisfied with, and she was adamant that she had no way of meeting a partner since she was not even employed. The marriage was a successful one and she grew close to her husband. The second marriage was not arranged, but neither was it entirely different, since she asked her friends to find her a potential partner. In this case, even though she thought she knew her future husband well, in everyday life he turned out to be a difficult man. She emphasized the importance of making sure you are compatible with someone in everyday life, since that is where problems begin. Perhaps it was the proximity and closeness of everyday interactions that made it more difficult for her and her husband to enjoy each other's company. Several years after her second husband's death, Fukuda-san decided she needed a change in her life, and after embarking on a more active lifestyle she became more outgoing. While her relationships were still long-term, she did not commit in the same way and felt free to break up when they did not suit her. She also came to expect a degree of verbal openness, and as one of the reasons for the break up with her previous boyfriend, she mentioned that he was not very good at "conversation," and that she often felt like she was doing all the talking. Her current boyfriend is married and while she is aware of the instability of their relationship she enjoys the time they spend together and believes they share a special connection and interest in learning new things.

Fukuda-san is proud of herself for being able to make this gradual transformation—from a shy woman toward the energetic, cheerful, open person that she is now—even though it amuses her that it mostly took place after she entered her fifties. Her personal transformation parallels the movement from so-called traditional marriage toward forms that more typically characterize modernity. An extreme form of this is what Anthony Giddens (1991) calls a "pure relationship": a close and continual emotional tie that lasts only as long as it provides the emotional benefits of shared intimacy and is a relationship for its own sake. However, Fukuda-san did not make a value judgement about these various kinds of relationship, never suggesting dissatisfaction with the traditional pattern. Rather than considering it constraining, and on this basis moving toward more modern forms, she believed that arranged marriage offered a feeling of security that she appreciated. It was a series of events in her life, rather than any dissatisfaction with potential constraints, that brought about the change in the types of relationships she entered.

Takahashi-san

Takahashi-san is a soft-spoken woman who is almost always smiling. She has dark hair and clear, dark eyes, and her tanned complexion has a healthy glow. She is seventy-four years old but still working to support herself. I noticed at first that Takahashi-san came to the salon regularly but infrequently, almost always on weekends. She works as a cleaner in an office building, so she starts her work around six and is usually finished by noon. As she often felt tired after finishing her job and housework, she would rarely come in during the week. She often told me about her previous job in Osaka, in a traditional Japanese-style restaurant (*ryōtei*), which she recalled happily. I asked her if she would tell me her life story, and she chose a small, quiet café in Shimoichi, several streets away from the salon to avoid running into anyone we knew so she could talk freely. After sitting down and ordering, I briefly explained that I would try not to interrupt her while she spoke, and Takahashi-san started her story.

Where to begin . . . Well, I was born in the eleventh year of Showa era (1936), and when the war finished in Showa 20, I was in the second grade of elementary school. . . . In third grade I was sent to a factory and started working. I wasn't going to school but worked in this weaving workshop. I worked there until the age of twenty and when I was twenty-one I got married. My oldest son was born when I was twenty-two [laughs]. Later, in Showa 35 [1960] my oldest daughter was born. And my younger son was born in Showa 38 [1963]. Well, back then, I had a husband [danna] who was working in construction, building houses and the like. That is what he did. . . . He worked, all that time . . . and then the [economic] bubble burst. And then there wasn't much work, so he stopped. We had fourteen to fifteen workers, living in [our house]. I was cooking for them, looking after all of them, just me. But after the bubble burst, he stopped working. And then one or two years later, he died. My husband died when I was in my forties. We lived in Gifu in Aichi Prefecture so I moved to Nagoya to work and then to Osaka. I had a friend who had worked here and through an introduction I got a job in the restaurant. . . . I worked there until I was sixty, for over ten years.

Takahashi-san described in detail the large and lively inn in which she served food, the kinds of customers they had, and the big parties they often held toward the end of the year. She recounted her memories of a time when the inn—the largest in Osaka, located in Souemonchō, near Dotombori River—was a famous establishment where wealthy customers would entertain their guests, often calling for dancers. Eleven years later, as the bubble economy in Japan burst, the place went out of business and she had to look for another job. It was those times, though, that she recounted gladly, and her descriptions were vivid and engaging:

Every day there would be around five geishas. They would come and wait and people would call them over to dance. Wearing beautiful kimonos, all, properly. . . . The largest rooms, we had two of them, were sixty jo,[1] and there were fifty smaller private rooms—some for four, some for ten people, and so on. All of them had karaoke, everything, they were spacious. . . . Everyone was eating and drinking, and some called up the maiko [apprentice geishas]. When it was bōnenkai[2] time we were so busy, some days we would have 1,100 guests, and one time

1,500—unimaginable. In one evening. And all would have banquet dishes, seven kinds [*kaiseki ryōri*—formal meals served on individual trays]. It was amazing.

Her description of her days working in the inn went on for quite a while, detailing the daily routines and the esteemed guests who were entertained there, including actors, and her memories of the loud and lively streets that surrounded the place, the gaudy river processions during Tenjin festival that they could see from the windows, with Kabuki actors passing on river boats.[3] She worked very hard, making preparations in the restaurant all afternoon, serving food all evening, preparing orders for the next day late at night at home, but she spoke cheerfully of those times, when she laughed every day, as she told me. She described how you could see the dancers while working. While she was serving food she would open the back door to the private room and would be able to see the customers and the dancers. She laughed mischievously when she told me that she looked a lot. The place she worked was a very interesting place, quite fun. It was a place with a flavor to it, and she felt it was a bit more of an experience than most other people would have had. Without a hint of regret, she said that she doubted that she would ever have a chance to have so much fun again, not just because of her age but because the times had changed—the economy is in recession and there is just not enough money around for such entertainment, geishas and so on. While the economy was growing, they were all spending money left and right, having fun. She then spoke in some detail about the closing of the restaurant, the fate of the owner, and the economic downturn in Japan. She only said a couple of sentences about her life in Osaka today, though she did tell me more about it on other occasions. She was still working, at the moment as a cleaner in an office building, and hoped to be able to retire soon.

When she indicated that she was finished and did not know what else to say, I decided to ask her for more detail, memories and events associated with certain times in her life, in the order she had mentioned them. I first asked about her childhood and wartime, and she told me about a large earthquake when she was in the second grade of elementary school, during the war. She was in school when it happened and the teacher sent them home. She was running, and suddenly the ground broke open and water started gushing through. Even now when she thinks of it, she gets scared, she told me. There were several smaller earthquakes in those times too, they happened quite frequently.

She also described the area where she lived, with the big river nearby that was used for watering the rice paddies. At the time it was clean and nice and people would go there to fish or to swim. All of that was built up now, she said with regret, but it was such a nice river back in her day. She remembered the times when she was going home from school and it would start to rain and they would pick the big leaves that were growing there and use them as an umbrella, running home as fast as they could. She happily recalled those times when she was little, emphasizing that things were good back then and the place was quiet. They lived in a rented house then, but later her parents bought some land and built a house of their own. Soon the war started and there wasn't much to eat, no rice. She said they were lucky, as there were lot of vegetables so they didn't starve and they ate sweet potatoes every day. In their village no bombs were dropped, but they could see the bombings of Nagoya. She said they could see it rise up to the sky, and then her father would comment, "they dropped it again." She talked a bit more about the war damage, and the stories she'd heard in the salon about what had happened in Osaka, with so many houses burned down and people forced to live in cramped conditions, sharing kitchens. . . . Eventually she indicated she was finished, and I asked her to tell me about the time when she started working, after World War II.

When she was in the third grade of elementary school, she replied, she went to do an apprenticeship as a weaver (*hataori*). She lived in a dorm with other workers, twenty of them, but they were all much older than her. She was still very little, she said, she could not work in the workshop but helped out instead by looking after the children and cleaning. She had to stop school, so she doesn't have much education, she confessed with some embarrassment. But there was no other way, as she had to work. When she was a bit older, seventeen or so, she started work in the workshop. At the time, they did not have bonuses in money but were given gifts for New Year's and Bon, such as a yukata or kimono, which the girls would put away, saving it for when they got married.

I asked her about her experience of living in the dorm, and after a moment of silence, she replied that her story is somewhat embarrassing, but that her mother had died when she was five. When she was six, her father remarried, and her "second mother," as she referred to her, had two sons and a daughter. But she was also very sickly and often unwell. When the youngest baby girl was born, Takahashi-san was in the first grade of elementary school and her stepmother was in hospital for four months. During that time Takahashi-san looked after the baby and the other children, being the oldest sister. There was no milk, not even cow's milk, so she fed her rice water. Her father had to earn the money, so he had to leave the house and leave her with the children. The stepmother came out of hospital, but after a few more months fell sick again. She was very weak. They never got along and always argued, so Takahashi-san left to do an apprenticeship. Her father was running a *kushikatsu*[4] shop at the time, and one of his customers who came often noticed this tension and offered to take her on, to take care of her, and she moved into the dorm. Takahashi-san thought that if the stepmother hadn't had the little daughter, perhaps she would have taken better care of her, but she wasn't her real child. So when her father came with the suggestion, she agreed, thinking it might be for the best.

She told me that she needed to look after the children and prepare the rice for all the workers in a massive pot, all on a fire oven. Together with the family and all the workers, there were thirty of them, so the quantities were enormous. It was quite hard, and they were a bit strict. She also needed to do the washing up, dusting, and other kinds of cleaning. The work in the weaving workshop later was not light either, but working with others was fun. When the work for the day was over they would sometimes go and see a play or a movie. There were three of them sleeping in a room, and they would always chat. That was lots of fun, she concluded.

After a short silence, I asked her to tell me more about getting married. Somewhat reluctantly, she told me she met her husband through *omiai*, it was an arranged marriage. But, she said, it was no good. He was the second son of a family acquaintance and her stepmother introduced them, but she did not put any effort into checking properly what kind of man he was. However, Takahashi-san was eager to be free of her family and accepted the first offer. "That was the origin of my failure," she laughed. Their marriage hadn't been a good one, and even though they did not hate each other, they argued a lot. He worked in the construction business and they ran an inn for their workers, for whom she had to cook and sometimes also help out on the construction sites, while looking after the household and their three children. She was always overworked, and he often had to entertain them until late, a task that involved alcohol. She would often complain, and he thought it was annoying, so they argued. She really wished she could just look after the household and children but she had to work, getting up before everyone else, often woken up by the workers on the days they had off because they wanted to eat something cooked. But she was young then, so she somehow managed.

She complained, and he would get upset at her, and they would argue. He would get angry that she was complaining when he was tired from working hard, but she thought it was pointless when they had nothing to show for it in the end, as he would just go out to drink all the time. His workers would invite him, "Boss, come and have a drink with us," so he joined them. But going out like that every night, she said, he got into the habit of drinking and started drinking on his own, spending all the money they earned, "until he died." He damaged his liver from drinking too much and died when he was forty-five years old. Her oldest son was in the third year of university and her husband did not leave them any money, so she had no choice but to start working to support the children. Her daughter was in high school and the youngest son was in year six of elementary school—"So I just worked and worked, to pay for the school fees." She moved to Nagoya, where she worked in a business hotel, a kind of residence for workers who were living away from home. The pay was good, but the work was very hard, preparing breakfast on her own for hundreds of lodgers every morning, cleaning, and the like. She felt like she couldn't move her legs or arms, it hurt so much, and she felt she couldn't go on like that. Luckily, while working there she met a friend who used to live in Osaka. Through her recommendation she got a job in Osaka. Her friend married and remained in Nagoya, so they lost contact.

At present, she is quite satisfied with her life and likes living in Osaka very much. She does hope she can stop working soon, as she is starting to notice it affecting her health. She enjoys living alone and socializing with her friends, although it is difficult to make friends later in life, as she told me on one occasion. It is easy to have acquaintances, but hard to create close friendships (*shitashii*). Older people seek comfort and they withdraw when they do not feel like doing something, she said, after mentioning one of her friends. Nevertheless, she would not like to move in with one of her children. Her daughters live in other prefectures, and she visits them a couple of times a year and enjoys those trips a lot. She talks to her daughters on the phone and feels quite close to them, but also values her independence and life in Osaka.

On several occasions, Takahashi-san's recollections focused on her life in Osaka and her work in the exciting environment of a high-end inn in the entertainment area of the city. She spoke vividly of her experiences there and of the responsibilities she was later given, having to do accounting every night. Even while explaining how hard she was working then, a smile did not leave her face, just as when she spoke of having fun with her friends. This part of her life was not just the most recent, she implied, but also the one that defined her, that made her who she is now: a sociable, confident person who meets new people with ease. The friendships she made, while numerous, are not very close but rather focus on spending time together cheerfully. In many of her later life relationships, the focus has been on conviviality rather than intimacy.

Living in Close Quarters or "Intimacy at a Distance"?

Takahashi-san's relationship with her children is close, but she does not want to live with them and values her independence. Yet she says she enjoys a close relationship, especially with her daughters, with whom she speaks frequently on the telephone. In this case, as in many other similar cases, it may be necessary to rethink conventional ideas of physical proximity and closeness of living together and intimacy, especially with respect of the coresidence of the elderly and their children's families. The three-generation household is no doubt still often considered an ideal, and while some older people are prevented by unfortunate circumstances from enjoying it, many, like Takahashi-san and Fukuda-san, simply choose not to live with their children. It is therefore essential to distinguish between isolation and living on one's own, just as it is necessary to differentiate between coresidence and intimacy—issues that are often conflated in relation to the elderly in Japan. For instance, many older persons living in new houses constructed as two-generation units (*nisetai jutaku*) felt increasingly isolated, since their friends and neighbors checked on them less frequently as they assumed that they are taken care of by their children, whom they would in some cases see as rarely as once a week (Brown 2003).

Writing about older women in the United States, Brian Gratton and Carole Haber (1993) noted that while the public discourse idealizes the situation of the elderly living with their family on farms as having most authority, and the urban pattern of separate residence is equated with neglect, their research showed that women living in three-generational households in rural settings had the least power. In contrast, women in urban settings often felt closer to their families while living in their own homes, which the authors label "intimacy at a distance." This is an important point that requires careful consideration in relation to the changing living patterns of the elderly in Japan.[5] Gratton and Haber further relate the possibility of "intimacy at a distance" with an increase in social security: "Rather than neglect, the living arrangements of the older women may reflect the impact of Social Security" (1993:183). While Takahashi-san's example may not be a good case in point for this, since she has to work to support herself, Fukuda-san's example supports this idea, along with numerous other cases I encountered in my fieldwork, some of which I describe in the following section.

To sum up, I argue that the close relationships of older people need not always include their family, especially their children. When they do, they are not necessarily based on coresidence, nor does living alone necessarily equal social isolation and loneliness. It often reflects a conscious choice and is connected with the high value placed on independence. Such independence, however, can often only be maintained with the help of friends and community ties or social security. Furthermore, close or intimate relationships in later life do not always take place within marriage, as illustrated by the case of Takahashi-san. The nature and meaning of intimacy can also vary significantly in these close relationships, ranging from the kind of implicit understanding that comes from living together to an emotional, verbal openness.

The case of Ikeda-san and Kato-san, the two coresident sisters who were frequent customers in the salon and therefore appear in these pages quite often, is particularly illuminating with respect to ideas of coresidence, interdependence, and intimacy. In her mid-eighties, Ikeda-san is a feminine, cheerful lady. Always well-dressed in dark trousers and a burgundy or lighter colored cardigan, Ikeda-san made sure that she never left the house without powder or lipstick. Several years ago, she had an operation for stomach cancer. Having partially recovered but still weak, she moved in with her older sister, who has a house a few minutes away from the salon. Ikeda-san has no children, and while she really likes her sister's company, she finds it difficult not to have her own house and her freedom. Ikeda-san's husband was a tobacconist, and she frequently helped out in the shop. While far from affluent, they had a comfortable life, occasionally going out and traveling with a group of friends from a society for people with disabilities where her husband held a position of responsibility. Having no children of their own, they took care of a young niece for a number of years while she was attending school in Osaka. On one occasion, Ikeda-san told me, not without pride, that she had raised her niece, who now lives in her own house with her family. Yet she chose not to live with her niece but with her older sister. Even though her sister is sometimes a bit strict and controls the household budget with a firm hand, she enjoys being in her company as the recipient of her caring attention, and the two of them could always be seen together, chatting or laughing.

Without children of her own, Ikeda-san led a fulfilling life and seems to have been quite close to her husband, with whom she often went out and traveled, often with a large group of friends and acquaintances. Unlike some women her age, she is therefore used to socializing in mixed company and enjoyed chatting to both men and women in the salon and making friends. This sometimes led to misunderstandings, as in the opening anecdote. But most of these relationships were not particularly close or intimate. At the same time, her relationship with her sister was quite caring and affectionate. Yet when I visited the sisters at their home, Ikeda-san's whispered confession to me while her sister was in the other room made it clear that sisters avoid certain topics with each other. Ikeda-san's eyes glazed with tears as she told me of her husband and the life they had together in their home, and how she missed her home and her freedom and was sometimes tired of her sister's authoritarian attitude. The sisters did not talk about their feelings for each other or their life together. Ikeda-san was grateful to her sister for her care and felt close to her and very fortunate to have her. Yet the close bond and intimacy that they share should not be equated with intimacy of the kind described by Shumway (2003), based on verbal openness about emotions.

Freedom and Intimacy in Older Age

The life stories of Fukuda-san and Takahashi-san, and the case of Ikeda-san, raise important issues of coresidence, freedom, and independence, and like so many other cases in the salon require us to rethink the link between coresidence and intimacy as represented in the ideal of the three-generational household. Although intimacy almost everywhere in the world, and perhaps especially in Japan, can be created through embodied practices such as sharing food, as well as bathing together,[6] coresidence is a balancing act between familial involvement and private, individual comfort: "Truly 'happy' homes are those that achieve a delicate balance between the need for intimacy among the family group and individual yearnings for relaxation and escape. One may relax during family oriented activities such as sharing a delicious meal, but activities such as soaking in the bathtub or sitting or lying on the floor with a cold beer in front of the TV are equally important for the wellbeing of the family and the production and reproduction of a home-like atmosphere"

(Daniels 2010:47). The issue of the well-being of individual family members extends beyond the boundaries of the home, for they may have various involvements with networks of people in the neighborhood, for instance. Many of my interlocutors, like Takahashi-san, mentioned ties to the area in which they lived as one of the main reasons for not wanting to move to their children's house. Of course, in situations of tensions within the home or even just restricted space and conflicting daily routines of older and younger generations within the household, this balance may be disturbed and the effort to maintain harmonious relationships can feel overwhelming. Kondo-san, the "vegetable expert" mentioned above, told me that she found living with her daughter too difficult because she always had to adjust and keep out of everyone's way. She eventually decided to move back to Osaka to live on her own, precisely in order to keep the relationship healthy. When Fukuda-san's first husband died, she decided not to accept her parent's offer to live with them and help out in their company but to look for a job instead. She decided against coresidence precisely because she so valued her warm and close relationship with her parents. "When you spend a lot of time together," she told me, "even the most beloved parent might feel tired and you might argue." In this light, it is necessary to distinguish the kind of embodied intimacy of people living together from emotional closeness and warmth. Yet the latter need not necessarily be based on revealing one's emotions verbally or discussing problems, as it too can take the subtle form of copresence, or of "being there for one another." The availability of support and "dependability" are among the more important features of relationships such as those cultivated by Fukuda-san with her son, her mother, and her brother, as well as with her lover—whom she had no interest in moving in with or marrying.

While some of my interlocutors obviously enjoyed living with their children and grandchildren, others were of a different opinion. For example, a short, grey-haired lady who came to the salon every day clearly enjoyed her grandchildren's visits and seemed always to be baking cakes to take over to their house. She mentioned that she preferred living on her own, as the young ones would stay up late and the children would play their video games and music quite loud. At the age of seventy-five, she was in good health and found that occasional support from her children living nearby and from her neighbors was sufficient for her, though were she to become weaker she would try to get home helpers and nurses through long-term care insurance (LTCI).[7] Similarly, Oku-san, a man in his late seventies who frequently visited the salon, clearly stated his discontent with his grandson living with him in his apartment. "I wish he'd return home, he's a nuisance [*jama ni naru*]," he told us on more than one occasion. Even though his daughter was of the opinion that it would be a good idea for them to live together, on the grounds that her son needed accommodation closer to his university and her father could no doubt use a hand with occasional shopping and the like, Oku-san insisted that it was in fact much more of a burden having his grandson stay. He had to do much more cooking, cleaning, and tidying, he said, and also shop for larger quantities than before, while his grandson was often oblivious to household costs such as heating or air-conditioning.

Many older people who I spoke with worried about becoming a burden to their children. One lady in her late sixties who I met in a workshop on housing options for the elderly, for instance, explained that she was looking for a serviced apartment or a small private nursing home because she did not want to become a burden on her children and "cause trouble" (*meiwaku*) to them. Such people were also explicit in their belief that living alone was better and more comfortable. However, to maintain their independence they were reliant on friends, neighbors, and/or social services. A similar case is described by Lynne Nakano (2005: 137): "After the death of his wife and his eldest son, the two people who are most closely associated with eldercare, Abe decided that the best way to live his life was to assert his independence. He would not be one of those old-fashioned elderly who stayed at home all day watching TV, nor would he burden his family. He would live on his own and make an effort to make friends and become involved in social life by participating in the eldercare programs. Becoming a recipient of social welfare was part of his strategy to demonstrate independence as an elderly person."

How is one to understand this kind of independence, which inevitably involves dependence on others? In the Japanese context, as perhaps elsewhere, the notions of dependence and independence form a complex relationship that may not be best understood in terms of a simple opposition. The idea of adulthood (*ichininmae*), for instance, implies a complex interplay between the two: to fully become an adult in Japan, and therefore an individual who is recognized as independent, one must recognize one's dependence on others (Rosenberger 2007:92). Similarly, for an elderly person to lead an independent life, maintaining social ties and related dependencies is essential. To further link this with existing ideas about personhood and responsible adulthood, it might be useful to draw on work in the field of childhood socialization in Japan emphasizing the idea that Japanese children are encouraged to feel dependent on their mothers, and are indulged by them (as expressed in the much-discussed term *amae*), while at the same time learning to accept authority—both emotions that are later transferred onto one's group and the need for social approval (Reischauer and Jansen 1995:144). This group-centered attitude of the Japanese is of course both well known and widely disputed on the grounds that it has been used to express some unique Japanese essence. Such criticisms notwithstanding, it remains a dominant ideology, another kind of story drawn on by Japanese people themselves.

The concept most often used (in writing) to refer to "independence" is *jiritsu* (dating from at least the fifteenth century), which literally means standing on one's own. In the case of young people it often refers to financial independence from one's family of upbringing (Okano 2009: 250). It also implies independent decision-making. Understanding of adulthood is underpinned by three main principles: "(1) having 'a sense of concrete and achievable purpose' (*mokuhyo*), (2) acceptance of responsibility, and (3) independence (autonomy). The last two were also generally agreed criteria for adulthood in the eyes of young adults in the West, but what these young Japanese meant by these terms seemed to differ slightly" (Okano 2009: 247).

In relation to responsibility, the ideas of responsibility for oneself and for others seemed equally important (Okano 2009: 248), which is particularly interesting in relation to ideas of independence and dependence on others. Autonomy (or self-direction) has been singled out as a key component of the concept of individualism (Lukes 1979 [1973]), a concept central to Western thought but which comprises many different ideas and intellectual traditions. Other important components are privacy, or the right to a sphere of existence that is not the concern of others, separate from the public; and self-development. The latter is an idea of Romantic origin that developed in two distinct directions. As Lukes (1979 [1973]: 71–72) writes: "The notion of self-development thus specified an ideal for the lives of individuals—and ideal whose content varies with different ideas of the *self* on a continuum from pure egoism to strong communitarianism. It is either anti-social, with the individual set apart from and hostile to society . . . , or extra-social, where the individual pursues his own path, free of social pressures . . . or highly social, where the individual's self-development is achieved through community with others." Interestingly, in the Japanese tradition, the idea of self-development is not at odds with the value placed on the community (Sawada 2004; Traphagan 2004).

The concept of independence as deployed in public discourse and in public policy is often restrictive. The elderly accepted into certain kinds of care homes are expected to be independent in the sense of being able to take care of their bodily needs. The restrictiveness of the official definition of independence was demonstrated in relation to policy for the homeless (Gill 2005). The policy makers coined the term *jiritsu-shien*, or independence-support (literally "support of self-reliance"), which has the pleasant connotation of not presenting the receivers as passive and also establishing a third category between dependent and independent in the state system. In practice, though, this often meant institutionalizing the homeless in restrictive settings and making them fully dependent on various social services: "Ironically, people who have been living self-reliantly—often in quite well-constructed shacks, some with petrol-driven electricity generators, often with incomes from recycling tin cans or magazines—emerged from the shelter to state-dependent lifestyles in various welfare institutions" (Gill 2005: 201–204).

The notion of independence, as used in the printed materials of various housing agencies, homes, or counseling services for the elderly, refers to a specific, bounded kind of independence: in the most restricted sense it refers to independence in caring for one's basic bodily needs; in a wider sense it includes independence of choice. When elderly people speak of thinking about where to live, they are talking about not becoming a nuisance to their family. Many who lived alone and separately from their children emphasized that they live independently. In fact, they either rely on support networks in their community or look for a place where support is readily available. Therefore, dependence and independence are clearly not mutually exclusive, even though they can seem opposed. Elderly can live independently because there are home helpers to support them, or community ties or institutional care to help them.

What, then, is the precise nature of the relationship between autonomy and dependence in Japan, especially with regard to older people? How can these seemingly opposed notions coexist without contradiction? In his well-known attempt to move beyond simple binary oppositions, emphasizing that every differentiation includes at the same time an act of valuation, Louis Dumont (1980) has suggested that certain pairs of concepts can best be understood as "hierarchical oppositions." In Dumont's seminal writings on ideology and hierarchy in Indian society, he defines hierarchical opposition as a kind of opposition in which the term with higher value (within an ideology) at the same time opposes and encompasses the lower one, as it stands for the whole. Thus, for example, in societies where economic activities are considered as less valued, their profanity stands in direct opposition to the realm of the sacred or of ritual activities. These economic activities are nevertheless important for ritual activities and are necessary for the latter to be carried out at all. The higher ideological level of ritual thus encompasses the seemingly opposed realm of the economical (Parkin 2009:5). Another example is the English concepts of "man" and "woman," considered to be opposing counterparts, but where "man" is accorded higher value and can also stand for all humankind (Parkin 2009:52).

It may therefore be revealing to consider the notions of dependence and independence in the Japanese context in terms of hierarchical opposition. Dependence, particularly in the form of mutual dependence, or interdependence, encompasses the notion of independence, which is seen as its opposite yet cannot exist without it. The value of dependence is high in a variety of different contexts in Japan. Take for example the aforementioned case of adulthood: to fully become an adult in Japan, and therefore an individual who is recognized as independent, one must recognize one's dependence on others.

Dumont's theory also allows for an inversion of value between the two poles in particular contexts, on a lower level of ideology. In this case, however, the previously lower pole takes on a higher value but cannot stand for the whole (Parkin 2009:52). The independence asserted by older people may therefore take precedence in some situations and be valued highly, but total autonomy can never be expected. Similarly, for an elderly person to lead an independent life, maintaining social ties and related dependencies is essential. Prompted by studies showing that women in Japan are much more autonomous than often represented, Takie Lebra focused on strategies for maintaining independence among older Japanese women, concluding that "the claimed autonomy of the Japanese woman, however, turns out to be grounded in her dependency, if not upon her procreative family, upon her mother or close friends" (Lebra 1979:337).

Ethnographic data seems to confirm that the priority of these two concepts can be inverted in some cases, but that independence cannot encompass dependence. One example of an inversion of the value of the two is described by Satsuki Kawano (2004) in her work on pre-funerals in Japan—celebrations organized by older people in which they express gratitude to their families, "ceremonies of later life celebrating their agency, self-sufficiency, and personal pleasure in steering the remaining years" (Kawano 2004:155). Kawano argues that these (still rather infrequent) ceremonies, organized by older people, represent a vision of their own later years different than the official policies, which tend to emphasize the dependency of the elderly on society and their families: "Older persons take charge, command attention, and enjoy being central figures. Sometimes going against the wishes of their children and those around them, they publicly announce egocentric orientations against cherished ideas of mutual dependence" (Kawano 2004:163).

Another useful perspective comes from Lebra's more theoretical work on the Japanese self, in which this Japanese anthropologist proposes a distinction between oppositional logic and contingency logic. If oppositional logic focuses on distinctions between concepts, contingency logic posits a contiguous relationship between terms, with the possibility of their partial overlap. The concepts placed in the contingency relationship are not independent or opposite but entwined, their existence conditioned by each other (Lebra 2004:8). Both kinds of logic are universally available, according to Lebra, and can coexist, but particular cultures may express a preference for one or the other, and while Westerners more readily choose oppositional logic, Japanese tend to employ contiguous logic more often, or at least more readily recognize when it is at work (Lebra 2004:9). With regard to dependence (*izon*), Lebra suggests that instead of pairing with its opposite, autonomy or independence (*jiritsu*), in everyday use dependence would more often be paired with nurturance or indulgence (*amae*) (Lebra 2004:19).[8]

Taking Lebra's theory in conjunction with Dumont's ideas about hierarchical oppositions may offer further insight into the dynamic between dependence and independence, if these are understood to operate alongside each other. Dependence can be related (through contingency logic) to nurturing care and to reciprocity (as embodied in the notion of mutual dependence and support or interdependence, based on a more generalized reciprocity enacted through a network of people rather than in dual relationships).[9] Dependence can also be related to burden, as expressed in the form of concern that one may become a burden on one's children (*futan*), or a worry not to become a nuisance or cause trouble (*meiwaku*). At the same time, on the level of ideology, as Dumont would put it, the norm of interdependence is in most contexts valued more highly than independence and can be understood to enable and encompass it.

To conclude, in order to lead a good life one needs to strike a balance between maintaining intimacy and a degree of independence. These two were sometimes in tension, but, as pointed out by my interlocutors, including Fukuda-san, at times it was precisely by maintaining a degree of independence that warm, intimate relationships were thought to be preserved. In addition, older people in Shimoichi were intent on cultivating various sources of support—as was Kobayashi-san, who had no children and made an effort to help out her friends whenever she could, in order to have more people she could rely in times of need. In this context, LTCI and state resources (including the pension) were understood as one among many possible sources of support, alongside family and neighborhood relationships, including those established through the salon. On various occasions people commented on the limited nature of these resources; a couple of ladies who attended the "*chotto tasukeai*" seminar aiming at giving a "little help" in the neighborhood told me one cannot expect that one will be able to get all the support covered by the LTCI (especially in times when the increase in the number of older people meant an increasing pressure on limited funds). Similarly, one man who was reluctant to rely on his family as his only source of support, lest he become a burden on them, was looking for accommodation in a serviced apartment with some support funded by LTCI. Lebra suggests that it may be fruitful to focus on dependability, which implies that "the more dependable people one has around, the more options one has for dependency and therefore the more autonomous one can be" (Lebra 2004:20). In fact, the systems in place may also be perceived as dependable, including the large-scale systems such as LTCI, as well as the small-scale networks of support such as those organized in the neighborhood.[10] My interlocutors made it clear to me that maintaining multiple sources of support or "dependability" is the best way to maintain a degree of independence: yet another necessary balancing act along the way to well-being.

Chapter 7

Life as a Path

From the moment I met Ueda-san and Murata-san, two volunteers in the salon, I immediately noticed the warm relationship they had with the salon's customers. Each in their own way enlivened the conversations and cheered up anyone who seemed to be feeling slightly down or isolated. Ueda-san was a smiling, mild, matronly presence who would converse on a wide range of topics and express her opinions openly, without hesitation. Murata-san was a short, slim man who would from time to time bring treats or photos from his recent hiking trips, including impressive landscape vistas and close-ups of rare mountain flowers. Both were active in a range of community endeavors, volunteering almost every day for a few hours, or supporting the older people in the neighborhood.

This chapter presents their life stories. Although I met both these people as volunteers, I deliberately seek to avoid reducing their stories to merely their experiences as volunteers, allowing them to instead provide a larger context within which their engagements with the salon can be better understood. As well as providing insight into important issues such as how people come to perceive themselves within a larger societal framework and face life decisions, I suggest that the accounts provide a somewhat novel perspective on volunteering and community involvement, different than that offered elsewhere. By giving an account of an entire life history, one can get a better sense of the place volunteering has within a person's life, including how it relates to other experiences and to important other people. In contrast to existing accounts that focus on the volunteer identity of those engaged in community volunteering and seek to provide an in-depth account of this engagement and its meaning for the actors (Stevens 1997; Nakano 2000, 2005), I believe that a different kind of meaning emerges when one places this engagement within the larger whole of a life experience or life story. Such positioning allows us to see relevant experiences—in this case volunteering—in relation to other events and aspects of the narrator's life, and to assess their meaning in this broader perspective, including their weight and relevance in relation to the other aspects of lived experience and the self-identity of the narrator. The issues of motivation and engagement with community life that emerge here are also explored with reference to extracts from conversations with NPO staff members, who see their efforts in the NPO neither as a job nor as volunteering.

"I Saw an Era Changing"

I arrived at Ueda-san's house slightly late and a little confused. Although her house was just a few paces away from the Shimoichi salon, it was difficult to find, as my directions instructed me to continue past the fishmonger's and turn into an alleyway. As it happened, there were several fishmongers in the shopping arcade at the heart of the neighborhood, and any number of small alleyways. When I finally arrived, I was surprised at the house's tranquillity in spite of its proximity to the bustling arcade. Ueda-san's house was an old, wooden two–story town house with a kitchen window facing the alley, a small living area and bathroom downstairs, and two rooms upstairs that could be reached by a narrow staircase. In all, a fairly typical size and layout in this old merchant area. Ueda-san made me a cup of cool yuzu tea, a popular citrus drink on hot summer days, and we sat in her living room looking out over a tiny garden, no more than two square meters, with pebbles and a miniature pine tree. She explained that the chairs on which we were sitting were made by Okada-san, a neighbor. He was handy with woodwork and made this furniture in such a way that it could be used on tatami mats, Ueda-san told me proudly. In return, she helped Okada-san and his wife with their computer and would print their photographs for them. Okada-san and his wife both sometimes volunteered in the salon.

After a short silence, Ueda-san started her story with some hesitation, wondering where to begin. A tall, stout lady of sixty-four with large glasses, usually smiling in a friendly and open manner, she was now serious and immersed in thought. More to herself, she recalled her life in a nutshell: "born as the ninth and last child in the family, I got married, lived as a professional housewife, and as I couldn't have children I went out to work. . . . I worked as a public servant in Osaka, for twenty-four years and eleven months." Having gathered her thoughts, she began to tell her story, slowly but unwaveringly.

Ueda-san was the ninth and youngest child born to parents who were of the Meiji (prewar) generation. The upbringing was different before and after the war, especially in terms of gender expectations; before the war women were expected to stay at home. One had to obey anyone senior, including one's older brothers and sisters. That was the way to bring up children, and that's how it was in her case. She was born in 1947 as a final, unexpected child after her father returned from the war. The war was a break, it marked a generational change; the teachers in her school were of the new generation, and so were the parents of the other children she went to school with, so she felt she was different from people born just three years later, especially in terms of gender equality. In her times, it was not an era of gender equality, and girls were sent to do *okeikogoto* rather than to school; after middle school she started working.[1]

She lived in Hiroshima Prefecture in her natal home until she was twenty-three, after which she moved to Osaka, where she got a job in a company. At that time women were expected to do particular tasks such as cleaning and making tea. After four years she married and left her work to become a professional housewife. As she didn't have children, after seven years she was encouraged mildly by her husband and neighbors to get a job. She found one with Osaka City Hall in a ward office. At first the workplaces were still unequal, women were still expected to come early and clean up the workplace before their male colleagues arrived, and serve tea during the day, even though the difference wasn't so pronounced for public servants. Gradually, after ten or fifteen years, one began to hear that women shouldn't be expected to serve tea, and the way of thinking emphasizing equality spread. Around Heisei year 3–4 (1992–1993) the new female employees declined to serve tea. This is the Japan we now live in, Ueda-san concluded, reflecting on the change in gender relations.

Born at the very beginning of the baby boom, whatever she did from then on, either looking for work or applying for a pension, was influenced by the large number of people in her generation. She felt she lived amid all the major changes of that time, while things were being rebuilt. In her case, she felt, she didn't live "within an ordered flow with everyone, somehow changing flow midway." For instance, at the time there was much American influence, to which she wasn't accustomed, though others from her generation took it in stride. Her parents (Meiji people, as she called them), being much older than most of her peers' parents, still had a prewar mentality and were quite old-fashioned, strict and authoritative. They always warned her about manners and the polite way of speaking to everyone who was older than her, including her teachers and older siblings. They made her sit in *seiza* (a formal way of sitting in a kneeling pose) for many hours, and wouldn't let her go out on New Year's Day; instead they would all eat together and on the following day would dress her in a nice kimono and let her go out. She was taught how to make *osechi ryori* (traditional New Year's food), which she continued to make every year until her husband died. All the traditional customs were truly observed at that time. Traditional festivities and food were important, until sometime around the Expo (World Exposition) in Osaka in 1970, when Ueda-san recalled there was a change in social customs and schooling. Before that time, families with nine children, like hers, were not uncommon.

Her parents might have been old-fashioned, but they let her do things she liked, such as traveling and hiking, which she enjoyed so much. But after marriage she stopped all that—she didn't do anything, she told me in an agitated manner. She didn't even think of doing things; in twenty-five years of working she perhaps went on company-organized trips less than ten times. "I didn't even think I'd like to go!" Ueda-san said strongly, in a raised voice. Well, after leaving her job she went a bit, when she was invited by her friends. But, she warned me, her story would not be representative, others might have had a very different life history. She felt that her life was interrupted, cut by the war, and that she was always witnessing transitions. "I saw the change of an era, I witnessed my parents aging," she said, as if summing up her youth, marked by care for her parents.

She was born when her mother was in her forties, and her father retired when she was in middle school. For that reason, she said, she doesn't know the concept of getting something done by your parents. If she wanted something done she would have to do it herself, she reiterated, since her parents were older. Ever since she was in elementary school she had to help with preparing food and participating in the kind of family obligations that young children were mostly unconcerned with, such as attending the funerals of neighbors and kin. She was the same age as her cousins' children, having been born after her father came back from the war. Her parents thought that they wouldn't be able to have any more children, but then she was born. Because of that timing, everyone else in her class was the oldest son or daughter. In terms of family circumstances, Ueda-san repeated once more, her childhood was very different. Her life was also marked by the number of people of the same age, during the boom. Even though there were many jobs, the salaries were low, because there were so many of them. Jobs were mostly for men, though, and unless a woman was a professional, like a nurse, she would usually marry after finishing school and become involved with the household, with the money the husband brought home, and that was the pattern she fell into. When did everybody (i.e., women) go back out to work, she started wondering. Maybe just before the Expo, everyone was buying houses (*maihomu*) and the wife would start a job part-time, to help pay off a mortgage. She also became a housewife in Shōwa 49 (1974), and went back to work in Shōwa 57 (1982). At the time there were very many housewives, but now many more women work. If you compare your mother's and your grandmother's way of life, she told me, many things have changed. In her case, social change was very rapid. She had experience of so many different things. She began to wonder what else to tell me.

She decided to tell me about her job, when she entered the ward office. She started part-time work at the ward office of the city hall and was soon offered permanent employment there. For twenty-five years she was in charge of services for people with disabilities and the elderly. At the time there were two kinds of jobs there, home helper and administrator, and she chose the former. As a result of an administrative reform seven years later, she became an office-bound administrative employee, a helper-coordinator. During her time, the system changed several times, and as she was working, various new tasks were assigned to her. Her position become a more general welfare-related position, and she was even placed in charge of all the public nurseries in the ward. After long-term care insurance was instituted in Heisei 12 (2000), she worked on that too.[2] Even before that time the ward office was dispatching home helpers to the elderly and disabled, through Shakai Fukushi Kyōgikai (Social Welfare Council). When the long-term care insurance law was enacted and independence support (*jiritsu shien*) payments for the disabled were started, she really took over everything not covered by those. Around Heisei 15 (2003), Osaka City started up neighborhood networks (*chiiki netowaku*), and the health care center (*hokensho*) came under the auspices of the ward office, and matters that had been dealt with elsewhere until then became the responsibility of these networks and network officers. It made sense, since they collaborated a lot before, but after that the job become very difficult. There were more people responsible for different things, but the service counter for customers was staffed on rotation, so that was added to her many duties. Finally, the use of computers was becoming more and more ubiquitous in her work, which she felt uncomfortable about as she couldn't really use a computer. (I was surprised to hear this, since she was the one person in the salon that all the customers asked to help them with computer-related issues, including burning CDs, searching the Internet, and printing photos or preparing presentations for events.) After an accident that made it hard for her to walk down the stairs and to walk much, she struggled more and more with her work tasks such as going out to other offices or people's homes, and she had to take a taxi. This proved unviable and, getting really tired of it all, she resigned, only later to realize she had resigned just a month before she met the minimum requirement for the state pension, which is twenty-five years of employment. To qualify, she would now have to work for one more year, which she didn't want to do.

Reminiscing about her times at work, Ueda-san remembered some difficult times dealing with people with dementia. In one case, a lady had a home helper who came to do house cleaning, but every time after the helper left the lady made an incredible mess. Whenever her daughter came over, sometimes soon after the helper left, she found the place in total disarray. She said to her daughter that the helper doesn't do anything, so the daughter filed an official complaint. Other times there were complaints about stealing money. One particularly difficult episode was when a helper came over to the apartment of a lady with dementia, bringing food. Having arrived there, she couldn't get in: the lady wouldn't open the door for her, having locked herself in and gone to hide on the balcony. Luckily, her next-door neighbor went in through the balcony and opened the door for them. When they got in they found the lady holding up a cushion, shouting, "The soldiers are coming, the soldiers are coming!" and leaning out from the balcony. The fire brigade arrived to help, but since she didn't have any relatives, someone had to calm her down. Ueda-san was called in. Suddenly the lady asked her who she was, and began to talk. From that moment until she finished talking, saying, "Thank you for listening to me," it took five hours. There was another difficult case, a woman with dementia who would wander away. Her wandering caused so much trouble to her family, they couldn't leave her alone without her leaving the house, sometimes without clothes.

It was harder back then. Before long-term care insurance, the ward office had to deal with all kinds of things. Toward the end of that time, before the insurance, the number of helpers in the Social Welfare Council branch in the neighborhood was constantly rising, until it reached around one thousand. The process of starting up a new system, the transfer of duties—that time was the hardest. Before long-term care insurance was launched it would have all been impossible without the volunteers, Ueda-san emphasized. Without their help, she thought, she wouldn't have been able to do her job. For instance, she was able to set up a rotation with helpers and volunteers to be with a blind young mother for twenty hours a day when her child was just born. Then she recalled a blind young mother who couldn't read picture books to her child. Having heard about her worries, Ueda-san recorded on a cassette the content of several books and got the lady's husband (who was also blind) to write it out using a Braille typewriter. Then she pasted it into the picture books so the mother could read to her child. She helped them make quite a few volumes this way. The girl really got to like reading books, and came to visit her many times afterward.

Another time, a young woman who knew her through her welfare job came to ask her for help. She was pregnant and bleeding, and even though her mother assured her she was all right, the young woman felt uneasy so she came to speak to her welfare worker whom she knew, Ueda-san. Ueda-san was concerned and took her to the local hospital, where she had an emergency delivery. Ueda-san knotted her brows thinking about what might have happened if she hadn't made it to the hospital. But the baby girl grew up healthy, she told me as her face brightened, adding with pride that the girl later decided she wanted to become a social worker and had just enrolled in a welfare course at the university. She also remembered the case of a young couple with disabilities, both of whom were in wheelchairs, and at the stage when their baby was crawling and just starting to walk it was very hard for them to look after it, to bathe it and the like. She sent out volunteers and helpers every day to help them out, especially with bathing. "Volunteers helped so much," Ueda-san said gratefully. "Even after I've left my work, I still think about how with the support from the volunteers the elderly and the people with disabilities could lead their lives, before the long-term care insurance law." The volunteer coordinator at that time was a marvelous person, organizing all kinds of events for the volunteers. "Those are the kind of things I remember of when I think of my work," Ueda-san said smiling, as if to finish. After a short silence, her expression stiffened a bit as she recited another summary of her life: "Other than that, we were a childless couple, we didn't go traveling. . . . There wasn't much interesting. . . . I came from a big family

[*kodaku san*], we played a lot outside with friends [and had to look after our-
selves]. . . . That's why I haven't been led much by self-interest."

After a short break I asked Ueda-san some questions, in the order in which
the themes appeared in her story. I asked if she could tell me something more
about her parents. Her mother became very sick and was unconscious for
forty-five days. Even though Ueda-san was already married she stayed in the
hospital with her mother, feeding her sticky rice until she regained consciousness. Because she hadn't been on an intravenous drip, she was strong and
her recovery was quick, and soon she was able to walk. Her father suffered a
stroke at the same time, so she looked after both of them and stayed with
them in the hospital in a double room. The nursing of both of her parents
lasted some six months in total. Her father was half paralyzed so she had to
give him water, take him to the toilet, and help with his rehabilitation and
exercise. She helped her father to practice using a drinking cup. After the
stroke he suffered a speech disability, and when he was finally back home she
would call him every day to practice speaking, doing speech therapy exercises for two or three hours a day. The bills were so high that one day she got
a call from the phone company asking if she was running a business from
home, suggesting that she switch her account to a business one. After two
years he really became quite like himself again, his speech mostly recovered.
His paralysis almost unnoticeable, her father was able to look after himself.
He would make his own meals three times a day until he died at the age of
eighty-three. When her parents were in the hospital for a long time and she
was looking after them, she fell ill from exhaustion and got a chill that made
it impossible for her to stand, her back hurt so much. Her husband then
came to get her. Because her parents were older, she never thought that parents are the ones who do things for you, she always thought that the child
was the one to do things. Looking after her parents like that made her do her
best. Even though she had other brothers and sisters, she cared for her parents, as the last child. She then made the decision she would look after them
until the end.

When that happened, she received a call. She had spoken to her father
that evening at around half past eight and he had mentioned he was a bit hun-
gry. She suggested he have a mandarin. After he ate the mandarin he started
feeling unwell and was taken into hospital. Some of her brothers and sisters
made it to the hospital, they were all there. Then Ueda-san received the phone
call: he had just died. She was told how he went: in the very end, as a nurse

was giving him a drip, she asked him how he was feeling. He told her that he was quite well, that he now felt much better, he livened up—Ueda-san described his last moments with a tear in her eye and a smile on her face. He got to live until the age of eighty-three. Her widowed mother lived for another ten years, on her own. Every day Ueda-san would check on her by telephone, or if she needed anything she would go over, that was the kind of life she was leading. Her mother lived until the age of ninety-three. Ueda-san thought of looking after her mother as a matter of course, she felt the obligation (*on*). And this feeling extended to the people who supported her when she assisted her mother, the volunteers and kind people in the neighborhood. They looked in on her mother, and so she was able to support her without having to live with her. What she couldn't do then, she feels that she would like to repay now, by volunteering. That was the beginning. One day, after retiring, she heard about this new activity (organized through the Fureai salon) and got involved, through Okada-san, a lady whose mother helped her mother. So she started a volunteer course run by the salon, feeling that everyone had helped her when her mother needed support. She felt she wasn't an especially good child to her mother, who really wasn't very demanding and never reprimanded her. She was married so she didn't live with them, and her parents returned to normal life after their illness. When her mother was approaching the end, she spent the last week with her. But her father passed away so suddenly she didn't have a chance to be there, Ueda-san said with some bitterness. All his children were there, but she, who cared for him for so many years, did not come in time.

After a moment of silence I asked about her time as a housewife. She smiled and replied that coming from a traditional family, and because she liked cooking, she would prepare all her husband's meals with care. She wouldn't think of serving him anything ready-made for breakfast. She got up early and made him a proper meal, including various different things. Her husband said that was too much and asked her to just give him bread and instant soup, regular food, that was by then considered normal. He asked her to sleep longer and not worry so much about his food, but she felt she couldn't do it. She would do all kinds of things around the house, and then one day someone suggested she take up a job at the newly opened branch of a shop owned by the same company her sister's husband worked for. She worked there in a cafeteria and met many other girls. The company made karaoke equipment, so she obtained a machine and would entertain her young colleagues at home. Then she became quite sick from exhaustion and after that she did not go back to work, though she continued to do karaoke at home for five years, as a job. Every night someone would come over, two or three people. She was also doing some childcare at home, the local children would come over to play and she would make treats for them. It was quite lively and noisy at times. Toward the end, she said that there were many things she had forgotten, like her three near-death experiences in various accidents as a child, of which she remembers just the stories, ending her story after a short pause with a smile and the words "and the rest was usual."

Living in a Social World

Ueda-san reflected a lot about her position in society and how her experiences reflected particular historical and demographic circumstances, such as being part of the large cohort of baby boomers. She placed her own life within a change of gender norms, which she described minutely and reflectively, emphasizing her understanding of herself as between generations, between "eras." It is useful at this point to cast a glance over the specific demographic and social circumstances that Ueda-san experienced firsthand and felt as directly influencing her life. While the demographic transition in Japan was by no means unique and is considered to be a feature of all industrialized countries, its pace was unprecedented as it happened in the space of merely three generations (Ochiai 1997). This resulted in specific demographic conditions that influenced the shape of social structures. The postwar generation of 1925–1950, which had a large number of siblings that survived into adulthood, unlike the previous and following generations, formed strong and large kin networks that were able to look after small children and aging relatives without external support (Ochiai 1997:71). This is the generation that formed the mainstream model and perhaps even made the "Japanese model" of welfare possible (Ochiai 1997).

Like Ueda-san in her account, Jennifer Johnson-Hanks (2008) insists that demographic conditions should be taken into account because of their close link with social, political, and technological changes, but particularly because demographic changes have contributed to the most radical changes in human lives. On the other hand, by focusing on the level of the population, Johnson-Hanks argues against methodological individualism, asserting that populations have systemic characteristics that surface only at the aggregate level (2008:310). These, in turn, have serious consequences for individual lives. Demographic conditions thus have important consequences on various levels:

the institutional, the level of family structure, and the level of the individual. As Emiko Ochiai (1997) shows, the level of predictability in postwar Japan achieved by low mortality rates, which meant that one could expect to live one's life course without fearing the loss of a partner or children, combined with financial security in times of economic growth, would have been likely to alter people's understandings of institutions such as family and marriage (Ochiai 1997:179). Ueda-san is strongly aware of this influence, as she stated several times explicitly, and of her particular situation as differing or conforming to the typical model.

Anthropologists focusing on life histories have warned against using them as tools for generalization about cultures or societies, questioning the legitimacy of treating the people narrating them as "types." In contrast, Sarah Lamb (2001) is interested precisely in this aspect of the narrative of a widow she spoke to, not least because she maintained that her interlocutor actively assumed such an identity and fashioned herself within this model: "All people, not only anthropologists, tell stories partly in order to make generalizations about the broader forces and conditions that shape and contain their lives" (Lamb 2001:27–28). She goes on to show that her interlocutor, by voicing her story, shows how different she is from what the cultural model would have her be (a widow, who is therefore a danger, a potential "slut"), but at the same time situates herself within this model by depicting herself as a "good wife." It is not impossible that this is the only way she can obtain legitimacy, to have the chance for her narrative, and therefore her questioning of the dominant model, to be heard.

I would argue that in order to criticize, expose, question, or even scrutinize the dominant model, the narrator of a life story feels the need to situate herself somehow within it, even if her own position is decentered or marginal. Ueda-san represented herself as a working woman who liked entertainment and socializing with her female friends; she valued her own engagement highly and did not consider her wifely identity to be the primary one. She rarely talked of her husband, who had passed away some time ago; his ancestral photo looked down on us as we talked. Yet she felt the need to say that she was a diligent housekeeper, a wife who rose early to prepare breakfast for her husband, almost as if that were the only way the other aspects of her identity could be legitimized. To be fair, this aspect of Ueda-san's story is not very strong, unlike in some of the other stories that more explicitly relate to the dominant life model. Nonetheless, Ueda-san felt that she needed to place her own life firmly within a social and historical context, precisely because she herself sometimes felt caught up within various, sometimes conflicting value systems.

Being raised by parents with traditional values, she felt she lived a life that was somewhat out of sync with everyone else's, that she didn't live (as she put it) within an ordered flow with everyone else. That said, Ueda-san's life course did not seem to diverge much from one we might consider typical, except perhaps for the fact that she had no children; she started work and left home in her early twenties, married and left work a few years later, returned to work several years later. The difference Ueda-san referred to was in terms of values: while other couples may have occasionally traveled together, it did not even occur to her that that was something she might have done, something she might have suggested to her husband. She was diligent and dutiful and focused on her obligations and care for her parents. Ueda-san felt she was caught between changing generational norms but that this allowed her to perceive the changes, always witnessing transitions (*itsumo kawari me wo mieru*). In this sense she felt that she was lucky, with an interesting perspective on things: "I saw the change of an era, I witnessed my parents' aging," she said.

It may seem somewhat unusual that she cared for her parents in old age rather than her older siblings doing so, in particular the family of her oldest brother. While they were not averse to giving parents some support, this came about naturally. As the youngest child, Ueda-san spent a lot of time helping her parents in her youth and developed a strong connection with them. The care in their later years, as they got sick, was something she decided to take on: she chose to feed her mother and practice speech with her father, and spoke of it as her own decision. Yet she also described it broadly in terms of obligation (*on*). This was not at all expected of her, as it is considered the duty of the oldest son and his wife, who are to inherit the parents' house. Ueda-san did not inherit her parents' property, as I found out later when I asked her, nor did she even think about it. Nevertheless, she described the caring relationship to her parents in terms of duty and obligation. In contrast, Daniel Miller describes the actions of young mothers in North London as based on the "modernist concept of freedom, where responsibility is felt to be an outcome of their own agency rather than merely an obligation . . . or unreflective compliance" (Miller 2004:36–37). Ueda-san might have stubbornly insisted on caring for her parents—up to the point of her own exhaustion, when her husband had to take her home to rest—but she framed her actions in terms of obligation. Moreover, by letting her mother live on her own and relying on help from neighbors, she managed to keep her job and continue working, which she considered important, and where she could perform other forms of care. Care may thus be seen as an obligation, though it is also a great deal more.

"My Life Was at the Crossroads"

Murata-san was a dark-haired man in his late sixties with a boyish look about him. Our interview took place in the quiet, pleasantly lit room upstairs from the salon in which we met as volunteers. When I asked him to tell me about his life, he didn't hesitate much: "Well, in my childhood, there were no particular problems, but since I started working, there were many things." When he was in his thirties, the company for which Murata-san was working started to struggle and he was told he would be transferred to another city. At that time, one couldn't decline a transfer, but Murata-san didn't want to leave Osaka, so he resigned and started working as a cook with his cousin. That period of his life was perhaps the hardest, he told me and laughed. It was a big company and there were all kinds of problems, different kinds of things to look after. He worked from the age of thirty until he was fifty-five, from early morning till late at night. Getting up and starting work while it was still dark, finishing work when it was dark again. In that manner, he worked for twenty-five years.

That was the time when Murata-san's mother started requiring full-time care. She had helpers coming, arranged through the Fureai salon, but he would take care of her when he was home from work. He looked after her until she passed away at the age of eighty-seven. At the very end she had gall bladder cancer and was admitted to hospital. Being of an advanced age she couldn't have surgery, she didn't have enough strength. So he wanted to take her home and had to make a sudden choice. Within three days he left his job. He was not yet fifty-six when he resolved to leave his job. His circumstances were such that he still needed to work, but he felt he would somehow be able to make do. He had some savings and somehow he managed to resign. When his mother returned home she was bedridden, so Murata-san had to look after her needs, including toilet care. A nurse told him around her birthday in early December that she might not live until Christmas. And just like she said, Murata-san's mother passed away in less than a week. She didn't like hospitals and said she would like to die at home. So that was it. Well, so Murata-san thought he would look after his mother until the end. In Japan even now, that is the way people want to go, in their own home, Murata-san told me, so one could look after them until the end.

For half a year after she passed away, Murata-san took it easy. Then his neighbor suggested that he find some work. His mother's friend from the neighborhood suggested a job in care for the elderly, which would be flexible so he could take time off. So he went to a course, obtained a home helper certificate, and started working through Fureai salon and at a day center for the elderly, doing those two jobs at the same time (*nisoku no waraji*). The work thorough the Fureai salon was about 10 percent of his overall commitment. Just a couple of months earlier he had left that job after working there for exactly five years. It was quite strange, Murata-san thought, that he worked for so long as a cook and then did care work for five years. "It was hard," he concluded.

Of course, it was emotional labor (*seishin rōdō*). Care involves a great amount of emotional labor and that exhausts one much more than physical labor. Murata-san really enjoys mountain climbing. On many occasions his friends would invite him to go climbing with them, but as he had to request days off one and a half months in advance at work, he sometimes couldn't go. Now that he had left his job, he could take it easy. From next year he will be eligible for a pension, though not a large one. So he's thinking of living like that—and of course of mountain climbing. One needs to consider one's health, Murata-san started to think recently. He is not sick, but has had some problems. When he was around the age of fifty-five he had some health problems, he had a lot of blood in his stool. That coincided with him leaving his job, and until then he had been too busy to go and see a doctor. Only after that did he start thinking about his health a bit more seriously. When his mother became unwell, he thought a bit more seriously about his own condition. The timing was good, he said, because if he'd continued working as before he'd probably have died soon, he would be ruined. He had surgery and part of his large intestine was removed. It took him around two years to recover, and even though he is still concerned about that, he tries not to worry. That time was hard, though, when he was fifty-five. He really felt his life was at a crossroads, Murata-san told me quietly, and he had to decide which way to take. But he made the right decision. Bleeding, himself; his mother sick; and wanting to let her be at home until the end . . . that time was the hardest for him, emotionally. But, he added with a smile—now he's enjoying himself.

Murata-san is conscious of his health now and tries not to eat or drink too much, not to eat meat, but to eat lots of vegetables every day. Once a week he takes a break, and he makes sure that every Monday he doesn't drink any alcohol, to give his heart a rest. Those are some of the things he thinks about. He lives on his own, so once a week he goes out to eat things that are more complicated to make or are not worth making just for one person. He tries to make the best use of eating out and making things at home, to find a balance in terms of nourishment. "That's the kind of life I lead," Murata-san concluded with a little laugh.

I decided to ask Murata-san a few questions about his story, in the order in which items were mentioned. I started by asking about his first job. He replied that he was working for a nylon stocking producer, dealing with general affairs. It was a very ordinary salaryman job, there was nothing in particular worth mentioning, it was a very boring life—Murata-san was almost apologetic. I asked if he nevertheless remembered any events from that period of his life. Well, there was nothing special; he went hiking in the mountains on occasion, but nothing much came to mind, Murata-san persisted, admitting that in his next job in a school cafeteria there were quite a few things. For instance, there were times when he would work without rest for two nights in a row, when they were making *obento* (boxed meals). He would really lose all the color in his face and become quite greenish. That was the most challenging time, he thought. He was in charge of stocking all the ingredients for the food, which was quite nerve-wracking at times, because if any of the ingredients were not available they wouldn't be able to work. Every day they made around one thousand meals. That was by far the hardest, Murata-san said, so after that everything was easier, nothing was as trying.

I asked him why, in his first job, he wouldn't accept a transfer to Nagoya. He replied that he needed to look after his mother and really didn't want to leave Osaka. Maybe if he was on his own he would have thought differently. Also, he really likes Osaka, there are so many good places to eat, it's an easy place to live. Public order is good too. A few miles south from this neighborhood, there used to be fields and that area used to change a lot, people moving in; areas that feel unsafe, unlike this area with many old houses and inhabitants from a long time ago. Some of them are quite old too, this is the area with the largest proportion of older inhabitants in all of Osaka—this and the neighboring ward, which is why there are so many jobs related to elderly care. Murata-san was born and raised in this neighborhood. Just once, when he was eighteen, he felt he would like to live on his own, so he moved away for a couple of years, but later he returned. His parents moved here after the war, into a dilapidated house, a bare skeleton, which they repaired. Twenty years ago, the local shopping arcade was so full you couldn't pass through; it was a well-known arcade back then. Gradually some of the shop owners passed away, supermarkets opened in the area, and the arcade began to decay.

I wanted to know more about Murata-san's work in the care sector, as a helper. He replied that he didn't work much as a helper, only helping one older man with his bathing once a week. That was hard during the summer, he would really be drenched in sweat. The man, his friend's father, who was in his nineties, had his bed on the second floor, but the bathroom was on the first floor, so he had to carry him downstairs and upstairs on his back, which was by far the hardest part of the job. He was not a heavy man, weighing some hundred and ten pounds, but later he gained a little weight, maybe ten pounds. Murata-san's back started aching, and he was thinking of looking for someone younger to take over, but in the meantime the old man passed away from pneumonia. He had led a long life—"living until ninety is quite a bit, it's heaven," Murata-san said. That friend of his was looking after his father at home, together with his wife, for five years. In any case, that was real physical labor, he concluded with a laugh.

I asked him about the day care center he worked in, so he described its daily routine. In the morning a van picks up the elderly from their homes and brings them to the center. Everyone in turn is given a bath, then there is exercise, lunch, and leisure time with playing games until 3 p.m., when the elderly are returned to their homes, and the center closes around five. The clients are people not too unlike those in the salon downstairs, but some were in worse shape and weren't able to walk. The fees were largely covered by long-term care insurance. Murata-san believes that the fact that Japan developed the system with helpers and day care for the elderly is very good, and something he would have never been able to imagine before. "During that time the family can get some rest, it really helps.'

It's a very good system, but it seems that the country doesn't have enough money, Murata-san worried. It's a great help for the beneficiaries and their families, but people working in the system receive very low salaries. Many leave their jobs because of that. For instance, as long as young people work in such a job, they don't have enough money to get married and start a family. It barely suffices for one person to live from that salary, so the future is a worry if they continue such a job. The salary might not increase much with seniority either, Murata-san said thoughtfully, almost to himself. In the day care center he worked in there was a lot of employee turnover. It was understandable,

Murata-san added: the pay was low and it's hard labor. Hard physical labor and emotional strain. One must stay alert so that no accidents occur. Once a lady fell over and she is still in hospital, and even though it wasn't the carer's fault, it was hard on her, she felt responsible since she was the one standing closest to her. That aspect is enormously emotionally straining. Then I asked him about his volunteering in the salon. He laughed cheerfully and replied that this takes no effort at all, he just needs to make hot drinks and chat, nothing particularly taxing. The conversation slowly moved on to everyday issues, gradually bringing the interview toward the end.

Care and Shared Lives

Despite gender and other differences (including the extent to which they felt happy to talk about their lives at length), there is something remarkably similar in Ueda-san's and Murata-san's accounts, not least in terms of their involvement with the local community. Both volunteer in the salon, serving coffee and tea to the elderly who come to enjoy some company or a quiet moment away from their (still) demanding families. Murata-san also helps out his elderly neighbor, a cheerful, lively lady in her nineties, by doing odd jobs around the house and taking out her rubbish, or taking heavy blankets to the dry cleaners—as I had found out from the lady in question. Ueda-san runs a small karaoke at her home as a side job but often entertains children and elderly in the neighborhood free of charge, always happy to chat and make a cup of tea, as well as organizing karaoke sessions for them. She took her "opening hours" for the community members quite seriously and would decline invitations to outings if they collided with the usual times when she was at home and available. Ueda-san also organized collections of old and used clothes for sale at a charity fair in the neighborhood and led craft workshops in the upstairs space in the salon, for example teaching young women from the neighborhood how to make *nuno zori*, slippers made from recycled fabric.

Over the course of their lives, both Ueda-san and Murata-san became involved in various forms of care, of which some were remunerated but many were not. When she married, Ueda-san organized childcare for the children in the neighborhood for a small fee; after that she worked as a home helper employed by the ward welfare department, at first on a part-time basis and eventually full-time. Several years later she worked as a social welfare worker in the ward office, when she was switched to desk work; during that time she performed many tasks that were not strictly part of her job but were a form of care, such as helping to adapt picture books for a blind mother. She cared for her parents full-time when they were sick and supported them in their later years while continuing to work. After leaving her job she started working as a home helper (helping with household chores such as cleaning, laundry, and airing the bedding) through the NPO running the Fureai salon, paid at an hourly rate; she also helps in the salon, which is not remunerated. Murata-san, on the other hand, left his job to care full-time for his mother; later he became a remunerated home helper once a week (helping to bathe a bedridden elderly man) while working part-time in a day care center for the elderly (helping with bathing, serving meals, leading exercise classes, and organizing joint entertainment for the elderly). The transitions between these various forms of care occurred gradually and sometimes overlapped, and unpaid care in the community and paid home helper jobs were not strictly distinguished by either Murata-san and Ueda-san, nor, for that matter, by my other interlocutors who were engaged in care. While their care-related appointments were circumscribed, both of them always stressed the importance of emotional support and warm relationships and did a number of additional small favors for the people they cared for. Murata-san eventually resigned from his day care job, precisely because it was taking a toll on his health, as it involved a lot of emotional and psychological labor. This lengthy yet merely cursory list of the care-related activities performed by Murata-san and Ueda-san indicates the amount and complexity of care relations in the community. Additional meanings emerge when such care activities are viewed in the context of a life story. For instance, movements across institutional and organizational boundaries indicate that exploring different forms of elderly care separately may contradict the experience of those involved in the provision of care.[3]

Involvement in caring for parents is significant here for a number of reasons. Murata-san became involved in elderly care after gaining the experience of caring for his mother. Many of my interlocutors confirmed that this was not unusual. One lady whom I met at a meal service for the elderly (Kavedžija 2015) mentioned that she became a home helper after many years of caring for her bedridden father. Three members of the salon's NPO management, and the founders of the NPO, were involved in care for their aging relatives, which increased their awareness of the problems faced by the carers and motivated them to organize some form of support. Furthermore, both Murata-san and Ueda-san felt that they were indebted to the community for helping them to care for their increasingly frail parents, as they had received various forms of support. Some neighbors would offer useful advice, tell them about a useful service or organization; others checked in on Ueda-san's mother, who lived on her own; this meant that on most days it was sufficient for Ueda-san just to phone her several times, and to visit her every couple of days, without the need to give up her job. Ueda-san connected her volunteering now to her feeling of debt incurred, as a way to repay it, at least in part. Care, in this sense, may best be understood as enmeshed in circles of reciprocity.

It may seem surprising that, having no children of their own, neither of my companions were particularly concerned with their own aging. When I asked Ueda-san about this, she said she was not really thinking about it much at all, but that she guessed that things would work out somehow, that people would help her and she would get by. Another childless lady whom I met in the salon, Kobayashi-san, told me once that she cultivated many friendships because she did not have any close family of her own. We were walking down the street together and Kobayashi-san was stopping every few minutes to greet someone and inquire about their health, or their daughter's English classes, or some such personal detail. She explained she had arranged a meeting with her doctor for the first lady, and introduced an English language teacher to the latter. She needs to build her community networks carefully, she said, to rely on in times of trouble. But many people, like Ueda-san, had a less consciously calculated approach. She helped a bit and hoped to be helped, just like the participants of the "A Little Help in the Community" volunteer seminar organized in the neighborhood in collaboration with Fureai (Kavedžija 2015), who explained that they wanted to contribute to creating and supporting an environment in which people help each other in the community. Rather than moving away, either to live with their children or into a care facility, they would like to be able to keep living in their familiar surroundings, for which the support of long-term care insurance alone may not be sufficient, especially as strain on its budget increases. The underlying ideas of expected reciprocity here are not straightforward, with people helping others to receive help in return, as a kind of repayment of debt. More broadly, they wished to support the existence of a system of community support.

Undoubtedly, the fact that neither Murata-san nor Ueda-san have children has influenced their attitudes toward community involvement. Nevertheless, as indicated by the example of a whole seminar room full of people, many of whom had children, they were far from alone in their way of thinking. More likely, I think, they provide a good case in which some of the important motivations for involvement in community care and volunteering are emphasized. This may be related to what Lebra (1976:102) labels "generalized reciprocity," referring to the obligation (*on*) that can never be fully repaid but must be always kept in mind by the receiver of kindness. Lebra (1979) mentions the strategy employed by some older Japanese women of inducing "generalized obligation" by caring for their grandchildren, hoping that they will accrue debt with their sons and daughters-in-law to be looked after if they become frail. It is not merely a reciprocity between a mother and child, but involves care for the grandchildren. The principle of generalized reciprocity in Lebra's work indicates an obligation that is not easily defined or singled out but which involves a variety of acts of care. I would like to argue that it could also be extended to a meaning that involves an exchange in a wider community, where the obligation does not rest with particular people but can be repaid to the community as a whole. By "helping out a little" (*chotto tasukeau*) one supports a system of support that may be there for one to rely on in times of need. Furthermore, it is possible that the family circumstances of my companions somewhat influenced their engagement in care as a potential source of purpose in life. While care for others provided them with a sense of meaning, they did not define themselves in terms of a narrow volunteer identity. These issues bring us back to the question of motivations of the people involved in the care of others, including their parents. The concept of obligation is undoubtedly relevant, but its meaning is broader than it might at first have appeared. One must also bear in mind the various meanings of care and its potential to provide a sense of purpose in life, as revealed in these life stories.

Involvement and Achievement

A similar set of issues emerged from my conversations with NPO staff members, who effectively receive a paid volunteer wage but do not think of their efforts quite in terms of a job or as volunteering. In this section I focus on issues of motivation, the difference between a job (*shigoto*) and activity (*katsudō*) and its relationship to remuneration and gratitude. Through the words of my interlocutors I attempt to paint a picture of the Fureai NPO as a workplace, with its leaderless structure, democratic decision-making, egalitarian relationships, and cooperative attitudes of staff in balancing their significant workload with their responsibilities as wives and mothers. They also speak of meaningful work and express feelings of pride and achievement, even if these are mitigated by the modesty of their aims and a sense of worry about the future.

Nakajima-san

Nakajima-san is a friendly and calm lady in her fifties with a motherly air about her. She was born in Shimoichi, the neighborhood where the salon is located today. Yet when asked if she was originally from the neighborhood she answered:

> Not at all, I am . . . my parents were traders from a neighborhood not too far from the entertainment are of Shinsaibashi, where they had a large house, until it burned down during the air raids in World War II—there was nothing left of it. This area wasn't struck and there were plenty of prewar houses left around here, so they bought a house in Shimoichi. So I am a second generation here, but it hardly feels familiar [*najimi no nai*]. I was born and brought up here, but I'm not a core member of the community, it feels more like I'm further out in the surroundings. So when people are talking about others, I don't know all the stories.

Here Nakajima-san presents us with an image of a community with ties spanning several generations, not quite closed to outsiders, but permitting them access only to the margins. The sense of community is enacted by referring to these links, knowing who people are and exhibiting knowledge of their background. I often witnessed this myself: people would often relate that, for example, "the son of that lady who used to make kimonos, whose grandfather was a fishmonger, came over from Tokyo," or give directions to someone's house in this vein: "It's past the *okonomiyaki* place that's around the corner down the street on the right, opposite the florists and past the post office, which stands where the old bathhouse stood, before the war, you know, not too far from Seo-san's house." This being the shopping district, there were several post offices, florists, and *okonomiyaki* stands down the street, so without knowing the detailed spatial relationships of one to the other, it would be truly impossible to decipher which one they referred to and which way to go (more abstract directions such as left, right, or fourth corner to the left were never given). As Nakajima-san's statement shows, the community itself is thus woven from the stories one knows of others—stories that are more important than names. One knows the others through stories.

After obtaining a university degree in social welfare, Nakajima-san worked in a hospital as a medical social worker. She married her boyfriend from her university days, who worked for a large electrical goods company. He soon received a transfer and they had to move to another prefecture, though twenty years ago he was sent back to the headquarters in Osaka, and they returned. Her parents had decided to move to the suburbs, so she and her family moved into the house where she grew up, where they still live today, with two adult daughters who are both single and who work in a bank. Twenty years ago, when they returned to Osaka, she tried to find a job, but "the system of reemployment for women, after they once leave to have children, is bad," as she once told me with a clearly unsettled expression on her face. The working hours of a medical social worker are very long, as one of the responsibilities includes meeting the patients' families, who can only come to visit after their working hours. While still single, Nakajima-san would often work as late as 10 p.m., starting at 9 a.m. With young children this kind of schedule would not be possible, and even though she tried to look for a similar job with flexible hours or part-time, this was hard to find. At that time, she started thinking that it might be a good idea to create a support group for sick people in the neighborhood, something of that kind. At that time Komatsu-san had heard of the Tasukeai system, and then it all began.

On one occasion I asked how she felt about her job at the NPO. She answered somewhat reluctantly:

> The social recognition [of our work] is very low, even though we work to make the neighborhood a more pleasant place for everyone to live in. The situation is difficult, economically speaking, there is no security. In a sense, it's not really considered a job. Although, recently the attitude of the public administration has finally started changing— they've begun to make more connections, doing things with NPOs, as they realized that that way things could be done at a smaller cost to the economy. In the beginning, when one interacted with local government officials, from the city hall for instance, they would really be reluctant and showed little understanding of the work of some small NPO. This disparaging attitude is slowly beginning to change, but even though we've been around for sixteen years now, I'm not sure if most of the people in the neighborhood really know what we do,

although they have a vague sense that Fureai is doing many useful things. One reason why this is so, is that we provide many services in the home, one volunteer comes and visits a lone person or a family and as they work inside, no one else knows that they are doing something useful. So, in a sense, the evaluation is impossible, the effort is invisible. That's why it's hard for them to understand what we do. So, while we know that the people we helped are happy and grateful for our support, that's a relatively small number—in the last sixteen years it might be some 750 people. But our neighborhood [*ku*] has some 100,000 inhabitants. Moreover, our users are the socially weak, so they don't get in much contact [with people], in the society, nor do they communicate widely about the support they get.

I wondered aloud if working at this NPO, which she established together with Komatsu-san and the others, had an impact on the way she thought about things and viewed society. Nakajima-san answered my question forcefully and clearly:

It had. How shall I put this . . . Japan is a male-dominated society, and while there are women working as CEOs of companies, while we were at university it was really hard to imagine women working in managerial positions. I hadn't thought that within my very ordinary life plan I could be involved with an NPO, or be running one. So I entered regular employment in my profession in the hospital, but later when I went back to work [things were different] we started this NPO. So on some level it seems strange to me that I'm in a managerial position. I wasn't even sure I'd be able to do this, that I'd have the abilities, so now when I look back I have a feeling: "so that's what I'm doing."

Mori-san

Mori-san, a slim, quiet lady in her fifties with a shock of curly, red-dyed hair, is in charge of accounts and the LTCI subsidies. She also works as an instructor with Sawayaka Fukushi Zaidan (Sawayaka Welfare Foundation) and presides over the annual meetings of the Osaka branch of the association affiliated to it. She was involved with Fureai from the very beginning. When Komatsu-san heard Hotta Tsutomu-san (the founder of Sawayaka Welfare

Foundation, who was mentioned by all the founders of Fureai) speak on television, she was immediately interested and ordered materials explaining the system setup in more detail. When she realized that this was quite complicated she decided to talk about it with her acquaintances. One day she brought the materials over to Mori-san's house to read, and she passed them on to Nakajima-san. They started the study group, and while the core membership shrank by the time of the establishment of Tasukeai, Mori-san emphasized the cooperative and egalitarian nature of the group: "Establishing a group and organizing its activities was, unsurprisingly, a very difficult task, so we were down to eight members when we started Tasukeai. Gradually the organization grew, but what matters is that no one was at the center—we all studied together and discussed matters and decided what we were able to do and how to do it. We looked into how Sawayaka did it and made our own decisions along the way, when we thought of different new activities or ways of doing things." Mori-san did not make much of this, but when asked, she told me that working in Fureai had indeed had an impact on her way of thinking and everyday life: "I had the chance to meet various people and gained many friends. I did lose some friends, too, but probably my circle of friends got broader. While I was a housewife I knew many people in the neighborhood, but through my involvement here I realized that people do many different things, which is really interesting. I also realized through the activities in Fureai that you can achieve a lot, things you wouldn't be able to do on your own." Mori-san thinks that from her family's perspective, she is not doing much at home at all. When her daughter was still in elementary school she was "properly" making meals and doing school-related activities, but now she has stopped preparing meals that are very time consuming, which her family sometimes mentions. But they do not express too much discontent and have been very supportive. Mori-san also pointed out that all of the staff at Fureai are wives (*shufu*) who know what it means to have family responsibilities, and they help each other out, covering for each other should they have to go to take care of some family business.

> When one receives such support at work, it becomes much easier for
> women to work. That said, the salary is very low, so this is not a place
> for everyone. It is not a company salary, we receive 600 yen per hour,
> like the paid volunteers. So no matter how much you work, that is not
> quite . . . strictly speaking, this cannot be thought of as a salary, as it's
> below the minimum wage, which is around 760 yen per hour in Osaka.

What we receive is not against the law, as we—the staff here—do not think of this as labor [rōdō]. It's a sum that we've decided upon ourselves, so we think it's all right. We think of it as of remunerated volunteering. The staff here [in the office] do not have labor contracts, unlike the helpers [through LTCI] who get paid 1,220 yen per hour. So we arrange proper contracts and insurance for them, that's the difference. . . . But if the women working in ordinary companies could somehow create an environment in which they support each other, many more women would be able to work, it would be easier to have and raise children. . . . It's sad that there's no such feeling in the society.

Komatsu-san

Komatsu-san is a petite lady in her late fifties sporting a short hairstyle and practical clothes. She was in the Fureai office all day every day, dividing her time between the helper (LTCI) organization and volunteer support, stressing that the staff share most of the work. She got involved in the Fureai organization through Sakamoto-san, whom she worked with in the cooperative—an organization that had operated in the community for a long while. Sakamoto-san suggested that she could talk to Nakajima-san and other people involved in the study group, and she got involved a couple of months before the group was formally established, although by then many things about its operation and its name were already decided. Before she had children, Komatsu-san had worked as a nurse in a hospital, where she became very aware of care issues:

While I worked in the children's ward, I thought it was strange that mothers whose children were in for prolonged tests or treatment would be expected to be with them at all times. . . . That's when I started thinking about the people from the neighborhood coming to accompany [tsukisoi] the children, to allow mothers to leave their bedside, at least for a short period of time. In the new hospital I worked in the cardiac illness ward. . . . A very famous surgeon worked there and many people brought their family members from far away. One elderly man had arrived here in Osaka for his surgery, but as it didn't go well he was hospitalized for a very long time. He was from Aomori and was really longing to see the sea, he kept saying he would like to die on tatami. I tried arranging his journey, as I knew he wouldn't be able to travel by train. But he would've needed constant care at home, and this wasn't possible to organize at that time. . . . Soon after that I got married and left the job, but that feeling, of wanting to do more than what the hospital can offer, really stayed with me. I wanted to do something socially involved [*sotomuki*] so I got involved in the co-op, just doing simple things in the neighborhood. But when I heard about the possibility of organizing home care, I thought that was interesting and wanted to hear more about it. You know, at the time when I worked in the hospital, we took it for granted that people who were dying were dying in the hospital, but I once went to this hospital in Tokyo that was starting its home-care service. That's something I was hoping to do, I thought there might be something I could do to help. Well, whether that was the motive [*kikkake*] of my involvement or not, I don't know, but many things coincided.

Komatsu-san is well aware of the problems in the health care system and the support that patients are given upon leaving the hospital. This is something that led to her involvement in the scheme run by the local hospital, introducing young nurses to the local welfare NPOs in the hope that they would be able to advise patients about support in the community, and generally raising their awareness of the problems. Komatsu-san likes her job and finds it worthwhile (*yarigai ga aru*), and she gets to meet people through it, in her job and in the salon. She told me that the salon really changed its relationship to the community: over ten years of engagement in volunteer activities there was little recognition, as one always talks to users in private. The salon gets visitors from different walks of life, something that they are actively supporting by hosting a variety of events for a range of audiences, so that people who visit gradually come to realize what their role is in the community. Komatsu-san now feels the physical effort taking its toll on her body (she fills in for the helpers when they suddenly cancel), but for the most part she feels enmeshed in her work so much she does not think about it.

Kuroki-san

Kuroki-san is a tall and youthful lady in her late forties, skillfully switching between a quiet and ladylike mode of communication and a teasing, friendly, and cheerful attitude with salon visitors when she would come down into the salon kitchen to make herself a bowl of fresh noodles for lunch. She does general office tasks and helps out with the accounts but feels most responsible for Tasukeai coordination and matching the users and volunteers. While she technically works from 10 to 5 on weekdays, she often comes at 9 and stays until 6, but this also means she can pop out to take care of household tasks. With the exception of an awareness of children with disabilities, she herself had no previous interest in welfare issues. She therefore emphasized that she got interested in the Fureai work through people she knew—Mori-san is her close friend's sister, and she knew Nakajima-san through the PTA. In the beginning, she didn't become a core member, as her children were still in kindergarten, but decided to help out a little on occasion. After the official opening, the local edition of the national newspaper ran a story about them, and suddenly they were receiving more and more calls, so they needed someone to be available in the office, and they divided up the duties. At first she helped two to three days a week, but when her children started school she became a staff member. As her involvement grew, so did her feeling of responsibility: "I didn't know this, but gradually a sense of responsibility developed inside me, it felt as if I can't just stop doing this, and this is how I still feel today. But at first, the only link was through the people [I knew], and a little bit of interest in children with disabilities." She also felt she has learned a lot, as she never had a "proper" job (*kicchinto shushoku*) before this, as she used to help out with the family business, so she felt she did not know much about the world and society (*seken to shakai*). It is common to refer to entering the world of work and employment as becoming a *shakaijin*, literally "a social being," but referring to an adult, a full-fledged member of society. It was clear that she considered her current work as different both from a job for a company (or as a public servant) and from work in the family business. In a sense, this was not a real job, but it was real work that induced a deep sense of responsibility in her, even though she had no particular passion for social welfare or support. She emphasized how satisfied she was with the way things worked out for her, as she learned a lot and developed her skills, met many people she would never have had a chance to meet if she was an "ordinary" housewife, and realized that there is a lot that she *can* do.

Sakamoto-san

Among the functionally dressed housewives of inner-neighborhood downtown Osaka, Sakamoto-san stands out: a well-groomed lady in her late forties wearing feminine outfits and red lipstick. She works in the salon two days a week and is responsible for the Golden Star Cleaning service, the newest activity in Fureai. As the organization of that service slowly became more routinized, some of her time freed up and she started to think about a new activity she could take up. Sakamoto-san also works as a career consultant three days a week. She was hired on a project in a "job café" for women organized by the city hall, which involved counseling and advice as well as organizing public lectures and seminars. Thus, it occurred to her that she could organize a weekly study program, which she started running a few months before I left the field in late November 2010. The program is intended for older people, with an aim of promoting mental agility and preventing the onset of dementia. Before the classes started, Sakamoto-san said that she was hoping to involve active elderly who are interested in such activities and want to become even more active and meet people, not restricting it to the salon visitors. The program envisaged various group activities, including mathematics, kanji, guided conversation about the past, reading out loud, and the like. While these activities at first seemed to me quite easy and as potentially infantilizing the elderly, some of my friends promptly joined the course in October 2010. Yoshimura-san, a lady in her early sixties, one of the younger ones on the course, told me enthusiastically about her experiences and showed me the materials. I was astonished at the difficulty and complexity of the exercises, especially since I had heard bursts of cheerful laughter from the room upstairs where the course was taking place and assumed it was more a social and a fun event. That said, not everyone in the salon thought that it was a good idea. A few of the older ladies in the salon politely accepted the flyers describing the course and listened to Sakamoto-san's invitation and explanation over a cup of tea, but as soon as she had left, commented wryly that they hardly have need of such a thing: "At the age of ninety, you're not so worried about dementia!"

Saito-san

Saito-san is a tall, quiet, and friendly young woman in her late twenties. She had been volunteering in the salon for several months when I started volunteering in October 2009 and helped me learn my way around the salon. Seven months later, she became the youngest member of staff, working part-time, mostly producing pamphlets, schedules, and the newsletter, as well as coordinating the volunteers at the open house in the neighborhood. Having worked for several years in a bank, Saito-san was tired of her restrictive working hours. Instead she was planning to attend cookery classes and pottery classes while waiting to be married to her longtime boyfriend, who was waiting to start a new job. She worked in a private medical clinic as a part-time receptionist and over time got more and more involved in Fureai, vaguely hoping that she might be able to continue this engagement even after marriage, if they managed to buy a house in the neighborhood. She was gradually taking over more responsible tasks and her suggestions were highly valued. While somewhat deferential to the older members of staff, who were of her mother's generation, Saito-san did not refrain from making suggestions and was treated with respect.

Saito-san, like Kuroki-san, did not get involved in volunteering because of intense interest in community issues but rather through her interpersonal relationships. She joined Fureai at the suggestion of her mother, who worked there as a helper. In contrast, Nakajima-san and Komatsu-san both had a long-standing interest in support and care but were nevertheless somehow surprised at their achievements: as women in what they perceived to be a male-dominated society, they never imagined they would find themselves in a managerial position. Ogawa (2004:55) has argued against the hopeful claim that NPOs and civil society could have positive effects on gender equality, since even though the majority of volunteers in the NPO he worked in were women, the managerial positions were mostly occupied by men. The situation in Fureai differs greatly from this description, as women not only managed but also founded the NPO, which did not come into being through state or local government intervention but rather as the result of their own efforts. In a way, these women created a workplace for themselves that allowed them to pursue the social values they endorsed while continuing their role as wives. This was made possible through a strong ethos of cooperation and organization based on sharing the bulk of daily work tasks. As Mori-san emphasized: "All of us staff here, we are all wives, aren't we?" The NPO is therefore a highly cooperative and quite egalitarian workplace; this sets it apart from the usual company workplace environment, which is hierarchical and gender-segregated (Graham 2003). Nevertheless, from the perspective of the staff working in the NPO, it is not a real job, nor is it considered as labor (rōdō), as it is not appropriately remunerated. In a sense, it is not just a job either; it is an effort or a mission, imbued with social value that they hope the wider community will recognize and thus help them to create a mutually supportive community. The efforts that are going on behind closed doors are not always readily acknowledged, but this is compensated for by the public activities aimed at raising the visibility of the NPO and its role, as much as creating networks in the community. The staff do not mind that they are not well paid, so long as they receive social recognition for their work. In other words, gratitude is not irrelevant.

From these accounts, an image ultimately emerges of the good life that staff members want for themselves and for others. At the heart of this vision is a community that is not indifferent and yet not suffocating, either; one to which they contribute and from which they themselves derive benefits. These women are no radical feminists, but they do strive for gender equality. Their vision embodies a sense of meaningful engagement in accordance with their values and results in recognition or gratitude for their efforts, just as much as it entails a place to work, a project that provides meaning while not conflicting with their roles or duties as wives and mothers.

Rethinking Life Choice and Social Action

Interestingly, while community involvement or volunteer identity was often exemplified in their narratives and in other conversations I had with these volunteers, this is not a pronounced theme in either of their life stories. In her excellent work on community volunteers in Japan, Lynne Nakano (2000; 2005) explores the creation of volunteer identity, volunteering as a lifestyle choice, and its relation to the self. She situates the volunteer identity in relation to the mainstream identities of salaryman and housewife and shows the different attitudes of her interlocutors to their volunteering efforts, ranging from significant identification of "professional volunteers," through "second-career" volunteers whose identification is secondary, to the "regular volunteers" who might spend a significant number of hours engaged in volunteer activities but for whom volunteering did not become their primary source of identification. Both Murata-san and Ueda-san, along with most other volunteers that I knew in both salons in Shimoichi and Awara, would belong to the last group in Nakano's classification. The exception would be the founders of the voluntary group, who now made the organization their full-time (paid) employment and whose accounts imply that they think about their activities as a job (even if not a "real" one) rather than as volunteering. On several occasions, when she was respectfully introduced as a volunteer to people she didn't know, Ueda-san felt uneasy and pointed out she was just doing her duty. Murata-san said that he would not call himself a volunteer (*borantia*), he was merely doing volunteering, or more precisely, "being al-lowed to do volunteering" (*borantia sashite moratteru*). I would argue that this absence of volunteer identification may be highly relevant for under-standing the kinds of community volunteer efforts that were most wide-spread in Shimoichi.

There are several interconnected reasons for the absence of volunteer iden-tification in these narratives. According to Nakano, "when people talk about their experiences of volunteering, they tell stories of how they had weighed the volunteer identity against competing commitments such as caring for their families, taking part-time jobs, or devoting themselves more fully to their careers" (2000:95). In contrast, the above accounts do not express a tension with other commitments but rather a continuity. In this sense it is most likely that the Shimoichi volunteers represent a somewhat different case, representa-tive of a particular kind of community volunteering (which was not the focus of attention of Nakano's work) that is perceived as an extension of family and neighborhood obligations. Furthermore, there is a conspicuous absence of other commitments: Ueda-san is widowed while Murata-san never married, and neither have children. In this way their situation could perhaps be seen as somewhat exceptional, though in terms of time constraints not too differ-ent from people with grown-up children. Nevertheless, the absence of family commitments may be significant, since it may imply that the importance of volunteering and community involvement becomes prominent in the ab-sence of family support and commitments. In many other ways, their ex-perience does seem to be quite representative of wider trends. For instance, they slipped seamlessly into these roles through local affiliations within their neighborhood. As Nakano (2000:96) observed: "In Japan, volunteers and recipients often live in the same middle-class neighborhood, where they are recruited through local networks." Their recruitment was gradual and perceived in continuity with other kinds of welfare responsibilities and ac-tivities, such as serving as a welfare official in the ward office, for Ueda-san, to which she proceeded from local volunteering with children and part-time employment as a home helper. The welfare involvement or the aspect of care for the elderly in the community was perhaps a stronger link, including a range of paid jobs, remunerated volunteering, and volunteering without pay. The transition occurred gradually, through local community contacts, and was not perceived as a strategic decision or a life choice per se.

Most often, people from the community—neighbors or acquaintances—would suggest taking up a job or getting involved in a project. A common suggestion, as recounted by several of my interlocutors, was along the lines of, "there is this thing . . . why don't you check it out?" More often than not, it was not a lack of activities, jobs, or projects that was a problem, since the abundance made it just as difficult to consider something seriously. Finding out about an opportunity from an acquaintance made it manageable and provided a personal recommendation. Ueda-san retired from her job and had free time on her hands when she ran into an acquaintance whose mother was a friend of her mother's, who told her about Fureai. Murata-san, on the other hand, was already involved as a home helper through the NPO when he retired from his day care center job and had more time to spend as a salon volunteer. This again seems in contrast with Nakano's (2000) account in which she emphasizes the strategic choice involved in becoming a volunteer. In most cases, Murata-san, Ueda-san, and other volunteers I knew do not appear to have chosen a particular path strategically but rather as a consequence of other life circumstances and in a more organic way, depending on the chances and opportunities offered. People rarely sought out community activities but were more often invited by an acquaintance; even in those cases where someone outright looked for a volunteering opportunity, this happened when a niche appeared in their biography, thus presenting itself as an opportunity. In this sense one should perhaps speak not so much of a calculated choice as of an opportunistic action. Focusing on life stories allows us to capture the intersections of lives, the directionality of which is often shaped by such encounters. That life paths may change directions under the influence of others is no surprise, but the fact that they are often influenced by distant acquaintances, people who are in no way our "significant others," may be something we are far less aware of. Life stories may reveal these encounters and the more haphazard aspects of a life path.

The concept of social action as an intention fulfilled has been criticized for its inability to account for actions not based on strategic thinking, especially at times when planning and the formation of intentions is difficult or even impossible. Johnson-Hanks (2005) made this point in relation to young women in contemporary Cameroon, but her argument has a broader value, since the model of social action as intentional, directed, and strategic does not seem to account for many people's life trajectories. As she acknowledges, in the more secure and stable societies such as those in the West, the model of intentional action and planning appears to work better than in the chronically and radically uncertain conditions of contemporary West Africa. In her view, this is partly due to the strong influence of numerous institutions and systems that reduce uncertainty, shape people's expectations, and in turn are shaped by cultural frameworks (Johnson-Hanks 2005). In other words, the presence of institutions that ensure a certain stability is just one part of the equation, the other being expectations and ways of framing one's experience that affirms one as a calculating, rational actor. I would argue that these frameworks influence our understanding of situations and impact our expectations, in a way providing us with a language to speak of our lives as meaningful wholes. It is likely, therefore, that in societies with a high degree of security and predictability, and in cultural contexts that value planning and intentional action, even when life choices are far from strategic decisions, people still tend to relate them or represent them in terms of choices.

In one case related by Nakano (2000:98), for instance, a man who served as president of the estate resident's association admitted that he had sacrificed the mainstream ideal of career and home ownership, though his own story seems to imply that this choice was never made explicitly between equally plausible options, since no employment is mentioned. Nakano's convincing argument notwithstanding, it is not inconceivable that he felt that his "failure" in certain aspects of his life was better accounted for by his making an altruistic choice, thus retrospectively making sense of his life. Such a retrospective evaluation is made by Murata-san, too, when he speaks of making the right decision to change his life and become a home helper and an elderly support worker. In fact, that choice arose within a niche of various social circumstances, including his health problem and his mother's need for full-time care, all of which led to him leaving his job. Johnson-Hanks's (2005) concept of "judicious opportunism" is useful here, since it emphasizes the importance of the opportunity without denying agency to the actors, or the capacity for rational or informed decisions. I argue that in order to understand people's life trajectories and the meanings they attach to them in their attempt to create a meaningful life story and, more broadly, a sense of purpose in life, it is necessary to examine the tension between planned, intentional action and judicious opportunism, within social institutions and the cultural context. Nonetheless, the tendency to represent one's life as a coherent, meaningful story is in tension with the sense that not everything fits together seamlessly, and that life is always messier than our accounts of it.

Chapter 8

Meaningful Life Inside and Outside the Story

Much remains unsaid about the lives of my companions in Shimoichi. This is a good thing: the stories of people's lives, messy and multifaceted, resist final interpretations. Amassing and enumerating facts about our interlocutors as protagonists of such stories implies that everything that matters has been told about them. This kind of finalization not only cannot do them justice but also silences them. The danger lies precisely in the power of narrative to impose order. Narrative provides us with an opportunity to present a life in a coherent form and to make sense of seemingly unconnected events and disjointed episodes, thereby rendering a life meaningful. Yet excessive coherence belies lived experience, which is often messy and inconclusive. Sometimes we are unsure of exactly how events and motivations have interacted with each other, while our own motivations and actions are often not transparent to us. As Judith Butler has shown, too much coherence in a narrative can screen off or hide "an acceptance of the limits of knowability in oneself and in others" (2005:63), while digressions, omissions, and contradictions may in fact tell us more about a person than a neat and polished, overly coherent narrative (Butler 2005:64; cf. Wengraf 2001).

While a narrative can be powerful and imbued with meaning, its very coherence can at the same time have a totalizing effect. The narrator feels a resistance to being fully known, or known in totality, with an outcome akin to the statement, "Oh now I know who you are" (Butler 2005:43), something that imposes an end to interaction, implying that everything worth telling has been told.[1] While narrators need to express their story in somewhat generalized terms in order to be comprehensible—as we have seen above, for example in Ueda-san's account—they also resist this kind of "finalization," to use Mikhail Bakhtin's term. This is quite different than the case of, say, the funeral chants of the Chilean Mapuche, which enumerate all the social relations of a recently deceased person, listing one by one all those that were important to them (Course 2007). By employing the totalizing power of narration, the funeral rites in this sense complete the person upon their death. The life stories presented here, by contrast, should not be interpreted exhaustively, with all the aspects of a life spelled out, and they resist any such attempt. They resist finalization precisely because they are alive, and therefore, by definition, unfinished.

Beyond the Boundaries of Life

Considering life as a whole inevitably requires a consideration of death and the departed.[2] Death is bound up with the ends of life, both in the sense of an ending that frames a life and its evaluation, and in referring to a sense of purpose. Such a notion of ends resonates with what Paul Tillich, writing about religion, calls the "ultimate concern." He refers to that which concerns us unconditionally—that "which determines our being or not-being" (Tillich 1951, cited in Traphagan 2004). In his work on aging in rural Japan, John Traphagan builds on Tillich's conceptualization of religion to argue that religious practice in Japan is entwined with the well-being of the living and the dead, focusing on the family and "the entities which give being meaning—ancestors" (Traphagan 2004:19). Death is thus closely associated with ends but is not always seen as an ending, for the ancestors are firmly a part of the circle of meaningful others. Furthermore, religious practice and ancestor worship, often performed by the elderly in order to ensure the well-being of the family, are seen as a way of expressing one's emotions and a concern for others—"the practice of concern."

Aging is not merely understood as approaching the end of one's life, for older people's everyday existence is marked by the loss of many of those people they cared for. In a moving and nuanced ethnography of aging in Kyoto, Jason Danely focuses on loss and memorialization practices. Older Kyoto residents repeatedly mentioned various losses that they experienced—of close friends and family members, of political status or roles of authority, of mobility or sight. Loss is not merely associated with a negative portrayal of aging as inevitable decline, but is better seen as something meaningful to older people (Danely 2015:24–25). Loss is further generated by the new configurations of Japanese welfare, which offers support services across the private, nonprofit, and public sectors, effectively distributing responsibility for elder care between family, state, and community. Danely argues that such distribution opens up spaces for abandonment, as many people fall through the cracks in the system (2015:156, 161). This "ideology of care through abandonment" produces a particular kind of subjectivity, one "unable to uphold human connections, recognition, and care without producing shame, isolation and estrangement" (Danely 2015:161).

The challenging circumstances that many older people face in Japan today nevertheless throw into stark relief a rather different question that lies at the very core of this book: How do people strive to live well? In other words, this book explores how people attempt (and often succeed) to craft social connections precisely in the face of loss, and how they come to see their lives as meaningful despite the many challenges they must confront.[3]

Narrative and Immediate Self

Not everyone thinks about their life in narrative form and certainly not all the time. That offering their story was not an equally easy task for all of my interlocutors transpires from the ways in which they were delivered to me: some made their stories very short, others began several times before getting the tone right, while still others began with a summary, a précis of their lives, as if reminding themselves of the key events, the bones of the story. Even if most of my interlocutors would not usually expect to recount their life story in its entirety—this is, after all, a rather peculiar genre—all of them enjoyed telling stories in the course of conversations, in the salon for instance, about events they had heard about or that had happened in the past, or relating to everyday matters, describing shorter episodes. Such stories helped to create and maintain social relationships, keeping salon conversations lively and often allowing for the presence of others who were physically absent. Care and concern for others were expressed by asking about them and expecting to hear stories about them. Narrative activity thus played an important role in salon sociality, as well as in the sense-making attempts of my hosts.

On the other hand, a tendency to be immersed in the moment seemed to carry equal importance in some other contexts. The sense of enjoyment to be derived from focused, immediate experience was reflected in the idea of "doing things properly," something my salon companions clearly considered to be especially important. Doing things properly implies a kind of practical mastery of everyday activities, even something as apparently straightforward as serving a cup of tea, and perhaps also of more specialized pursuits such as photography or calligraphy. While the insistence that things should be done "the proper way" might be experienced by some as constraining, my hosts showed me how doing things according to a set of rules or customs can lead to a sense of control and joy that comes from immersion in the activity. The pleasing feeling that stems from it, even when the activity in question is as mundane as preparing a small origami rubbish box for the coffee tables in the salon or cutting spring onions for the soup, can be a form of aesthetic enjoyment.[4] Besides skillful activities, taking a moment to observe changes in the weather, a flower arrangement, or the color of tea is something that my older companions would tell me they enjoyed, and as they thought less about what they can expect in the future, this gradually became an increasingly important source of enjoyment in their lives. Such moments, less verbal and thus less often discussed within conversations in the salon, were seen as no less important for leading a good life.

What emerges from these different contexts are two distinct ways of being in the world, which I refer to as the *narrative orientation* and the *immediate orientation.* The former is a state of being in the world that can involve narration but more broadly involves sense-making and reflection. This orientation is analytical; it involves paying attention to a course of events or a comparison of one situation to another, a concrete event to an imagined outcome, for example, or various aspects of problem-solving. In the immediate orientation, by contrast, one's attention is held by the immediate experience of one's surroundings and sensations, without comparing these to what is expected or to some ideal, or relating them to memories, and without trying to order them into a sequence. The distinction between these in everyday life is not rigid or absolute, and they do not refer to distinct kinds of persons but rather different types of attention that can be experienced by anyone at different times.[5]

What are the implications of these two orientations for leading a good life?[6] The stories we know of others and from others teach us about how to lead a good life, sometimes directly or by example, and at other times by making us aware of what we would rather avoid. The capacity of stories and the storytelling process to create a meaningful sequence from apparently disconnected events makes them an important part of the sense-making process (Ochs and Capps 1996). The narrative orientation, then, promotes a good life to the extent that it helps to transform daily events and happenings, including traumatic or difficult ones, into a meaningful sequence, thereby creating a sense of a meaningful existence. By allowing a comparison with other stories we know, this orientation can facilitate the assessment of what we want and where we would like to go, guiding our choices and (moral) actions. Yet to the extent that reflection and comparison with others—as in the case of Tokuda-san—can make one's life more miserable and increase a feeling of isolation, the narrative mode can also have negative consequences for leading a good life. Tokuda-san faced a fear of loneliness as her husband was hospitalized with a serious heart condition. The stories of other ladies in the salon who were living on their own and praised their freedom upset her and made her feel even more alienated and lonely. The comparison of her own story with the stories of others kept her in a state of discontent.

Narrative activity, in this broader sense, is without doubt an important activity and can contribute to an understanding of one's life as a meaningful sequence. Nonetheless, the narrative may present a threat to one's ability to lead a good life. To the extent that viewing one's life in narrative terms likens it to a biographical project in the making, as theorists of late modernity have suggested, one may feel an increased sense of responsibility for one's life choices and decisions (e.g., Giddens 1991). While this means that one is increasingly liberated from traditional social institutions, the process is accompanied by a rise in risks and personal insecurities (Beck 1992). Shaping one's life, just like a story, is cast as one's own responsibility, and this may lead to anxiety—ultimately an existential anxiety that links freedom and responsibility (Yalom 1980). The interest in "mindfulness" as a mode of therapy for depression, helping people to find "peace in a frantic world" (Williams and Penman 2011), is indicative of the type of problem created by the late modern condition. Mindfulness in this sense refers to a type of meditation practice that focuses on the flow of one's own breath. The intention is to focus on immediate experience and to assume an attitude of observing what is transpiring in one's mind and body as a way of countering the tendency to compare one's current state to an ideal and to treat the disjuncture as a problem to be solved, leading to the questioning and restlessness that characterize depressive thinking (Williams and Penman 2011).[7] In short, the narrative quest for coherence and meaning has both benefits and dangers, as does mindful presence in the moment. A fulfilling life, a life that is meaningful and good, requires a careful balance between the narrative and immediate orientations.

Despite a certain similarity, the good life and the meaningful life do not map neatly onto the immediate and narrative modes; for instance, a focused experience of the present moment while gardening, accompanied by a sense of immersion, can be seen to make one's life more meaningful. The concepts

of the good life and meaningful life overlap significantly but cannot be re-
duced to each other—for example, a life can be rendered meaningful by understanding how events within it lead from one to another, but could still
be considered morally problematic and thus not be seen as a good life either
by the person who lived it or by others. I hope that others will take up the
challenge of exploring the mutual constitution of these two concepts, both
theoretically and ethnographically. A thread that joins them in this case,
sometimes pleated neatly together and sometimes merely stitched loosely,
linking individual lives to others, is involvement in care. Care, at its best,
powerfully aligns our own well-being with a concern for others. Living well,
for my companions in Shimoichi, involves caring and being cared for, receiving and giving care. In a way, this may be seen as the core existential
challenge they faced.

The Good Life

Anthropologists have concerned themselves for many years with the different ways in which people live, think about their lives, and negotiate social
models and personal preferences. While many ethnographies may have been
guided by an underlying concern with what the good life is or what it represents for a given group of people, questions of well-being, happiness, and ideals of the good life have rarely been explored explicitly by anthropologists.[8]
Neil Thin (2008) attributes anthropology's evasion of the topic of happiness
to four influences in the social sciences: besides "anti-hedonism" and "moral
relativism," he mentions "clinical pathologism" and "anti-psychologism."
Clinical pathologism refers to the attitude of social scientists based on the
conjecture that pathologies and problems are more worth studying than the
good aspects of life. Anti-psychologism has constrained discussions of emotions, either through the social constructionist rejection of psychologists' uni-
versalist assumptions about the unity of human psychological makeup, or
through a cognitivist resistance to the study of emotions (Thin 2008:138–150).
If one were to turn one's attention to the topic of living well, there are several
concepts in use in social sciences and comparative psychology, including
well-being, happiness, subjective well-being, and the good life.

What is the relationship between well-being, the good life, and happiness?
Some authors conceive them as basically different expressions of the same
notion, or at least do not make an explicit distinction (cf. Thin 2008:134;
Diener and Suh 2000). On the other hand, and as indicated by cross-cultural

contributions by psychologists in the volume edited by Ed Diener and Eunkook Suh (2000), happiness seems to be both differently conceived in different cultural contexts, and differently valued in relation to its contribution to well-being. In other words, what happiness means for people and how important it is considered to be for their well-being varies in different contexts and perhaps for different individuals (Kavedžija and Walker 2016). This has been explored by philosophers through the notion of "prudential value" or "final value," which refers to a good as an end in itself. If the good life or well-being is formally defined by philosophers in terms of what has a final value for a person, then one should ask what these values are. Is the happiness the only final value? It is possible that there are other final values, like meaningful work, social relations, or friendship, among others (Brülde 2007:1–2). From an anthropological viewpoint that focuses on substantive accounts rather than formal definitions of well-being, happiness cannot therefore be equated with the good life, even though it could represent a central value for some.

One of the main differences between the concepts of well-being and the good life is the evaluative dimension of the first, referring to people's evaluation of the quality of their own lives, while the good life would be more focused on the content of the ideals concerning how one should live: one does not have to live a good life in order to think about what a good life would or should be. By using the term "good life," the question shifts: "What is the level of your well-being?" becomes "What makes a good life (for you)?" While the notion of well-being seems to be focused on the individual, the notion of a good life as held by persons implies the relation to societal values and ideals, the interplay and dynamics of which emerge as central. As has been argued by Wendy James (2008), this dimension is partially obfuscated in the notion of well-being. Furthermore, a person can consider their life as "good," in moral terms for example, even if they are not satisfied with their well-being, perhaps due to poverty or lack of health. People can think of their life in terms of sacrifice for their family or "a larger cause." In extreme cases, ideals of the good life can be envisaged in opposition to personal well-being, as in the case of the Jain renouncers described by James Laidlaw (2005). Jainism "devalues worldly well-being to the extent of institutionalising, and recommending for the spiritually advanced as a telos of religious life, the practice of fasting to death" (Laidlaw 2005:158). I would therefore argue that for all the reasons mentioned above, the concept of the good life is the one best suited as a point of departure in existential anthropology.

The notion of the good life has perhaps figured most prominently in Amazonian anthropology and is a theme associated particularly with the work of Joanna Overing and her students. In her writings about Amazonian sociality, Overing has stressed the importance of conviviality (literally, from the Latin, to live together, to share a life) and the "aesthetics of community," a notion that refers to the emphasis these people place on "achieving a comfortable affective life with those with whom they live" (Overing and Passes 2000:2). At the same time, there is a very strong notion of an independent, autonomous self who belongs to the collective, while autonomy itself is linked with intersubjectivity. The importance of this work lies in part in its attempt to understand Amazonian ideas of the good life in terms that reintegrate morality and aesthetics, along with the social and the political—as implied in the expression "the art of social living"—since the spheres of aesthetics and ethics are not considered autonomous or separate for the peoples of this region (Overing 1989, 2003). The notion of the good life is closely related to that of living well together with others, which invokes the concept of the good person or even the good citizen. In this sense, the good life emerges as a powerful concept for bridging the moral, aesthetic, and political spheres of human activity.

The Good Life in Balance

In their attempts to live well, my companions in Shimoichi resorted to stories, reflection, and narrative, as well as quiet immersion in tasks or repetitive engulfing activities, thus balancing the narrative and immediate modes. Striving toward a good life they faced several countervailing tendencies, which they carefully and caringly sought to keep in balance.

Chapter 3 points to a tension between leading a life with rich social relationships and a multitude of links to other members of the community, and maintaining a desired level of separation in which the social "burden" of these relationships is minimized. In other words, the good life requires maintaining ties to others without being fully absorbed into the thick social fabric through its excessive demands, minimizing the intrusive aspects of those social relationships. Chapter 4 indicates the need to navigate a tension between politeness or formality as distancing mechanisms, and as a sign of respectfulness that allows social relationships and indicates concern for others. Furthermore, it is important to judge the amount of politeness and formality so that one does not offend by distancing someone too much or appearing overly intimate. This in turn is closely related to the balance between autonomy and dependence, which, as Chapter 6 shows, can take the form of a tension around achieving intimacy (and avoiding a sense of social isolation) while maintaining a sense of freedom. Being careful to preempt the reactions of others and to be considerate may take a toll on one's own sense of health and diminish the feeling of being able to do as one pleases. It also shows that maintaining a sense of independence relies somewhat paradoxically on cultivating multiple dependencies on others. In conjunction, these three elements reveal the complexity of interactions of people with the community, or in a sense, of negotiating the boundaries between the self and others, boundaries that can be seen as more or less permeable and that need to be kept open to a degree, but guarded.[9]

Chapter 5 illustrates how the stories that are available to people, such as the "model life" story of the salaryman and housewife, provide them with raw materials for making sense of their own lives. The ways in which they position themselves in relation to these stories can be very different. A person may, like Kato-san, construe their life as being in alignment with this "model" story line and derive meaning from the sense of having fulfilled their duty or role. Someone else might view their life as diverging from this path and see that as a failure, or as an achievement and mode of resistance, or both. Kawasaki-san navigated this middle ground, between a sense of disappointment with himself and a sense of pride, all in relation to this expected model life course. Indeed, the divergences from the model life were presented and understood as part of his *ikigai*, which he described as seeking challenges. In other words, the way the good life or meaningful existence is narratively constructed may differ significantly—one can make the most of full identification with one of the stories available, or seek to make the points of divergence into precisely that which makes life meaningful. The life events that make up a life story are often understood in terms of choice. As Chapter 7 shows, some of these life choices have been thoughtful decisions, carefully planned, while others were made in more haphazard ways through the exercise of "judicious opportunism," and only interpreted as "choices" retrospectively, narratively brought back into the meaningful flow of life. Emerging from these two chapters is a sense of a tension between experiencing and interpreting one's life as a collection of accidental, haphazard, or externally determined events, and as choices that one has actively made. People must negotiate this tension regarding the location of agency in their lives, in terms of control over the events in their lives and control over the interpretation of these events.

Existentially Situated Care

Care is central to understanding the good life: it makes life possible and creates spaces for meaning. As an attitude orienting people toward others, to activities and objects, it overlaps closely with meaning, a sense of doing something worthwhile. What one cares about is what has meaning. The kinds of care one is involved in, whether as a carer, a recipient, or a facilitator, as well as what one cares about and for whom, tell us much about what is meaningful and how a sense of meaning is created in the everyday. This is not to say that care is always positive or nurturing: caring and care work can involve toil and can make one question the way one lives. Nonetheless, I am interested in the moments when—against the odds or despite the challenges that face them—people manage to hold things in balance, and care works. By studying the practice of care within the existential context of efforts to live a good life, rather than focusing on clinical settings or relationships of care alone, I suggest we can understand something specific and important. Locating care in its multiple incarnations within efforts to live well offers a different perspective, one deeply embedded in everyday life, not without its challenges, but not always in extremis.[10]

The balance between engaging in a community and maintaining a sphere into which others do not intrude; balancing desired intimacy and excessive or stifling proximity; keeping dependence and autonomy in check; negotiating agency in one's life: in a certain sense these all concern the boundaries of the self, envisaged as more or less separate from others depending on context, with boundaries that are never completely sealed but need to be guarded and negotiated. Such blurred boundaries are a reflection of the existential drive to reach out to others and extend the self. A focus on this disposition of care, as the bridge between "self" and "other," may help to redirect our attention from their separation to their various modes of coexistence and interpenetration. The task ahead, then, is to explore the diversity of forms this disposition can take, in different places and at different times in life.

Notes

Chapter 1

1. Gordon Mathews usefully translates *ikigai*, perhaps with more precision, as "that which makes one's life seem worth living" (1996:51).

2. For a more detailed discussion of the use of *ikigai* in the public discourse see Kavedžija 2016.

3. This is just one of many examples in which *ikigai* is situated between self and society, and indeed, while *ikigai* is a personal choice, it also depends on commitment to those others either involved in it or with a similar interest, and thus "tacitly indexes one's involvement in socially oriented activities" (Traphagan 2004:69). John Traphagan suggests that one's maintenance of an *ikigai* is in the interest of the wider community (as in the case of the fear of senility in Japan) and that one has a responsibility to maintain it. This responsibility toward the community is implied in the notion of the "good person." He concludes that having an *ikigai* indexes an individual's focus on self-cultivation and discipline, which in itself benefits the community. In the case of elderly people this means showing an effort to maintain mental and physical health in order to avoid burdening the family and community (Traphagan 2004:74). The well-being of group and individual are, therefore, conceived as closely linked through the idea of the "good person." In this way, *ikigai* is contextualized in political as well as ethical realms.

The idea that self-cultivation is at the basis of community development has a long history in Japan. It can be traced to the seventeenth and eighteenth centuries, which witnessed a proliferation of religious and ritual practices considered to lead to material and social well-being and focused on personal cultivation (*mi o osameru*; *shūshin*; Sawada 2004). The idea of self-cultivation as a path to the advancement and prosperity of the community is an ideologically potent one and has been exploited in various ways—for example, by the state in the Meiji period as a part of an ideology based on Shinto and Confucian principles. Similarly, although undoubtedly with less problematic aims, it might be possible to understand the mobilization of ideas about self-development in the context of the contemporary "Japanese-style welfare state," which relies on community support and volunteering, and in which the role of the family is central (see Goodman 1998:141; Ben-Ari 1991; Nakano 2005). This political and moral dimension of well-being as mediated through the concept of the "good person," which is differentiated by age and gender, provides an important background for an analysis of *ikigai* in public discourse.

4. This is clearly related to the dis-embedding mechanisms of modernity, which marks off retirement and separation from working roles more clearly than ever before. *Ikigai* talk often attempts to blur this boundary by calling for various kinds of social involvement, including employment for the elderly and volunteering activities.

5. Relations of care are not simple or unequivocally positive; instead they are often inflected by power (Drazin 2011) and increasingly by the market context in which they take place (Hochschild 2000). Much has been written in the burgeoning anthropology of care about the way care plays out in the context of healthcare systems (e.g., Heinemann 2014; Seo 2016) and the state (e.g., Ticktin 2011), at times taking on the guise of "anonymous care" delivered blindly and equally to everyone, without consideration given to who they are (Stevenson 2014). Such "commodified" relations of care are not necessarily "uncaring," nor is the care provided by close relatives necessarily "warm," of course (see also Thelen 2015:3). Elana Buch (2013) writes about the efforts of paid home helpers to make their elderly clients feel at home by performing sensory work for them, paying attention to smells, for instance. Whether provided by family members or otherwise, care does not always promote well-being; it takes its toll on the carers, and it is not always necessarily "good" for those being cared for. In a radical example, Garcia writes about the families of drug users (2010), resembling a discussion of codependence of alcoholics in Japan (Borovoy 2005). No matter who it is performed by, care is a moral endeavor with consequences for both sides (Kleinman 2009; Mol 2008; Taylor 2008). More recently, there have been attempts to move discussions of care beyond illness and the clinic, such as Emily Yates-Doerr and Megan Carney's (2015) analysis of care through nutrition in family homes. Care has also been portrayed as fundamental to the construction of kinship ties (Borneman 1997), but it is perhaps best understood as socially generative, producing a range of social connections (Thelen 2015).

6. The attitude of care, as I use the expression here, refers to an orientation to others that is underwritten by concern: a performance of consideration for others. It does not assume that there is a correct emotional attitude to performing care work that precedes it, either because it is based on empathy (Slote 2007) or the right kind of motivation (Held 2006), as writings on the ethics of care suggest. In a recent study of everyday care in Northern Thailand, Felicity Aulino (2012) problematizes the idea of "sincerity" in care and the performance of care as a right kind of inner feeling. Aulino argues that a focus on care as some kind of universal human attitude risks obscuring cultural and historical differences: "A fundamental problematic of my work lies in the question of whether 'caring' is a pan-human way of understanding the role of the caregiver, or if, instead, particular sets of emotional and practical ways of being with people, with specific historical lineages, can be differentiated as caregiving in various contexts. In turn, I push forward a phenomenological understanding of care that traces how social and political structures get embodied in practices of providing for others" (Aulino 2012:4). Aulino describes the performance of care as akin to a ritual, where the action matters more than the presumed emotional state of the actor. In fact, we could add, the performance itself *affects* us, thus fostering a particular emotional state. Finally, I do not think that the attitude of care is best understood as pertaining to the caregiver. It is instead a relational field binding two or more people together (and this was especially true in Shimoichi).

7. To be sure, many of Yalom's observations may not have a direct counterpart in some non-Western contexts. Rather than taking for granted that this framework will work

wherever it is applied, I wish to use it as a point of departure for questioning the forms taken by existential concerns in a Japanese context. I am convinced that on a certain deep level there is a universal aspect to human experience, which at a minimum concerns how to live well in the world with others. I will use the term "existential" in this broader sense, referring to various aspects of human existence in the world. This brings us to one of the central questions explored in this book: What do the experiences of older people in Japan, and of those caring for them, tell us about how people discern for themselves the kind of life worth living?

Chapter 2

1. *Sokushinjōbutsu* can refer to an ascetic practice of self-mummification, denying oneself food or drink, in an attempt to become a Buddha.

2. Some examples of such urban ethnographies based in Tokyo area include Dore (1999 [1958]), Bestor (1989), Thang (2001), and Robertson (1994). For a discussion outlining the relevance of this work today see Daniels (2010).

3. The names of the two neighborhoods described in this chapter have been changed, in part so that the two organizations in which I conducted research could not easily be recognized or located. Both of the organizations are well known in their respective neighborhoods. Both organizations granted me open access and insight into their organizational matters with good knowledge of what my research project entails. All but the most infrequent visitors of both salons were informed of the nature of my research project, but as the salons are open-access public spaces that can be entered by any interested passerby, it was not possible to explain the details to newcomers in all cases. For this reason, only prearranged interviews were voice-recorded, and the rest I attempted to reconstruct in my field notes as soon as I left the field site each day. Some of my informants revealed a large amount of personal information, including their feelings about others, which provides important context for many of the issues I discuss. In order to protect their identities, I have chosen to rename the areas and organizations as well as the people whom I mention.

4. The neighborhood is situated in a ward of the city of Osaka with and above average proportion of elderly population (above the age of sixty-five).

5. Children (under fifteen years of age) made up around 12 percent of the population in the South Osaka ward in question, people between the ages of fifteen and sixty-four make up around 64 percent, the elderly (over the age of sixty-five) around 24 percent, and those over the age of seventy-five 12 percent. By comparison, Osaka City as a whole has the following proportions of these groups: 11.7 percent, 65.7 percent, and 22.7 percent (Ministry of Internal Affairs and Communications 2010).

6. In Suita City, children (under fifteen years of age) made up around 14 percent, people between the ages of fifteen and sixty-four around 66 percent, and the elderly (over the age of sixty-five) around 19.6 percent of the overall population (Suita City 2011).

7. Nonprofit organizations and voluntary organizations are discussed in more detail in Chapter 3.

8. Bon dance or Bon Odori is performed during Obon, a festival in honor of the spirits of one's ancestors, which are returning to the family altars.

9. For a discussion of urban communities and their traditional networks that have been said to resemble village community life, see Knight (1996:220).

10. For a discussion of these issues in Shimoichi, see Chapter 3.

11. Most of Chapter 3 is dedicated to a description of the NPO Fureai and its workings and history, as well as the foundation of the community salon and its operation.

12. Perhaps the issue of power and gatekeepers is worth mentioning here: if the permission was granted by the group some members might feel obliged to agree or be reluctant to disagree openly. The organizers and managers of the organization were in any case more likely to be interested in naming their organization as a way to promote its visibility.

13. It is argued that with the number of the elderly growing and the medical expense per capita on the increase, health insurance in Japan was facing a serious crisis (Murashima et al. 2003:407).

14. In effect, this meant a turn away from the Scandinavian model, which seemed to be a direction in which the Japanese welfare system was moving (with a broad entitlement financed by taxes), toward a German model of social insurance (Campbell and Ikegami 2000:29).

15. According to data from 2007, the largest proportion of all households with people aged sixty-five or over (which make up over 40 percent of the total number of households) was "couple only households" (29.8 percent), followed by "one-person households" (22.5 percent), "three-generation family households" (18.3 percent), and "parents and unmarried children only households" (17.7 percent) (Cabinet Office 2009:6).

16. A number of books and publications advising on the topic have the same unusual title, and so did a lecture in the Osaka prefectural consumer life center (*Ōsakafu shōhiseikatsu senta*) I attended in November 2009. The title of that lecture might provide a hint as to why this expression is often used in this way: "Where Is the 'Final Abode'? To Live a Senior Life with Peace of Mind" (*Tsui no sumika' wa doko de? Anshin dekiru shiniaraifu wo okuru tame ni*). As some of my interlocutors pointed out, peace of mind, or living free of worries and anxieties, is what most people seek when deciding on a place to spend their later years.

17. Tatami mats, used as floor coverings in traditional Japanese houses, come in several standardized sizes, with a width half the length of one mat, overall measuring a bit less than 1 by 2 meters. It is common to express the size of a room by stating the number of tatami, or in *tsubo*, a unit that equals two tatami mats.

18. At times, these expectations have not been satisfied for the older couple, who felt more isolated within such living arrangements, as the younger couple, who was available on a daily basis, made less of an effort to make weekly visits, and other people in the neighborhood assumed that the older couple had company because they lived with their family (Brown 2003:63).

Chapter 3

1. *Okonomiyaki* is a Japanese-style pancake with cabbage and pork or seafood; *takoyaki* are small balls made of batter with pieces of octopus in them.

2. Hina Matsuri (the Doll Festival) or Girl's Day is celebrated on the third of March. Ornate dolls representing the emperor and empress with attendants in court costumes from the Heian period are displayed on a stair-shaped platform.

3. NPO is pronounced in Japanese as *enu-pi-o*. For discussion of this term and its status see Ogawa (2004).

4. Hospitals in Japan allow patients to wear their own nightgowns and pyjamas and in most cases do not provide laundry services on the premises. For more detail about hospitals see Ohnuki-Tierney (1984:189–210).

5. The organization provides an emergency phone line available 24-7 to all their members.

6. For more detail on LTCI in Japan see Chapter 2.

7. Many users, especially if they live alone, prefer them to come on weekends, to keep them company.

8. I have not collected detailed data on income levels, as this was not considered an appropriate question to discuss, and people were clearly uncomfortable when asked and mostly evasive.

9. Whether it is even useful to think of the state and civil society as in opposition is questionable, not least because the voluntary sector is not homogenous and includes the NPOs closely collaborating with the government, as well as civil movements opposing government policies. Ogawa goes so far as to call volunteers under the NPO system apolitical (2004:114, see also pp. 99–100, 125). Furthermore, the state itself is not monolithic and comprises a number of actors and local governments that have a degree of autonomy (Schwartz 2002:199).

10. This can be viewed as a cost-saving mechanism and lead to exploitation of volunteers by the state, as they are not receiving adequate compensation and may even feel constrained in their actions (Ogawa 2004:30, 37, 66–67).

11. While Japan has often been described as a classless (and indeed, homogeneous) society (e.g., Nakane 1970), issues of class in Japan have been tackled in the work of William Kelly (2002), who points out a discrepancy in attitudes toward the term "class," contrasting the theorizations and analyses of class by social scientists with the avoidance of the term by public officials and the majority of people, who do not conceive themselves in terms of class position. The class structure in Japan as described by social scientists is based on a distinction between blue-collar and white-collar workers, albeit complicated by differences in company size, as well as by the fact that the distinction is not consistent in all dimensions—for example income, education, and home-ownership (Robertson 2003:128). A much more pervasive term is *chūryū* or "mainstream," identification with which is widespread and unrelated to the objective differentials used by sociologists to define social classes (ibid.:234). Kelly traces the rise in identification with "mainstream consciousness" (*chūryū ishiki*) to the 1960s, when white-collar occupations expanded, at the same time noting that these never reached the point of forming the majority of the working population. Nevertheless, "it was in the 1960s that certain key elements of middle-class life and location became nationalized into a model of 'mainstream' life that has since powerfully represented designs for living" (ibid.:236). This can in turn be linked to the creation of mass culture in the 1960s. During this period of economic growth and media expansion, Japan witnessed the formation of "uniform and standardized taste groupings" (Ivy 1993:241). As Ivy notes in her article about the formation of "mass culture" in Japan, these groupings were differentiated along the lines of gender and age and not so much of region or class, which led the majority of Japanese people to identify themselves as being in the "middle" or as "middle class" (Ivy 1993:241).

12. This term (*kōkyōshin)* is a compound of three characters—*kō* "public," *kyō* "together," and *shin* "spirit"—and refers to fostering a communal feeling in the public. This rhetoric of fostering relationships in the community resonates with a number of official discourses: the call for creation of participatory (*sanka-gata*) welfare in which most people would be able to spontaneously and freely participate in welfare, and the related notion of New Community

(*aratana kōkyō*) emphasizing self-reliance of the citizens (for more about the policies promoting these concepts see Avenell 2010:83). No doubt, this little presentation was prepared for official situations, where referring to official discourses would be seen as clearly showing why the activities of this NPO are relevant. In fact, staff members of NPO mentioned on other occasions that they participated in some events organized by government officials and needed to submit written reports on a regular basis.

13. The importance of distance in crafting social relationships and a further discussion of Nakajima-san's statement can be found in Kavedžija 2018.

14. The Japanese word that was repeatedly pointed out to me as the most similar is *otagai sama*, referring to a mutual relationship (of support), implying equality, usually within a local community.

15. The introduction of the NPO Law has been described in great detail by Pekkanen (2000).

16. In a broader sense, this use of terms like "community" and "tradition" as discourses for the creation of an image of stability in changing urban communities is nothing new. Thus Bestor argues that "apparent continuities... are the results of a process of traditionalism—the interpretation, creation, or manipulation of contemporary ideas about the past to bestow an aura of venerability on contemporary social relations" (1989:4).

17. A similar point regarding the less positive aspects of "traditional" sociality has been made by Ben-Ari (1998:70); he refers to earlier works by Dore ([1978]1994) and Bestor (1989) that show how local community discourses emphasize the positive images of the past as harmonious but gloss over the negative aspects, such as conservative and antidemocratic attitudes toward authority.

18. The "free gift," as conceptualized by Derrida, could only exist if there is no reciprocity (past, present, or future), and in order to prevent this neither the recipient nor the donor can acknowledge the gift or recognize it as such (Derrida 1992; Laidlaw 2000:621).

19. The agency of the weaker or dependent should not be neglected (see, e.g., Mahmood 2011; Walker 2012).

Chapter 4

1. A price of 100 yen was relatively low, as typical café prices ranged from 180 to 250 yen. According to Nagafuku-san, even the salon price was not low for many of the older salon visitors with limited incomes.

2. For a discussion of this see Matsumoto (2011:51).

3. This proposition seems to be supported by examples given by Diana Bethel (1992) in her work about the residents of a home for the elderly in Japan. Many residents were ashamed to admit to their friends and neighbors that they had moved to an institution of the elderly, while others believed that they had brought shame onto their children, in spite of the latter's disapproval of the move, since the children ended up being condemned by the community being insolent and egoistic (Bethel 1992:131). In other words, those who do not have the "social capital" of well-being are in a difficult situation.

4. These conversations show a range of interactions or "styles of relating" (Overing and Passes 2000:xi): some involve a larger group and are very open, while others are conducted quietly in smaller groups or pairs, usually among closer friends, and appear more exclusive and private in character.

5. Parts of this chapter, and in particular the following anecdote, have been used in an article published elsewhere (see Kavedžija 2018) to develop an argument about the ethics of "doing things properly" (*chanto suru*).

Chapter 5

1. Contributions to the volume entitled *Men and Masculinities in Contemporary Japan*, while exploring a diversity of masculinities, mostly locate these in relation to the "ideological and representational dominance of hegemonic masculinity embodied in the middle-class, white-collar, heterosexual salaryman" (Robertson and Suzuki 2003:12). In his discussion of manual day laborers, Tom Gill explores the negotiations of masculine role on the margins of society. Day laborers, though, have a relative freedom and mobility envied by many other Japanese men, especially salarymen, "whose lifestyles are generally static and intellectual, . . . where permanent is valued over temporary, and brainwork over bodywork. When men do move, it may well be involuntarily, in the form of forced transfers (*tanshin funin*) to distant branches of their company" (Gill 2005:145). His analysis concludes with a stress on the starkness of the choice faced by Japanese men between having freedom in work and having a family.

2. In her ethnography of a Tokyo hostess bar, Anne Allison analyses attitudes of salarymen toward various aspects of their work and reveals subtleties of differentiations between generalized expectations and roles and their personal opinions. Salarymen are often expected to work overtime, not take days off, and participate in the company entertainment in the evenings. Company drinking and entertainment is depicted as "human," as a unifying process between workers of different ranks, but is clearly recognized as work, in opposition to personal life, by some of her interlocutors (Allison 1994:99). Some are absent from home on most nights, spending an evening with the family once a month or even once in six months, but in the jocular male setting of a hostess bar they would take pride in their absence from home, as a representation of hard work and devotion to the company (Allison 1994:102).

3. *Uyoku dantai*, Japanese right-wing nationalist groups, are sometimes affiliated to yakuza syndicates.

4. The interview situation can nevertheless be perceived as threatening to some extent, and therefore "the self-representation of the interviewee is also a self-preserving self-presentation" (Wengraf 2001: 117).

5. In some cases, narrative and story are understood to be quite distinct entities (cf. Frank 2010: 121).

6. The process of understanding works in a similar way, by situating the new information in relation to what we already know (see Gadamer 2004).

Chapter 6

1. *Jo* is a size unit, 60 *jo* equaling 91.83 square meters.

2. *Bōnenkai* are end-of-year parties, or literally "forget-the-year parties," usually with coworkers and often organized (or even sponsored) by the company, but sometimes also among friends, with an aim of forgetting the problems of the past year.

3. Tenjin Matsuri or Tenjin Festival, held every summer (July 24 and 25) in Osaka, is considered one of the three largest festivals in Japan and is sometimes described as one of

the world's largest boat festivals. It is associated with the Tenman shrine and involves three thousand people dressed in eighth- to twelfth-century-style court costumes in a land procession followed by a boat procession (Japan National Tourism Organization 2011).

4. *Kushikatsu* is a Japanese-style snack made from deep fried meat, seafood, or pieces of vegetables on skewers.

5. The number of older people living in single households in Japan has increased to nearly a quarter of all households with occupants over the age of sixty-five (Cabinet Office 2007).

6. Importantly, this kind of embodied intimacy achieved through communal bathing, for instance, is not connected to privacy (Daniels 2010:47).

7. Unlike receiving welfare benefits or needing to be housed in a nursing home prior to the introduction of LTCI, which were stigmatized and implied a lack of support from one's family (Bethel 1992; Traphagan 2004), the compulsory character of participating in LTCI and pervasiveness of its use meant that most of my interlocutors were not hesitant to claim support through it.

8. For more on notion of *amae* see Doi (1973).

9. A relevant discussion of generalized reciprocity can be found in Sahlins (1972).

10. The addition of the state and LTCI to the list of sources of support that one can depend on is very relevant, as they expand what Lebra wrote in 1979: "Autonomy and dependency are compatible insofar as the latter is based on well-balanced reciprocity" (Lebra 1979:350). It may appear that with the possibility of relying on LTCI for support, one's reliance can become entirely one-sided, but it is important to bear in mind that the perception of LTCI as a system that is compulsory for everyone (see Chapter 2) means that one is seen as being involved in long-term generalized reciprocity.

Chapter 7

1. *Okeikogoto* refers to learning traditional skills and arts, playing a musical instrument, or, more recently, learning a foreign language as a part of the practice of self-improvement, particularly appropriate for young women that are to be married.

2. For more detail on the long-term care insurance law see Chapter 2.

3. See Kavedžija (2015) for a discussion of care provision.

Chapter 8

1. Arthur Frank discusses the dangers of a narrative's totalizing effect, drawing on Bakhtin's idea of finalization. He highlights the moral problems implicit in an overly ordered and rounded narrative, notably the implication that that there is "nothing more to be said about you" (Frank 2010:97).

2. Anthropologists and social scientists have written a good deal about death in Japan, particularly regarding the ideas of the good death and the afterlife (e.g., Smith 1974; Long 2003; Connor and Traphagan 2014), as well as the funeral practices and the relationship between the living and the dead (e.g., Shimane 2002; Kawano 2010; Rowe 2011; Suzuki H. 2013; Boret 2014).

3. See also Joel Robbins's (2013) call for an "anthropology of the good," which, while not neglecting suffering, might well examine how people make their lives purposeful in difficult or hostile circumstances and thereby reveal how "the good" is fostered in social relationships.

4. This aesthetic disposition, which really just means a tendency to observe beauty in everyday things and activities, is certainly not a uniquely Japanese trait. See, for example, Overing (2003) for a discussion of the Amazonian aesthetics of everyday life.

5. The distinction between these is not clear-cut, so I separate them for heuristic purposes only. They might be best thought of as tendencies, as these states in their pure forms may be impossible. For example, an extreme case as close as possible to the state of pure immediacy is that of experienced meditators who manage to achieve a state of focus on the here and now in which they barely react to distractions in the outside world by trying to understand them. Most people can rarely expect to experience this kind of state for more than a few seconds (see Williams and Penman 2011).

6. For a fuller discussion of these two orientations see Kavedžija (2016a), in which I discuss the limits of narrativity and importance of balance for living well among older Japanese.

7. It remains to be seen whether the recent, marked increase in cases of depression in Japan (Kitanaka 2011) can be related to the tendencies associated with late modernity, to take responsibility for one's own life and life trajectory and to internalize blame and dissatisfaction. Yet this seems like a question worth serious exploration.

8. For a more extensive discussion of happiness and anthropology see Walker and Kavedžija (2015).

9. For a discussion of the porous boundaries of self in relation to well-being see Kavedžija (2012).

10. A body of new and stimulating literature on the anthropology of care, drawing especially on insights from medical anthropology, brings this topic sharply into focus (see also notes 5 and 6 in Chapter 1). This literature primarily attends to clinical care, dementia, bedridden people, and end-of-life care. The relatively extreme situation of dependency presented in this work brings multiple social and political tensions into relief and offers nuanced insights into our understandings of personhood as well as the political and economic underpinnings of contemporary worlds. The present work, by contrast, in focusing on the more mundane and ordinary challenges of caring relationships, expands the focus somewhat and offers a broader perspective, not too dissimilar from Tatiana Thelen's (2015) invitation to consider care as constitutive of social relationships in general, beyond the clinic and kinship.

Bibliography

Allison, Anne. 1994. *Nightwork: Sexuality, Pleasure, and Corporate Masculinity in a Tokyo Hostess Club*. Chicago: University of Chicago Press.

Asahi Shinbun. 2010a. "Chōkorei shakai no kowashisa jikakushiyō." *Asahi Shinbun*, 15 May, p. 16.

———. 2010b. "'111sai' no kazoku taiho chō to magomusume, nenkin kishu no utagai Tokyou-Adachi no Hokkotsuitaijiken." *Asahi Shimbun*, 28 August, p. 39.

———. 2010c. "Minseiiin kaisen jōhō no kyōyū de chiiki wo mamoru." *Asahi Shimbun*, 6 December, p. 3.

Aulino, Felicity. 2012. "Senses and Sensibilities: The Practice of Care in Everyday Life in Northern Thailand." Doctoral dissertation, Harvard University.

Avenell, Simon A. 2010. "Facilitating Spontaneity: The State and Independent Volunteering in Contemporary Japan." *Social Science Japan Journal* 13(1): 69–93.

Bardsley, Jan. 2011. "The *Oyaji* Gets a Makeover: Guides for Japanese Salarymen in the New Millennium." In *Manners and Mischief: Gender, Power and Etiquette in Japan*, ed. Jan Bardsley and Laura Miller, 114–135. Berkeley: University of California Press.

Beck, Ulrich. 1992. *Risk Society: Towards a New Modernity*. London: Sage.

Ben-Ari, Eyal. 1991. *Changing Japanese Suburbia: A Study of Two Present-Day Localities*. London: Kegan Paul International.

Bestor, Theodore. 1989. *Neighborhood Tokyo*. Stanford: Stanford University Press.

Bethel, Diane L. 1992. "Life on Obasuteyama, or, Inside a Japanese Institution for the Elderly." In *Japanese Social Organization*, ed. Takiye Sugiyama Lebra, 109–134. Honolulu: University of Hawaii Press.

Bloch, Maurice. 1975. *Political Language and Oratory in Traditional Society*. London: Academic Press.

Boret, Sébastien Penmellen. 2014. *Japanese Tree Burial: Ecology, Kinship and the Culture of Death*. London: Routledge.

Borneman, John. 1997. "Caring and Being Cared For: Displacing Marriage, Kinship, Gender and Sexuality." *International Social Science Journal* 49(154): 573–584.

Borovoy, Amy B. 2005. *The Too-Good Wife: Alcohol, Codependency, and the Politics of Nurturance in Postwar Japan*. Berkeley: University of California Press.

Brown, Naomi. 2003. "Under One Roof: The Evolving Story of Three-Generation Housing in Japan." In *Demographic Change and the Family in Japan's Aging Society*, ed. John W. Traphagan and John Knight, 53–88. Albany: State University of New York Press.

Brülde, Bengt. 2007. "Happiness and the Good Life. Introduction and Conceptual Framework." *Journal of Happiness Studies* 8(1): 1–14.

Buch, Elana D. 2013. "Senses of Care: Embodying Inequality and Sustaining Personhood in the Home Care of Older Adults in Chicago." *American Ethnologist* 40(4): 637–650.

Burgess, Ernest W. 1960. *Aging in Western Societies*. Chicago: University of Chicago Press.

Butler, Judith. 2005. *Giving an Account of Oneself*. New York: Fordham University Press.

Cabinet Office. 2007. "Annual Report on the Aging Society 2007." http://www8.cao.go.jp /kourei/english/annualreport/2007/2007.pdf. Accessed 10 Nov 2012.

———. 2009. "Annual Report on the Aging Society 2009." http://www8.cao.go.jp/kourei /english/annualreport/2009/2009pdf_e.html. Accessed 10 Nov 2012.

Cai, Deborah, Howard Giles, and Kimberly Noels. 1998. "Elderly Perceptions of Communication with Older and Younger Adults in China: Implications for Mental Health." *Journal of Applied Communication Research* 26(1): 32–51.

Campbell, John C., and Naoki Ikegami. 2000. "Long-Term Care Insurance Comes to Japan." *Health Affairs* 19(3): 26–39.

Connor, Blaine P., and John W. Traphagan. 2014. "Negotiating the Afterlife: Emplacement as Ongoing Concern in Contemporary Japan." *Asian Anthropology* 13(1): 1–17.

Constable, Nicole. 2009. "The Commodification of Intimacy: Marriage, Sex, and Reproductive Labor." *Annual Review of Anthropology* 38: 49–64.

Coulmas, Florian. 2007. *Population Decline and Ageing in Japan: The Social Consequences*. Abingdon: Routledge.

Course, Magnus. 2007. "Death, Biography, and the Mapuche Person." *Ethnos* 72(1): 77–101.

Danely, Jason A. 2008. Departure and return : abandonment, memorial and aging in Japan. UC San Diego. https://escholarship.org/uc/item/1dv4s2nb (permalink).

———. 2015. *Aging and Loss: Mourning and Maturity in Contemporary Japan*. New Brunswick, N.J.: Rutgers University Press.

Daniels, Inge. 2010. *The Japanese House: Material Culture in the Modern Home*. Oxford: Berg.

Derrida, Jacques. 1992. *Given Time: I. Counterfeit Money*. Chicago: University of Chicago Press.

Diener, Ed, and Eunkook M. Suh. 2000. *Culture and Subjective Well-Being*. Cambridge, Mass.: MIT Press.

Doi, Takeo. 1973. *The Anatomy of Dependence*. Tokyo: Kodansha International.

Dore, Ronald P. 1994. *Shinohata: A Portrait of a Japanese Village*. Reprint. Berkeley: University of California Press.

———. 1999 (1958). *City Life in Japan*. London: Routledge.

Drazin, Adam. 2011. "Towards an Anthropology of Care: Cleanliness and Consumption in Urban Romanian Homes." *Slovensky Narodopis* 59(5): 499–515.

Dumont, Louis. 1980. *Homo Hierarchicus*. Rev. ed. Chicago: University of Chicago Press.

Frank, Arthur W. 2010. *Letting Stories Breathe: A Socio-Narratology*. Chicago: University of Chicago Press.

Fuess, Harald. 2004. *Divorce in Japan*. Stanford: Stanford University Press.

Gadamer, Hans G. 2004. *Truth and Method*. London: Continuum.

Garon, Sheldon. 1997. *Molding Japanese Minds*. Cambridge: Cambridge University Press.

———. 2003. "From Meiji to Heisei: The State and Civil Society in Japan." In *The State of Civil Society in Japan*, ed. Frank J. Schwartz and Susan J. Pharr, 42–62. Cambridge: Cambridge University Press.

Giddens, Anthony. 1991. *Modernity and Self-Identity: Self and Society in the Late Modern Age*. Cambridge: Polity.

Gill, Tom. 2005. "Whose Problem? Japan's Homeless People as an Issue of Local and Central Governance." In *Contested Governance in Japan: Sites and Issues*, ed. Glenn D. Hook, 192–210. London: Routledge Curzon.

Goodman, Roger. 1998. "The 'Japanese-Style Welfare State' and the Delivery of Personal Social Services." In *The East Asian Welfare Model: Welfare Orientalism and the State*, ed. Roger Goodman, Gordon White, and Huck-ju Kwon, 139–159. London: Routledge.

Graham, Fiona. 2003. *Inside the Japanese Company*. London: Routledge Curzon.

Gratton, Brian, and Carole Haber. 1993. "In Search of 'Intimacy at a Distance': Family History from the Perspective of Elderly Women." *Journal of Aging Studies* 7(2): 183–194.

Hamabata, Matthews Masayuki. 1991. *Crested Kimono: Power and Love in the Japanese Business Family*. Ithaca: Cornell University Press.

Hann, Christopher Michael, and Elizabeth Dunn, eds. 1996. *Civil Society: Challenging Western Models*. London: Routledge.

Heinemann, Laura L. 2014. "Care: Deviation." *Cultural Anthropology* website. http://www.culanth.org/fieldsights/519-care-deviation. Accessed 09 Apr2018.

Held, Virginia. 2006. *The Ethics of Care: Personal, Political, and Global*. Oxford: Oxford University Press.

Hendry, Joy. 1995. *Wrapping Culture: Politeness, Presentation, and Power in Japan and Other Societies*. Oxford: Clarendon Press.

Hochschild, Arlie R. 2000. "Global Care Chains and Emotional Surplus Value." In *On the Edge: Living with Global Capitalism*, ed. Anthony Giddens and Will Hutton, 130–146. London: Jonathan Cape.

Imamura, Anne E. 1987. *Urban Japanese Housewives: At Home and in the Community*. Honolulu: University of Hawaii Press.

Ivy, Marilyn. 1993. "Formations of Mass Culture." In *Postwar Japan as History*, ed. Andrew Gordon, 239–258. Berkeley: University of California Press.

Jackson, Michael. 2005. *Existential Anthropology: Events, Exigencies and Effects*. Oxford: Berghahn.

———. 2011. *Life Within Limits: Well-Being in a World of Want*. Durham, N.C.: Duke University Press.

James, Wendy. 2008. "Well-Being: In Whose Opinion, and Who Pays?" In *Culture and Well-Being: Anthropological Approaches to Freedom and Political Ethics*, ed. Alberto Corsín Jiménez, 69–79. London: Pluto Press.

Japan National Tourism Organization. 2011. "Tenjin Matsuri." JNTO website. http://www.jnto.go.jp/eng/location/spot/festival/tenjinmatsuri.html. Accessed 10 Nov 2012.

Johnson-Hanks, Jennifer. 2002. "On the Limits of Life Stages in Ethnography: Toward a Theory of Vital Conjunctures." *American Anthropologist* 104(3): 865–880.

———. 2005. "When the Future Decides." *Current Anthropology* 46(3): 363–385.

———. 2008. "Demographic Transitions and Modernity." *Annual Review of Anthropology* 37: 301–315.

Kavedžija, Iza. 2012. "Singing on an Empty Belly." *Anthropology of This Century*, no. 5 (October). AOTC Press. http://aotcpress.com/articles/singing-empty-belly/.

———. 2015a. "Frail, Independent, Involved? Care and the Category of the Elderly in Japan." *Anthropology and Aging* 36(1): 62–81.

———. 2015b. "The Good Life in Balance: Insights from Aging Japan." *HAU: Journal of Ethnographic Theory* 5(3): 135–156.

———. 2016. "The Age of Decline? Anxieties About Ageing in Japan." *Ethnos* 81(2): 214–237.

———. 2018. "Of Manners and Hedgehogs: Building Closeness by Maintaining Distance." *Australian Journal for Anthropology.* Early view, available online on https://doi.org/10 .1111/taja.12274.

Kawano, Satsuki. 2004. "Pre-funerals in Contemporary Japan: The Making of a New Ceremony of Later Life Among Aging Japanese." *Ethnology* 43(2): 155–165.

———. 2010. *Nature's Embrace: Japan's Aging Urbanites and New Death Rites.* Honolulu: University of Hawaii Press.

Keane, Webb. 2002. "Sincerity, 'Modernity,' and the Protestants." *Cultural Anthropology* 17(1): 65–92.

Kelly, William. 1993. "Finding a Place in Metropolitan Japan. Ideologies, Institutions and Everyday Life." In *Postwar Japan as History*, ed. Andrew Gordon, 189–217. Berkeley: University of California Press.

———. 2002. "At the Limits of New Middle-Class Japan: Beyond 'Mainstream Consciousness.'" In *Social Contracts Under Stress: The Middle Classes of America, Europe, and Japan at the Turn of the Century*, ed. Olivier Zunz, Leonard Schoppa, and Nobuhiro Hirowatari, 232–254. New York: Russell Sage.

Kitanaka, Junko. 2011. *Depression in Japan: Psychiatric Cures for a Society in Distress.* Princeton: Princeton University Press.

Kleinman, Arthur. 2009. "Caregiving: The Odyssey of Becoming More Human." *Lancet* 373 (9660): 292–293.

Knight, John. 1996. "Making Citizens in Postwar Japan: National and Local Perspectives." In *Civil Society: Challenging Western Models*, ed. Christopher Michael Hann and Elizabeth Dunn, 222–239. London: Routledge.

Koyano, Wataru. 2009. "Ikigai no tankyū: Kōreishakai no kōreika ni ikigai ga hitsuyōna wake to ikigai taisaku." [Exploring ikigai: The necessity of ikigai for elderly in the aging society and ikigai measurement.] *Ikigai kenkyū* [Healthy and active aging] 15: 22–36.

Laidlaw, James. 2000. "A Free Gift Makes No Friends." *Journal of the Royal Anthropological Institute* 6(4): 617–634.

———. 2005. "A Life Worth Leaving: Fasting to Death as Telos of a Jain Religious Life." *Economy and Society* 34(2): 178–199.

Lamb, Sarah. 2001. "Being a Widow and Other Life Stories: The Interplay Between Lives and Words." *Anthropology and Humanism* 26(1): 16–34.

Lebra, Takie Sugiyama. 1976. *Japanese Patterns of Behavior.* Honolulu: University of Hawaii Press.

———. 1979. "The Dilemma and Strategies of Aging Among Contemporary Japanese Women." *Ethnology* 18(4): 337–353.

———. 2004. *The Japanese Self in Cultural Logic.* Honolulu: University of Hawaii Press.

Long, Susan Orpett. 2004. "Cultural Scripts for a Good Death in Japan and the United States: Similarities and Differences." *Social Science and Medicine* 58(5): 913–928.

Lukes, Steven. 1979 (1973). *Individualism.* Oxford: Basil Blackwell.

Mathews, Gordon. 1996. *What Makes Life Worth Living? How Japanese and Americans Make Sense of Their Worlds.* Berkeley: University of California Press.

Mathews, Gordon, and Bruce White, eds. 2004. *Japan's Changing Generations: Are Young People Creating a New Society?* London: Routledge Curzon.

Matsumoto, Yoshiko, ed. 2011. *Faces of Aging: The Lived Experiences of Elderly in Japan*. Stanford: Stanford University Press.

Mattingly, Cheryl. 1994. "The Concept of Therapeutic 'Emplotment'." *Social Science and Medicine* 38(6): 811–822.

McCreery, John L. 2000. *Japanese Consumer Behavior: From Worker Bees to Wary Shoppers*. Richmond: Curzon.

Miller, Daniel. 2004. "How Infants Grow Mothers in North London." *Consuming Motherhood*: 31.

Ministry of Health, Labour and Welfare. 2002. "Aims of Establishing Long-term Care Insurance." http://www.mhlw.go.jp/english/topics/elderly/care/1.html. Accessed 10 Nov 2012.

Ministry of Internal Affairs and Communications. 2010. "National Census 2010—Preliminary Population Count." http://www.stat.go.jp/data/jinsui/pdf/201212.pdf.

Mol, Annemarie. 2008. *The Logic of Care: Health and the Problem of Patient Choice*. London: Routledge.

Murashima, Sachiyo, Azusa Yokoyama, Satoko Nagata, and Kiyomi Asahara. 2003. "The Implementation of Long-Term Care Insurance in Japan: Focused on the Trend of Home Care." *Home Health Care Management and Practice* 15(5): 407–415.

Nakane, Chie. 1970. *Japanese Society*. Berkeley: University of California Press.

Nakano, Lynne Y. 2000. "Volunteering as a Lifestyle Choice: Negotiating Self-Identities in Japan." *Ethnology* 39(2): 93–107.

———. 2005. *Community Volunteers in Japan: Everyday Stories of Social Change*. London: Routledge Curzon.

Nakata, Toyokazu. 1996. "Budding Volunteerism." *Japan Quarterly* 43(1): 22–26.

Nussbaum, Jon F., and Carla L. Fisher. 2011. "Afterword. Successful Aging and Communication Wellness: A Process of Transition and Continuity." In *Faces of Aging: The Lived Experiences of the Elderly in Japan*, ed. Yoshiko Matsumoto, 262–272. Stanford: Stanford University Press.

Ochiai, Emiko. 1997. *The Japanese Family System in Transition: A Sociological Analysis of Family Change in Postwar Japan*. Tokyo: LTCB International Library Foundation.

Ochs, Elinor, and Lisa Capps. 1996. "Narrating the Self." *Annual Review of Anthropology* 25: 19–43.

Ogawa, Akihiro. 2004. *The Failure of Civil Society? The Third Sector and the State in Contemporary Japan*. Albany: State University of New York Press.

Ohnuki-Tierney, Emiko, 1984. *Illness and Culture in Contemporary Japan: An Anthropological View*. Cambridge: Cambridge University Press.

Ota, Hiroshi, Howard Giles, and Cindy Gallois. 2002. "Perceptions of Younger, Middle-Aged, and Older Adults in Australia and Japan: Stereotypes and Age Group Vitality." *Journal of Intercultural Studies* 23(3): 253–266.

Overing, Joanna. 1989. "The Aesthetics of Production: The Sense of Community Among the Cubeo and Piaroa." *Dialectical Anthropology* 14(3): 159–175.

———. 2003. "In Praise of the Everyday: Trust and the Art of Social Living in an Amazonian Community." *Ethnos* 68(3): 293–316.

Overing, Joanna, and Alan Passes. 2000. *The Anthropology of Love and Anger: The Aesthetics of Conviviality in Native Amazonia*. London: Routledge.

Parkin, Robert. 2009. *Louis Dumont and Hierarchical Opposition*. Oxford: Berghahn.

Plath, David W. 1980. *Long Engagements: Maturity in Modern Japan*. Stanford: Stanford University Press.

Reischauer, Edwin O., and Marius B. Jansen. 1977. *The Japanese Today: Change and Continuity*. Cambridge, Mass.: Belknap Press.

Robbins, Joel. 2013. "Beyond the Suffering Subject: Toward an Anthropology of the Good." *Journal of the Royal Anthropological Institute* 19(3): 447–462.

Robb Jenike, Brenda. 2003. "Parent Care and Shifting Family Obligations in Urban Japan." In *Demographic Change and the Family in Japan's Aging Society*, ed. John W. Traphagan and John Knight, 177–202. Albany: State University of New York Press.

Robertson, James, and Nobue Suzuki, eds. 2003. *Men and Masculinities in Contemporary Japan: Dislocating the Salaryman Doxa*. London: Routledge Curzon.

Robertson, Jennifer. 1994. *Native and Newcomer: Making and Remaking a Japanese City*. Berkeley: University of California Press.

Rosenberger, Nancy. 2007. "Rethinking Emerging Adulthood in Japan: Perspectives from Long-Term Single Women." *Child Development Perspectives* 1(2): 92–95.

Rowe, Mark Michael. 2011. *Bonds of the Dead: Temples, Burial, and the Transformation of Contemporary Japanese Buddhism*. Chicago: University of Chicago Press.

Rupp, Katherine. 2003. *Gift-Giving in Japan: Cash, Connections, Cosmologies*. Stanford: Stanford University Press.

Sahlins, Marshall. 1972. *Stone Age Economics*. Chicago: Aldine-Atherton.

Sawada, Janine A. 2004. *Practical Pursuits: Religion, Politics, and Personal Cultivation in Nineteenth-Century Japan*. Honolulu: University of Hawaii Press.

Schwartz, Frank. 2002. "Civil Society in Japan Reconsidered." *Japanese Journal of Political Science* 3(2): 195–215.

Seale, Clive. 1998. *Constructing Death: The Sociology of Dying and Bereavement*. Cambridge: Cambridge University Press.

Sennett, Richard. 2002 (1974). *The Fall of Public Man*. London: Penguin.

Seo, Bo Kyeong. 2016. "Patient Waiting: Care as a Gift and Debt in the Thai Healthcare System." *Journal of the Royal Anthropological Institute* 22: 279–295.

Shumway, David. 2003. *Modern Love: Romance, Intimacy, and the Marriage Crisis*. New York: New York University Press.

Slote, Michael. 2007. *The Ethics of Care and Empathy*. London: Routledge.

Smith, Robert John. 1974. *Ancestor Worship in Contemporary Japan*. Stanford: Stanford University Press

Stafford, Charles. 2000. *Separation and Reunion in Modern China*. Cambridge: Cambridge University Press.

Stevens, Carolyn S. 1997. *On the Margins of Japanese Society: Volunteers and the Welfare of the Urban Underclass*. London: Routledge.

Stevenson, Lisa. 2014. *Life Beside Itself: Imagining Care in the Canadian Arctic*. Berkeley: University of California Press.

Sugimoto, Yoshio. 2010. *An Introduction to Japanese Society*. Cambridge: Cambridge University Press.

Suita City. 2011. "Kihon kōsō–jinkō." Suita city webpage. http://www.city.suita.osaka.jp/home/soshiki/div-gyoseikeiei/kseisaku/seisaku/3rd-soukei-06.html. Accessed 10 Nov 2012.

Suzuki, Hikaru, ed. 2013. *Death and Dying in Contemporary Japan: Shifting Social Structures and Values*. London: Routledge.

Suzuki, Nanami, ed. 2013. "The Anthropology of Aging and Well-Being: Searching for the Space and Time to Cultivate Life Together." *Senri Ethnological Studies* 80.

Taylor, Janelle. 2008. "On Recognition, Caring, and Dementia." *Medical Anthropology Quarterly* 22(4): 313–335.

Thang, Leng Leng. 2001. *Generations in Touch: Linking the Old and Young in a Tokyo Neighborhood*. Ithaca: Cornell University Press.

Thelen, Tatiana. 2015. "Care as Social Organization: Creating, Maintaining and Dissolving Significant Relations." *Anthropological Theory* 15(4): 497–515.

Thin, Neil. 2008. "'Realising the Substance of Their Happiness': How Anthropology Forgot About Homo Gauiusus." In *Culture and Well-Being: Anthropological Approaches to Freedom and Political Ethics*, ed. Alberto Corsín Jiménez, 134–155. London: Pluto Press.

Ticktin, Miriam. 2011. *Casualties of Care: Immigration and the Politics of Humanitarianism in France*. Berkeley: University of California Press.

Traphagan, John W. 2000. *Taming Oblivion: Aging Bodies and the Fear of Senility in Japan*. Albany: State University of New York Press.

———. 2004. *The Practice of Concern: Ritual, Well-Being, and Aging in Rural Japan*. Durham, NC: Carolina Academic Press.

Traphagan, John W., and John Knight. 2003. *Demographic Change and the Family in Japan's Aging Society*. Albany: State University of New York Press.

Tsukada, Takashi. 2012. "The Urban History of Osaka." *City, Culture and Society* 3: 1–8.

Viveiros de Castro, Eduardo. 2004. "Exchanging Perspectives: The Transformation of Objects into Subjects in Amerindian Ontologies." *Common Knowledge* 10(3): 463–484.

Vogel, Ezra F. 1971 (1963). *Japan's New Middle Class: The Salary Man and His Family in a Tokyo Suburb*. Berkeley: University of California Press.

Wada, Shuichi. 2000. "Kōreishakai ni okeru 'ikigai' no ronri." [The logic of 'ikigai' in aging society.] *Ikigai kenkyū* [Healthy and active aging] 12:18–45.

Walker, Harry and Kavedžija, Iza , 2015. "Values of Happiness." *HAU: Journal of Ethnographic Theory* 5(3): 1–23.

Watson, Lawrence C., and Maria-Barbara Watson-Franke. 1985. *Interpreting Life Histories: An Anthropological Inquiry*. New Brunswick, N.J.: Rutgers University Press.

Watts, Richard J. 2003. *Politeness*. Cambridge: Cambridge University Press.

Wengraf, Tom. 2001. *Qualitative Research Interviewing: Biographic Narrative and Semi-Structured Methods*. London: Sage.

Williams, Mark, and Danny Penman. 2011. *Mindfulness: A Practical Guide to Finding Peace in a Frantic World*. London: Piatkus.

Yalom, Irvin D. 1980. *Existential Psychotherapy*. New York: Basic Books.

Yates-Doerr, Emily, and Megan A. Carney. 2015. "Demedicalizing Health: The Kitchen as a Site of Care." *Medical Anthropology* 35(4): 305–321.

Index

Acknowledgments

This book, like every story, could not exist without its protagonists. But I am indebted to them for more than just allowing me to write about their lives. The community salon in Shimoichi was a welcoming field site and a warm home away from home. Without the patience and kindness of all the people associated with it—the staff, volunteers, and visitors—this research would not have been possible. Many others, in Osaka and elsewhere in Kansai, have given me their time and attention, generously allowing me to ask numerous questions and watch them go about their everyday lives, for which I am very grateful.

The Graduate School of Human Sciences at Osaka University provided a friendly academic base in Japan, and Professor Naoki Kasuga's support was much appreciated. Beverley Yamamoto and Fuyuko Nagarekawa helped in numerous ways. I was lucky to have Laura Dales, who introduced me to many of her friends and some of my valuable interlocutors, to share the time in the field as a colleague and a friend. With Tomohiro Morisawa I shared many of my fieldwork woes and joys. Many stimulating conversations with Leslie Fesenmyer, Ammara Maqsood, Ivan Constantino, and Brett Clancy made writing exciting and certainly less solitary. I am indebted to Inge Daniels, Roger Goodman, and Robert Parkin for their support, encouragements, and numerous useful comments.

The fieldwork and writing were generously supported by a variety of sources, including the Clarendon Fund, the Japan Foundation, and the Wenner-Gren Foundation. Without this support, this work would not have been possible.

My family and their encouragement made it easy to remember what makes life worth living. I am grateful to my parents, Jolanta Sychowska-Kavedžija and Boris Kavedžija, for their unwavering support, and to my sister Nel Kavedžija for her joking encouragement. Many pages of this book were written in beautiful, serene locations, thanks to my parents and parents-in-law, David and Felicity Walker. Very special thanks are due to Harry Walker, in conversations with whom many ideas took shape, who accompanied me in the field and whose comments on earlier versions of the chapters were invaluable. His patience and numerous forms of support made this work possible, and his companionship made it thoroughly enjoyable.